You have a real talent for promotion and writing advertisements.

Albert Gore, Vice President
United States of America

There are a lot of great copywriters, but Joe Sugarman is the best. He knows how to build a story and close the sale. Anyone who wants to sell better will enjoy Advertising Secrets of the Written Word.

Richard Thalheimer, President
The Sharper Image

I have been a fan of Joseph Sugarman's copywriting and marketing ideas for years and have benefited greatly by imitating his long-copy ads. Now he is letting us all in on his secrets in a book that should cost $2,000 because it contains so much detailed information. Thank you, Joe. I really liked the book!

Jack Canfield, Author
Chicken Soup for the Soul

Every trade has its role models. And for me, there is no better model for ad copywriters or magazine editors than Joe Sugarman.

Ray Schultz, Editor
DIRECT Magazine

Joseph Sugarman is brimming over with creative ideas. That isn't so unusual; many of us are. But Joe's ideas rocket into our marketing consciousness like shooting stars with one triumphant difference: His ideas invariably work. They motivate. They sell. So this isn't a book for theoreticians. It's aimed like an exquisitely polished arrow into the heart of writing to sell. New to marketing? Read this book. Been in the business for thirty years? Read this book.

Herschell Gordon Lewis, Chairman
Communicomp

From the participants who attended my seminar and learned what you are about to:

I enjoyed the seminar, and I learned a lot. I am more determined than ever to start and succeed at running a mail order business.

Lee R. Herrington III, President
Herrington's Catalog

Your seminar has really opened my eyes to a realization of what makes effective mail order advertising. I am sure that attending the seminar will pay dividends many times over in the years ahead.

J. M. Robinson
Atlantic Richfield Company

I told you I'd summarize the 6 or 8 major things, new to me, that I got from the seminar. Going over the notes I find it's 36 major things I'll be doing differently.

Gordon T. Beaham III, President
Faultless Starch/Bon Ami Company

Not only did you teach me some fundamental new concepts in space advertising, but you planted some seeds that may well change our marketing program and perhaps even our way of doing business.

Frederick J. Simon, President
Omaha Steaks International

I would recommend your seminars to novices to gain the degree of confidence necessary to write super ads almost instantaneously. Old timers will also benefit because what they'll learn is that you can help them make their ordinary ads super successful. Although I've been in mail order for more than 15 years I soon found, as a result of your 5-day seminar, that there was more I didn't know than I did know.

> Ed Axel
> Energy Group of America, Inc.

I know that if I can implement any portion of the knowledge you imparted to us, my company cannot help but be more efficient and successful.

> Gayle McClean
> Toronto, Ontario, Canada

You did two things right. First, you charged $2,000. This clever device guaranteed the quality of the participants and assured you of their rapt and undivided attention. Second, you gave them their money's worth. I only did one thing right. I came.

> Joe Karbo
> Huntington Beach, California

The depth of knowledge and the skill with which you organized and presented it was far above what I anticipated when I signed up for the seminar. But the real payoff was what the course covered that was not in the outline. I feel that the content relating to the philosophy of achieving success in life and the numerous examples you provided to prove this philosophy will have the greatest payoff for us in the long run.

Ed Scofield
Garden Way Associates

When you're a farmer you always worry about the crop. It's growing too slow—you worry. It's growing too fast—you really worry. I find it to be about the same when a farmer gets into space advertising. The orders are coming in so good from our space ads, I'm beginning to worry. A high class worry, I'll admit.

Frank Schultz
Alamo, Texas

I most enjoyed your openness in revealing, in depth, how you run your company. Few businessmen have the confidence to give away their "secrets" as you did!

C. L. Schaldenbrand
Word Processing Exchange

At times the seminar combined high drama, "made for TV" movie serialization, and mail order technique in an unbeatable blend of education and excitement. It was the best class I have taken since Harvard Business School.

John E. Groman
Epsilon Data Management

On my way back, on Friday night I stayed at the Sheraton Centre Hotel in New York. My two bags with my clothes were stolen in the lobby of the hotel. I don't care about the clothes, but I can't tell you how much I regret the loss of the seminar material, which is of an "inestimable" value for me, and which was also in the bags.

Herman Van Hove
Brussels, Belgium

It has given me a fresh perspective and the insight I had sought when I first decided to attend your seminar. I now have a much clearer picture of why our successful promotions succeeded and our failures failed.

Richard J. Guilfoyle
Limited Editions Collectors Society

Advertising
Secrets

At his exclusive marketing seminar,
Joseph Sugarman taught copywriting, marketing and
creativity to a group of mail order enthusiasts who
went on to achieve incredible success. This book
reveals many of the same advertising secrets that he
shared with his students, each of whom paid
thousands of dollars to attend.

Books by Joseph Sugarman

Advertising Secrets of the Written Word
Marketing Secrets of a Mail Order Maverick
Television Secrets for Marketing Success
Success Forces
Triggers

Advertising Secrets of the Written Word

Joseph Sugarman

*The Ultimate
Resource on
How to Write Powerful
Advertising Copy
From One of America's
Top Copywriters and
Mail Order
Entrepreneurs*

Publisher's Note: This publication is designed to provide accurate and authoritative information in regard to the subject matter covered. It is sold with the understanding that the publisher or author is not engaged in rendering legal, accounting, or other such professional services. If expert assistance in such fields is required, the services of an appropriate professional person should be sought.

Printed in the United States of America

Publisher's Cataloging-in-Publication Data
(Provided by Quality Books, Inc.)

Sugarman, Joseph
    Advertising secrets of the written word : the ultimate resource on how to write powerful advertising copy from one of America's top copywriters and mail order entrepreneurs / Joseph Sugarman.—1st ed.
        p.   cm.
    Includes bibliographical references and index.
    ISBN: 1-891686-00-3 CL
    ISBN: 1-891686-01-1 PB
        1. Direct marketing. 2. Advertising copy—Handbooks, manuals, etc. 3. Advertising, direct-mail. I. Title.
    HF5861.S84 1998   659.13'3
                                             QBI97-41618

Attention: Schools, Ad Agencies and Corporations. DelStar books are available at quantity discounts with bulk purchases for educational or business use. For more information, please contact DelStar Books at the address below.

06 05 04 03 02 01   10 9 8 7 6 5 4 3 2

Cover design: Ron Hughes
Cartoonist: Dick Hafer

DelStar Books
3350 Palms Center Drive
Las Vegas, NV 89103
Phone: (702) 798-9000
Fax: (702) 597-2002

*To Wendy, April and Jill
with love and affection*

The truly creative mind in any field is no more than . . . a cruelly delicate organism with the overpowering necessity to create, create, create—so that without the creating of music or poetry or books or buildings or something of meaning, his very breath is cut off from him. He must create, must pour out creation. By some strange, unknown, inward urgency he is not really alive unless he is creating.

—Pearl Buck

Contents

Advertising Secrets of the Written Word

Foreword	xiii
Acknowledgments	xvii
Introduction	1
Section One: Understanding the Process	
Preview	9
1. General Knowledge	11
2. Specific Knowledge	15
3. Practice, Practice, Practice	23
4. The Purpose of All the Graphic Elements of an Ad	27
5. The First Sentence	31
6. Creating the Perfect Buying Environment	35
7. Resonating with the Reader	39
8. The Slippery Slide	45
9. Assumed Constraints	55
10. Seeds of Curiosity	59
11. Copy as Emotion	65
12. Selling the Concept, Not the Product	71
13. The Incubation Process	77
14. How Much Copy Should You Write?	81
15. The Art of Personal Communication	87
16. The Copy Sequence	93
17. The Editing Process	101
Section Two: Understanding What Works	
Preview	111
18. Powerful Copy Elements Explained	113
Typeface	113
First Sentence	114
Second Sentence	114
Paragraph Headings	114
Product Explanation	115

New Features	116
Technical Explanation	116
Anticipate Objections	118
Resolve Objections	118
Gender	119
Clarity	120
Clichés	120
Rhythm	121
Service	121
Physical Facts	123
Trial Period	124
Price Comparison	125
Testimonials	126
Price	127
Offer Summary	127
Avoid Saying Too Much	128
Ease of Ordering	128
Ask for the Order	128
19. The Psychological Triggers	131
Feeling of Involvement or Ownership	131
Honesty	134
Integrity	136
Credibility	136
Value and Proof of Value	138
Justify the Purchase	139
Greed	139
Establish Authority	140
Satisfaction Conviction	143
Nature of Product	146
Current Fads	146
Timing	149

Desire to Belong	151
Desire to Collect	152
Curiosity	154
Sense of Urgency	155
Instant Gratification	157
Exclusivity, Rarity or Uniqueness	158
Simplicity	160
Human Relationships	163
Guilt	165
Specificity	166
Familiarity	167
Hope	170
20. Getting the Mind to Work	175
21. Selling a Cure, Not Prevention	179
22. Telling a Story	185
23. Rating Your Writing Level	189

Section Three: Proving the Points—Ad Examples

Preview	195
24. The Lazy Man's Way to Riches	197
25. A Fluke of Nature	205
26. Lingerie for Men	213
27. The More You Learn	219
28. A More Stimulating Way	223
29. Magic Baloney	225
30. Pet Plane	229
31. Mail Order Mansion	233
32. Hungarian Conspiracy	237
33. Vision Breakthrough	241
34. Gold Space Chains	245
35. Consumers Hero	249
36. Nautilus Spelling Sale	253

A Note: The Power of Your Pen   257

Epilogue   Some Final Thoughts   259

Appendix A   Assumed Constraints, Continued   263

Appendix B   Seeds of Curiosity, Continued   265

Appendix C   Summary of Axioms and Major Points   267

Appendix D   Recommended Reading   271

Appendix E   Classic JS&A Ads   279

Index   299

By Ray Schultz, Editor, *DIRECT* Magazine

Every trade has its role models. And for me, there is no better model for ad copywriters or magazine editors than Joe Sugarman.

Bandleader Artie Shaw had a standard question for musicians who wanted to join his band: "Who do you listen to?"

A similar question might be asked of writers applying for work: "Who do you read?"

Sugarman is the guy who sells BluBlocker sunglasses on TV. He also happens to be one of the most amusing and prolific writers in the United States, as I discovered when I started reading his JS&A catalog in 1985.

He was totally out of the box. He cracked me up with the sheer exuberance of his copy approach.

He offered readers $10 for every spelling error they found in his copy. ("Please don't correct my grammar.")

He offered "loaner" watches to customers as part of a service guarantee.

He offered a $6 million home for sale in the airline magazines, accepting American Express, Visa, MasterCard or any negotiable hard currency.

He sold a $240,000 airplane in a single mail order ad.

And he did it all with a very special tone. It's like Nelson Algren said about John Cheever—that he was the one writer you could identify "without turning the pages of *The New Yorker* back to see who wrote it."

Not that Sugarman is the most colorful rogue ever to write great mail order copy. There were others. Louis Victor Eytinge, a convicted murderer who learned how to write in prison. Or Gene Schwartz, the art collector, who made his living writing stuff like "She Fled the Table When the Doctor Said Cut Her Open."

But Joe surpassed those guys in a few very important ways—the sheer volume of his writing, the trends that he set and my favorite—the personal catalog—one in which the copy and the product reflect the quirks of the owner. And Joe has a lot of imitators who have personalized their catalogs using Joe's catalog as their inspiration.

How did Joe learn his trade? He claims he learned it from his failures and not from the mail order greats who preceded him. Greats like David Margoles, who sold 4 million garlic crushers in the 1950s.

Then there was Max Sackheim, co-founder of the Book-of-the-Month Club and another great pitchman who lived by his wits. As Lester Wunderman in 1996 reflected about Sackheim, "When he talked to clients, he promised a breakthrough—not as we have now, minuscule improvement."

Then there was John Caples, who entered American folklore by writing "They Laughed When I Sat Down At the Piano." The late Larry Chait asked Caples why he stressed the social benefits instead of just selling the virtues of the course.

"You don't understand," Caples answered. "Learning the piano is tough. You can't sell that. But you can sell the idea of social success and overcoming whatever deficiencies you have in order to become popular."

Though he may never have met them, Sugarman knows on a gut level what these guys knew. And that's important, because he's one of the last of a breed.

Now for the good news. He's passed the tradition down in *Advertising Secrets of the Written Word*, the best book ever done on the subject of mail order writing.

Besides the advice on selling, it stresses basic truths about writing, in language anyone can understand. I've even given the manuscript to my new reporters to read.

I'm sad to report that Sugarman doesn't write as much copy as he used to—no more catalogs and very few space ads. He's followed the money into infomercials and home shopping.

Until they reissue old JS&A catalogs (the way they've reissued the 1909 edition of Sears, Roebuck), this book will have to stand as Joe's legacy in print. But it's a fine legacy.

So here is it. Enjoy. As Walter Winchell said when he introduced Damon Runyon, "The next act is better."

Ray Schultz is one of the top writers and editors in the direct marketing industry and editor of DIRECT *magazine, a Cowles Business Media publication.*

Acknowledgments | To Those Who Made It Possible

Many people have contributed to my copywriting skills and to the creation of this book, and to all of them I am very grateful. Mary Stanke, President of JS&A Group, Inc., whose direction, commitment and 26 years of service allowed me the creative freedom to express myself through my writing and who helped me build a substantial business in the process. To Wendy and our two children, April and Jill, for their understanding and support during the many seminars we held—always behind the scenes, but their presence was very important and always felt. Judy Sugarman, my sister and copyeditor for 25 years—always there to correct my spelling, undangle my modifiers and give me very candid feedback.

I also wish to acknowledge the thousands of customers who gave me a tremendous education and for whom I have an unwavering respect. I wish to acknowledge my many competitors, too. I hated it when they copied me but in the process of trying to outwit them, my copywriting skills grew even stronger. There are hundreds of other people I could mention—too numerous to list here—who have played a vital role in my success and growth. A special thank-you to the people who played a role in the production of this book: Lyn Chaffee, Doug Easton, Ron Hughes, Virginia Iorio and Nancy Kleban. And finally, I wish to give a special mention to Dick Hafer, whose cartoons were created specially for this book.

A special acknowledgment to all my wonderful seminar participants who learned from me and went on to create or build successful businesses—all through the power of their pens. I learned a great deal from them. Finally, I wish to thank, with humility and gratitude, all who have exchanged their hard-earned money for this book. May you too learn and prosper.

| ## The Origins of This Book

This is a story about a seminar. It was a copywriting and marketing seminar I presented in the '70s and '80s during a time when I was actively involved in both writing copy and marketing a range of products that included everything from electronics to collectibles—from Bone Fones to Picasso tiles.

I was a prolific writer, often writing complete catalogs, print advertisements and direct mailings. And I owned the company, JS&A Group, Inc., that sold these products, so I experienced the direct consequences of my successes and failures.

Failures Outnumbered Successes

My failures far outnumbered my successes. In fact, I have yet to find anybody who has experienced the number of failures I experienced during the early stages of my career. But it was through these failures that I received a very costly education that to this day has guided me through a successful career in advertising and direct marketing.

To the public, I was a big success. Babe Ruth is remembered for his home run record and not for the fact that he also held the record for the most strikeouts. And so it was with me. Most people just saw my successes, as they were quite visible. And they just saw my successful innovations because they were the ones that worked. So to the general public and to others in direct marketing, it appeared that I had the Midas touch.

I didn't see myself running seminars. I was busy enough running my business. And to share my secrets with the industry was only asking for competition. But it was a series of coincidences that prompted me to offer seminar courses and I'm glad I made the decision to do them. And many of my participants are glad too—people whose seminar experience made an enormous difference in their lives.

My seminar was different. First, I was an actual practitioner—not an educator or a consultant who never had to make a major marketing gamble or cover a payroll. I was out there on the firing line, making sure each day that the copy I was writing and the marketing decisions I was making were going to be accepted by the marketplace.

Second, it was during a time when my success was reaching a peak. Our mail order ads were appearing everywhere. They appeared in newspapers, magazines and on airplanes and with such regularity and frequency that the format was attracting a great deal of attention and creating an entire flock of imitators.

Finally, I realized what people were willing to pay just to hear me as a speaker or talk to me as a consultant. Bernie Pargh, an entrepreneur and owner of B.A. Pargh, a business equipment sales company, flew from Nashville to Los Angeles one day just to hear me speak to a direct marketing group. "Joe, I've spent over $1,000 just to hear you speak for 45 minutes," he told me.

I would also get calls from people who had marketing problems and would want to fly to visit me in the Chicago suburb of Northbrook, where our company was based, just to sit and talk to me for 15 minutes.

The Fateful Visit

But the seminar would have never taken place had it not been for a small vacation I took up to northern Wisconsin to visit my sister and her family.

It was during that trip that I discovered the beauty of the north woods and made the decision, with my family, to find a second home there. The home I eventually found was a 10,000-square-foot, two-story building on a 16-acre site overlooking one of the most beautiful lakes I had ever seen. The property was filled with virgin timber—tall stately pines and oak trees that had escaped the lumbermen who cleared most of the trees from northern Wisconsin during the 1800s.

But the home was costly and at the time something I couldn't afford. The price in 1977 was $350,000 and I couldn't really justify it until my lawyer and close personal friend, George Gerstman, suggested I could use the facility as a seminar site. "Hold marketing seminars at the place, turn it into a business and you could write off the entire property and even make a profit," he suggested.

The idea really appealed to me. It was a very unique setting.

It was isolated, quiet, and the fresh northern Wisconsin air at Minocqua was stimulating and invigorating.

I spent a great deal of the summer going up there with my family and furnishing the facility for a seminar. I cleared away a number of the odd buildings that dated back to the 1800s but were in such disrepair that I had no choice but to remove them. My wife, Wendy, helped pick out the furniture and dishes. She also hired a cook, housekeepers and the support staff needed to run the seminars while Mary Stanke, my operations chief at JS&A, assisted with registering the participants and preparing all the materials for the seminar. And so within a few months the facility was transformed into an enchanting seminar site—a learning center that I called "Nature's Response."

The Most Expensive Seminar

Back in 1977, I was charging $2,000 for five days—a price that made it, at the time, the most expensive seminar in the direct marketing business. For my last seminars toward 1988, I charged $3,000. I announced the seminar in *Advertising Age* and *Direct Marketing* magazines in the format of one of my typical ads. And the response was immediate. If Bernie Pargh was willing to spend $1,000 to fly to Los Angeles to hear me speak for 45 minutes and several people were willing to fly from different parts of the U.S. to talk to me for just 15 minutes, I had a value that certainly was worth $2,000 for five full days.

Within a few weeks, I had a full class with participants from all over the world. We had somebody from Germany, several from California and quite a few from the East Coast. We had a farmer from Texas and a dentist from Carmel, California. Richard Viguerie, the conservative Washington fund-raiser, enrolled and of course Bernie Pargh attended. I actually had more participants than I wanted so I created a reservation list for my next seminar.

To get to Minocqua, the seminar participants had to fly to Chicago, board a commuter plane there and fly to the town of Rhinelander, Wisconsin, where they then took a bus for the 40-minute ride to their motel. To get to the seminar site, the participants took a pontoon boat from the motel and landed at our boathouse where they walked up a path to the house.

And at the house, they would find several rooms outfitted as classrooms, a large dining room, kitchen and a very large wooden balcony where they could look out at the lake, relax and enjoy the clean north-woods air.

It was an idyllic setting in a remote part of America—a place where my students would learn a form of copywriting and marketing that they could not learn anyplace else.

Book Contains Many Lessons

This book will share many of the lessons and experiences that were taught at these seminars. You'll learn how to mentally prepare yourself to write copy, how to write effective copy, and how to present your product, concept or service in a novel and exciting way. You'll learn what really works and what doesn't and how to avoid many of the pitfalls that marketers fall into and much more.

I convey my unique approach to copy by demonstrating my thought process on everything from how copy should flow to the elements every ad should have—from the psychology of copy and its motivational triggers to the emotions generated by words. But the seminar was certainly more than learning about copy and marketing.

The seminar turned into a motivational experience for many who went on to become quite successful. Others, who were already successful, couldn't wait to get back to work and implement their newly learned knowledge. And they too grew in the process.

You too will understand how to relate what you've learned about copywriting to other forms of marketing and you'll see how many of the same principles apply.

The Goal of Copy

Throughout this book, I talk about the eventual goal of writing effective copy, namely: "To cause a person to exchange his or her hard-earned money for a product or service." It's really as simple as that.

Direct marketing is truly the tool of the next century. Using direct marketing, you can move millions of people to reach into their pockets for millions of dollars—all from the power of your pen or the message you convey on a TV screen.

For most of what I teach in this book I use a print ad as a reference point. Print ads are among the most difficult of all forms of direct marketing. On a single page, in two dimensions, located in a medium with hundreds of competing messages and without sound or motion, you've got to entice a person to start reading your ad, convey the complete story of your product or service and then convince the person to reach for the phone and order. To understand this process and to effectively implement it requires a lot of experience and skill. But once you have mastered the skills, you will have the ability to build a business from just the power of your pen.

When Mike Valentine attended my seminar, he was operating his radar detector company out of his garage. Later, using many of the skills I taught him, his company, Cincinnati Microwave (developer of the Escort Radar Detector), grew to a $140 million public company. Jimmy Calano was a young 20-something entrepreneur who had been giving small management seminars when he attended my course. He eventually became a major force in the seminar business with CareerTrack—a multi-million-dollar company. Victoria's Secret sent two of their top marketing people when the company consisted of just two stores and a catalog. They eventually were acquired by The Limited and became a powerful retail chain throughout the country.

From a UPS driver who had a fascination with direct marketing and came to the seminar with his last $2,000 to Joe Karbo, author of *The Lazy Man's Way to Riches*, who already was a very successful mail order entrepreneur—they all came with great anticipation and they all left with valuable knowledge which helped them continue to grow and prosper.

16 Seminars Given

I had 312 students attending 16 seminars—from the first one in the summer of 1977 to the last one given in Maui, Hawaii, in the spring of 1988. Immediately after my last seminar, I wrote a good portion of this book. The rest of my writing and marketing insights come from several years of experience since then in the visual medium of TV—infomercials, TV spots and home shopping.

Regardless of your current educational level or knowledge of marketing, this book will give you fresh insights into the world of copywriting, marketing, human behavior and other lessons taught at my seminar.

Even if you are not interested in writing copy, you'll have a better appreciation and understanding of the copywriting process—so much so that you will be confident that you too can write good copy or, at a minimum, critique copy.

So pull up an easy chair, prop up your feet and sink into one of the most comprehensive contemporary books on the subject of copywriting, marketing and creative expression—a treasure chest of insights that will entertain as it teaches.

Section One

As the pontoon boat pulled up to the boathouse and the group slowly disembarked, there was a sense of excitement. The seminar that each had traveled thousands of miles to attend was finally in sight. What kind of value would they get? What kind of experience would they go through? And indeed, what would they learn?

They were the first group of attendees to participate in my seminar. And on the very first day I promised them that they would learn how to write great copy. They would understand the thought processes you go through to prepare to write that great piece of ad copy. They would also learn the basic underlying concepts of how to structure a great advertisement.

The Very First Day

But more importantly, what they were going to learn the first day was to eventually lay the foundation for learning about every form of communications—from print to TV, from direct mail to catalogs.

As the group assembled in the three-story vaulted living room, I introduced the staff to the participants. There was the cook, the servers, the housekeepers, the groundskeepers and the entire seminar staff. I then introduced my wife and two young children—April, six years old, and Jill, only three. My family was going to be there just as if I were at home. Ironically, each of my children played a small but important role in the seminar.

The first day was indeed one of the most important. And from the many lessons learned and the experiences shared, that first day prompted many of the participants to come up to me and tell me what an impact it had not only on their copywriting ability but on their understanding of the entire field of advertising and marketing. As Harvey Cinamon from Boston told me that first day, "I could leave right now and know that I've gotten my full value."

Richard Viguerie, the Washington fund-raiser, told me that the lessons he learned that very first day were invaluable in his business. "Just one slight change prompted by what I learned here today would pay for the entire seminar."

So get ready to experience what cost me millions of dollars to learn and what seminar participants paid a great deal to be taught. Welcome to a unique learning experience.

Chapter 1 | General Knowledge

The preparation to become a copywriter involves knowledge. There are two types. The first is a very broad or general knowledge and the second is a very specific or targeted knowledge. Let me explain.

The best copywriters in the world are those who are curious about life, read a great deal, have many hobbies, like to travel, have a variety of interests, often master many skills, get bored and then look for other skills to master. They hunger for experience and knowledge and find other people interesting. They are very good listeners.

Look at my background. I'm an instrument-rated multi-engine commercial pilot, an amateur radio operator, a professional photographer; I love computers, music, reading, movies, travel, art and design. I've done the complete catalog for my company including everything from setting the type to doing the layout. I've done all the photography and even some of the modeling. (My hand became quite famous, but more on that later.) I've tried many sports—golf, tennis, football, baseball, basketball, scuba diving, skiing, and snowmobiling. I've traveled to every continent on the globe with the exception of the Antarctic and I know I'll eventually get there. I've mastered a second language—German—during the three years I spent with the military in Germany. I've had hundreds of failures and many successes, with each representing a learning experience.

The best copywriters have a variety of interests and master many skills.

The thirst for knowledge, a tremendous curiosity about life, a wealth of experiences and not being afraid to work are the top credentials for being a good copywriter.

If you examine the lives of some of our greatest writers, you will see that they experienced a great deal and wrote about their experiences. Hemingway, Steinbeck—both lived and then wrote about their adventures. The more we experience, the more knowledge we have, the easier it is to come up with that big copy idea or marketing concept.

But more significantly, it is important to experience as much in life as possible and not to fear failure. It's not whether you win or lose in life that's important but whether you play the game. Lose enough and eventually you will win. It's only a matter of time. Edwin Land, the inventor of the Polaroid camera, said it best when he described his definition of a mistake: "A mistake is a future benefit, the full value of which is yet to be realized."

I can remember when I was very young and failed at something I tried very hard to accomplish. I'd often say to myself, "No big loss—it's in my back pocket. One of these days I'll use what I've just experienced simply by reaching into my back pocket and presto, I will have the answer just when I need it."

Experiences Create Ideas

Our minds are like giant computers. Every experience that goes into your brain—both good and bad—becomes more program material and data to recall and assemble in new ways in the future. Remember when the first Apple computers came out with their big 64K memories? You might also remember the slow speed and the poor graphics compared to the high-powered personal computers we have today. Today's computers are faster, more efficient, can accomplish more and can interrelate information faster and more easily. So it stands to reason, the more we've experienced, the more we can draw upon when it comes time to relate those experiences to new problems or opportunities.

There is nothing really new in life. It's simply a matter of taking previous pieces of knowledge and putting them together in a unique and different format. Matter is not created and destroyed. Everything on earth that was here a billion years ago is pretty much here now. The only difference is that it has taken new forms.

The more you have in your brain from experiences and knowledge and the more you are able to interrelate that knowledge and come up with new combinations of old material, the greater an idea person you will be and the more powerful your capabilities as a copywriter.

There is a saying that goes, "If all you have is a hammer, you look at every problem as a nail." The more tools you have to work on a problem in the form of experiences or knowledge, the more new ways you can figure out how to solve it.

Lateral Thinking for Ideas

Edward de Bono, one of the great creative thinkers of our time, came up with the term "lateral thinking" to describe the process of coming up with ideas by not focusing or thinking of just the problem. Often, by relating the problem to something that has nothing to do with the problem, a new idea emerges.

De Bono created a small product that he called his "Think Tank" which encouraged people to think more laterally and consequently more creatively. It was a small 8-inch sphere mounted on a platform with a small window. Through the window you saw a selection of 14,000 small words located on small plastic pieces. You shook the Think Tank and then looked into it and wrote down the first three words you saw.

You then tried to relate the three words to your marketing problem, to come up with a fresh perspective toward solving your problem. For example, let us say I wanted to sell my airplane. Typically, I would run an ad and focus on just the airplane, its features and equipment. But in using the Think Tank for lateral thinking, I drew three totally unrelated words, 'farm,' 'salesman' and 'compassion' and had to create an ad incorporating those three words. This process would cause me to search my brain, my data bank, and all my past experiences for some way to relate the three words while keeping in mind that I had to sell the airplane.

The Dictionary as a Tool

Lateral thinking is simply a tool. So is your dictionary. And so is your mind. Probably one of the most important keys in copywriting and conceptualizing is the ability to relate totally divergent concepts to create a new concept. Once again, the more data you have to work with from your life experiences and the more your mind can relate this data to a problem, the better you are going to be at coming up with that really great idea.

Running Your Own Company

Another factor that makes a great copywriter is the experience of running your own company and being responsible for every word you write. The really great direct marketing copywriters often don't work for advertising agencies, but rather run their own companies and experience their own successes and failures. Ben Suarez, Gary Halbert, the late Gene Schwartz and dozens of others recognized as top copywriters have owned their own companies and learned over years of trial and error—years of both big mistakes and great success. You can't beat that type of experience.

In my case, I have been presented with thousands of products, written ads for hundreds of them and have had to come up with that big idea hundreds of times a year. Even as I look back at my advertising, I see a learning curve that would not have been possible had it not been for that immense wealth of broad experience. Ironically, you're going to read about many of those experiences throughout this book. You'll be able to avoid many of the pitfalls and mistakes I made climbing my way up the ladder and you'll understand why these mistakes were indeed learning experiences.

The preparation for becoming a great copywriter is a lifestyle. It's a hunger for knowledge, a curiosity and a desire to participate in life that is broad-based and passionate. If you have this personality, you are already well on your way. If you don't, simply being aware of it is often enough to start a mental process and movement that will take you to where you would like to be. But being a great copywriter is more than just having a lot of experience in life. What you will learn in the next chapter is just as important.

Chapter 2 | Specific Knowledge

I was sitting in the laboratory of the Sensor Watch Company in Dallas, Texas, looking through a microscope and learning everything I could about how a new digital watch was designed, produced and assembled.

I was becoming an expert on digital watch technology, on integrated circuits, quartz crystals and oscillator circuits. "Why are all the contacts gold-plated?" I asked the engineer. "They're gold-plated in every integrated circuit. It's part of the technology," was the reply.

The conversation continued. It had been two days and I was still delving into every aspect of this new digital watch I was planning to introduce. I still hadn't reached the point where I could write an ad on the advantages of the new product. At the time, most digital watches had liquid crystal displays, and in order to see the time, you had to press a button to illuminate the display. On the new Sensor watch, the display glowed constantly, thanks to an inert but radioactive substance that was placed in a small flat capsule behind the display.

New Technology Required Powerful Presentation

This new technology meant that you could glance down at your watch and, in an instant, tell the time—even at night—without pressing any buttons. But I felt that there had to be a powerful way of presenting the product and I still wasn't comfortable with what I had.

The Sensor 770 was very expensive to make and sell. So I knew that I needed something that made the watch I was selling really different and special.

"Why didn't somebody think of this radioactive material for watches before?" was my next question.

The engineer looked at me, paused for a second and then said, "We haven't had the technology to seal the radioactive material in a transparent capsule without it leaking out until somebody developed a technique with a laser. The laser is what seals the capsule. Without the laser, there is no way you could completely seal the capsule."

That was all I needed. The concept was clear. And the ad headline that I wrote for the new Sensor Digital Watch was, "Laser Beam Digital Watch."

The story told of how the watch was made possible thanks to a laser beam and how its new technology benefited the consumer. That single concept resulted in millions of dollars in profitable sales for the digital watch.

When I had reached the point about the laser beam sealing the capsule, I knew I had found that unique headline concept that made the watch stand out from the rest of the competition. But it took a few days of very intensive learning and study before the concept emerged. Sometimes this can happen in a few minutes, sometimes it can happen in a few hours and sometimes it may take weeks. This time it took a few days of patience along with specific knowledge.

You Must Become an Expert

You need to become an expert on a product, service or anything you write about to really be effective. Becoming an expert means learning enough about a product to obtain enough specific knowledge so you can communicate the real nature of what you are trying to sell. Say to yourself, "I am an expert or have learned enough to be able to effectively communicate this product to the consumer." That's what we mean by "specific knowledge."

This doesn't mean that you have to learn everything there is to know about a subject every time. There have been times when I simply looked at a product or service and came up with the big idea from my own past experience or specific knowledge in a particular category. Remember, I'm a pilot, ham radio operator and photographer. I already had not only vast knowledge of the gadgets I would sell in my business, but knowledge of my customer, as well. I myself was my typical customer. I was the type of individual I had to sell products to because I was as gadget-oriented as the person I was trying to appeal to.

You Must Know Your Customer Too

And that's another point. In addition to knowing your product or service, you've really got to know your customer. You've got to be an expert on who your customer is by gathering specific information on whom you are selling to. You may already be an expert by virtue of being a typical customer. You know your likes and dislikes, what excites you and what you yourself would expect from a company selling you a product. But if it is your assignment to write copy for a product or service that you really don't have a feel for, then you have a great deal of studying to do to make sure you understand who your customer is and what motivates him or her.

You Must Understand a Product's Nature

And even if you understand your customer and understand your product, you must realize one more thing. There is a specific way that each product should be presented to your customer. In short, the product has a nature of its own and it's up to you to discover what the nature of that product is in the mind of the consumer.

Let me cite a good example. Back when I first started JS&A in the basement of my home, I met Howard Franklin. Howard was an insurance salesman from Chicago who bought his first calculator from me from an ad I ran in *The Wall Street Journal*. He loved his calculator and stopped by one day to buy a few more of them. After that, Howard would stop by every once in a while and buy more calculators as gifts for his better clients.

One day, Howard stopped by and said that since JS&A was a growing concern, I should buy insurance. "You want to protect your family because if anything ever happened to you, there may be quite an estate and lots of taxes to pay before your family would realize anything."

"Thank you, Howard. I appreciate the offer, but I don't really believe in insurance," was my standard reply.

But Howard was a good salesman. Every once in a while Howard would clip out an article on calculators from a local paper or an article from some magazine on some new gadget and send it to me with his card. And every once in a while, Howard stopped by and picked up a calculator and again dropped the comment, "Joe, you should really have insurance."

"Thanks, Howard. I appreciate the advice," was my typical comment.

Then one day I heard a siren in front of my next-door neighbor's house. I looked out the window and within a few minutes, my neighbor was being carried out of his home on a stretcher with a white sheet over him. He had died that morning from a massive heart attack. He was only in his 40s. I was 36 at the time.

The next day I called Howard on the phone. "Howard, remember our many discussions on insurance and protecting your family and stuff? Well, I think that we should sit down and work out some sort of program for an insurance plan for my family and me."

I had finally made the plunge. Was it Howard's salesmanship? Was it his persistence? Maybe. But I realized from that

It took an event close to home to make me take action.

experience a really effective way to sell a whole series of products. Howard succeeded because he had planted enough seeds in my mind for me to realize what insurance was for, who should sell it to me and who was a good friend and customer. When it came time to buy, only I, Joseph Sugarman, would know. And only when there was an immediate experience that hit close to home would I see the value of insurance. I went through the experience and I responded.

Some of the implications from this example will be referred to later in this book, but the point concerns the nature of a product. Every product has a nature to it that you must understand to be successful when creating a marketing concept behind that product. For example, from the insurance experience, I soon realized how to sell burglar alarms and became one of the largest burglar alarm sales companies in the country, protecting more homes than any other company.

The alarm was called the Midex and my thoughts went back to Howard as I created the ad. I knew that to scare people into buying a burglar alarm was like Howard coming into my basement and saying, "Joe, when you die, are you going to leave your wife and kids in financial disaster?" That would never sell me insurance. Nor would a similar technique of quoting crime statistics work to sell burglar alarms.

I realized that if I were to buy a burglar alarm, I would first have to recognize a need for one. Perhaps if my neighbor was robbed or crime in my community was on the rise or I had recently purchased something expensive.

Once I had a need for a burglar alarm, I would look for one that really made sense for my situation. The first thing I would insist on is that it worked. After all, the first time I really need my alarm to work may be the only time it would be called upon to work, and I'd want to make sure it worked flawlessly.

The second thing that would be important to me is the ease of installation. It would have to be so easy to install that it wouldn't require any outside person stringing wires all over my house. So when I wrote the ad on the Midex burglar alarm, I made sure that I spent several paragraphs on the reliability of the product and the testing each unit went through before it was shipped. And I used astronaut Wally Schirra as my spokesperson for the alarm. He was quoted as saying, "I'm very pleased with my unit."

Scare Tactics Don't Usually Work

Never did I try to scare the prospective customer with crime statistics. It would look as ridiculous as Howard screaming or warning me in my basement to get insurance because I may die. All I did was realize the nature of the product I was selling, bring out the points that were important in the product to the consumer and then wait until the consumer saw the ad enough times or was threatened close enough to home before he or she bought.

We received many orders from people who had cut out the ad and put it in a file. When indeed they were threatened, they then called and placed their order. Fortunately, there were enough people who wanted a unit when they saw the ad to earn us a nice profit, but we also received orders months after we stopped running our ads. And despite the fact that many of the electronic products of the time were obsolete just a few months after they were introduced, we managed to run our ad for over three years before sales slowed down.

I have one other example on the importance of becoming an expert on the product you sell by gaining specific knowledge in order to write outstanding copy on a subject. It happened in 1975, right at the start of the CB boom in the United States. Back then, the U.S. government had imposed a reduced nationwide speed limit of 55 miles per hour to conserve fuel. The lower speed limits really affected those 18-wheel long-haul truck drivers. Truck drivers responded by buying citizens band radios to communicate with each other.

The truck drivers would travel in caravans and truckers ahead of the caravan would signal if there was a "Smokey" (police officer) in the area. Soon CBs became so popular that the average motorist started buying them and a whole new fad emerged in the U.S.—a fad so big that songs, movies and a variety of products were created to capitalize on it. The CB units themselves were in such demand that you couldn't even get one without a wait, and thieves were stealing them out of cars and turning a very hefty profit reselling them.

As a ham radio operator, I knew of the fun in radio communications and the advantages of having a unit in my car. This was my general knowledge. So I wanted to experience the fad and I decided to get a CB radio. I then became somewhat of an expert on it. There was a lot less to master with CB than there was with ham radio, where I had to learn the Morse code at 13 words per minute and a great deal of technical information before passing my operator's test.

During the early stages of the fad, I was attending the Consumer Electronics Show in Chicago when I bumped into Mike Weschler, a salesman, who showed me a new product. "Joe, here is a miniature walkie-talkie."

The Product Was Not Unusual

I looked at the small sliver of a product he handed me and realized that a small walkie-talkie was no big deal. You could get them at any Radio Shack store. But Mike then pointed out that the unit had an integrated circuit—it was one of the only units using this new type of technology and it indeed was smaller than any of the other products on the market.

The product seemed a little more interesting after Mike explained its features. It was so small that it could easily slip into a shirt pocket. "What frequencies can you broadcast on and what is the power?" I asked, calling on my knowledge of ham radio.

"The unit has two frequencies. One takes a crystal for any of a number of frequencies and the other would be permanently set to a frequency around 27 megahertz."

I looked up at Mike as he was demonstrating the unit and asked him, "Mike, isn't 27 megahertz near one of the CB frequencies?"

"Right. It's channel 12 but don't worry, there is not that much radio traffic on channel 12. It's normally reserved for walkie-talkies," Mike answered rather sheepishly as if I had discovered a fault with the unit.

"No, Mike, I think that will turn out to be an advantage." And indeed it was. I took the unit, called it a Pocket CB and sold over 250,000 of them at $39.95. It was a huge success and fully attributable to my general knowledge combined with the specific knowledge of the unit and the discovery of that unique feature that might have been overlooked by somebody else.

Realize how important it is to know your product and know your customer. It is this specific knowledge that will make a dramatic difference in your ability to communicate your thoughts in copy.

Chapter 3 | Practice, Practice, Practice

One of the first things I would ask my seminar students to think about was the definition of good copywriting. Is it the skill of being able to accurately put words on paper? Can it be taught? What sort of background do you need to be a good copywriter?

We would then talk about both general knowledge and specific knowledge. But I explained that there was more to the art of copywriting.

Copywriting is simply a written form of communicating facts and emotions. It is a mental process. Some copywriters will tell you that many of their greatest works were well thought out in their minds even before they put them on paper.

Joe Karbo wrote one of the most successful income opportunity ads ever written for his book, *The Lazy Man's Way to Riches,* in one draft and without corrections. It just poured out of his mind onto a sheet of paper. And it was one of the few ads he ever wrote.

Some copywriters will tell you that they just sit down and start writing. Some find that sitting in front of a computer does the trick and others need something mechanical like a pen and a pad of paper.

My greatest ads were written during a variety of circumstances. Many were well thought out before I put the first word to paper and they flowed out with hardly a correction. Other times they would flow but you wouldn't recognize the first draft from the last because of the number of corrections I made. Sometimes I would sit in an airplane and just write from takeoff to landing and come up with great copy. And other times, I used my computer with great success.

It's All a Mental Process

The bottom line for all these approaches is that copywriting is primarily the mental process of first getting your thoughts organized in your mind and then eventually transferring them onto paper. There is no best method—just what works for you.

But the best place to start, without question, is to start. That's right. Pick up a piece of paper and a pen, and start. Do enough of it over a long enough period of time and I guarantee you, you'll improve each year. Write articles for a local newspaper. I started writing for my high school paper. It gave me experience and confidence. Write letters, write postcards—just plain write every opportunity you can.

I look over my very first JS&A direct response ads and can't believe I wrote them. They were horrible. But I matured and I learned with each ad I wrote. In my first ads, I used clichés— "It's the product the world has been waiting for." And my sentences weren't flowing as they do now. Sheer volume and experience will do wonders. As they say to anybody wanting to make it to Carnegie Hall, "Practice, practice, practice."

Don't Worry about the First Draft

Another fact to realize about writing copy is that the first draft of an ad is often terrible and the real skill in copywriting is taking that rough draft and polishing it. You might add words, delete entire sentences, change the order of sentences or even paragraphs. It's all part of the copywriting process. I often pointed out to my students that if everybody in the class were given the assignment of writing a draft of an ad for a product, the first draft of my ad would quite likely be terrible compared to everybody else's. It is what I do with the copy after my first draft that really makes the difference.

In that first draft the goal is to put something—anything— on paper, the emotional outpouring of everything you are trying to convey about your product or service. Don't worry about how it reads. Just get it down onto something you can work with like a computer screen or a piece of paper and then go from there.

To define exactly what copywriting is, I often presented the following axiom:

Axiom 1

Copywriting is a mental process the successful execution of which reflects the sum total of all your experiences, your specific knowledge and your ability to mentally process that information and transfer it onto a sheet of paper for the purpose of selling a product or service.

And in this book you will learn some of the valuable techniques to use to expand your knowledge of the copywriting process so you can write copy that motivates people to take an action—specifically to take their hard-earned money and exchange it for your product or service.

Copywriting is the key to any successful direct marketing venture. You can have the world's best product or service, but if you can't communicate your ideas, you have nothing. I will give you the skills and insights you need to successfully write copy. I've already personally taken the most expensive course ever. If you would add up my failures and their cost to me, add the insights I received mostly from my failures, and then add the experiences I've had in copywriting and marketing, you would see that it has indeed been an expensive education. And you're about to share in it.

Chapter 4 | The Purpose of All the Graphic Elements of an Ad

You are now ready to start to learn the techniques I use to write copy. You already understand the importance of having a broad general knowledge. This takes time and is a lifelong quest. And you understand the importance of obtaining specific knowledge on a project you are working on. This I hope is quite clear from Chapter 2.

But what you are about to learn in this chapter and the chapters that follow is the specific knowledge you will need to understand my copywriting approach and to become a top copywriter.

In these chapters, I will present several axioms. Each one will be in bold type and each one is critical to your understanding of my philosophy. The axiom presented in this chapter is very important and very difficult to believe at first. Understand this concept, believe in it and it will give you a good foundation for your future writing skills. Don't believe in it and you'll fall into the trap that many copywriters typically fall into.

To introduce the concept, let's look at the CB radio ad on the next page, which ran from 1975 through 1977. The ad has all the elements you would expect any space ad to have. And to understand this first axiom, I would ask my students to define the purpose of each element in an advertisement. The following is what we finally decided:

1. Headline: To get your attention and draw you to the subheadline.

2. Subheadline: To give you more information and further explain the attention-getting headline.

3. Photo or Drawing: To get your attention and to illustrate the product more fully.

4. Caption: To describe the photo or drawing. An important element and one that is often read.

5. Copy: To convey the main selling message for your product or service.

Headline

Subheadline

Paragraph
Heading

Photos
& Drawings

Captions

Copy

Price

Logo

Response Device

Pocket CB

New integrated circuit technology and a major electronic breakthrough brings you the world's smallest citizens band transceiver.

SMALL ENOUGH FOR YOUR POCKET

Scientists have produced a personal communications system so small that it can easily fit in your pocket. It's called the PocketCom and it replaces larger units that cost considerably more.

MANY PERSONAL USES

An executive can now talk anywhere with anybody in his office, his factory or job site. The housewife can find her children at a busy shopping center. The motorist can signal for help in an emergency. The salesman, the construction foreman, the traveler, the sportsman, the hobbyist—everybody can use the PocketCom—as a pager, an intercom, a telephone or even a security device.

LONG RANGE COMMUNICATIONS

The PocketCom's range is limited only by its 100 milliwatt power and the number of metal objects between units or from a few blocks in the city to several miles on a lake. Its receiver is so sensitive, that signals several miles away can be picked up from stronger citizens band base or mobile stations.

VERY SIMPLE OPERATION

To use the PocketCom simply turn it on, extend the antenna, press a button to transmit, and release it to listen. And no FCC license is required to operate it. The PocketCom has two channels—channel 14 and an optional second channel. To use the second channel, plug in one of the 22 other citizens band crystals and slide the channel selector to the second position. Crystals for the second channel cost $7.95 and can be ordered after receipt of your unit.

The PocketCom components are equivalent to 112 transistors whereas most comparable units contain only twelve.

A MAJOR BREAKTHROUGH

The PocketCom's small size results from a breakthrough in the solid state device that made the pocket calculator a reality. Mega scientists took 112 transistors, integrated them on a micro silicon wafer and produced the world's first transceiver linear integrated circuit. This major breakthrough not only reduced the size of radio components but improved their dependability and performance. A large and expensive walkie talkie costing several hundred dollars might have only 12 transistors compared to 112 in the Mega PocketCom.

BEEP-TONE PAGING SYSTEM

You can page another PocketCom user within close range, by simply pressing the PocketCom's call button which produces a beep tone on the other unit if it has been left in the standby mode. In the standby mode the unit is silent and can be kept on for weeks without draining the batteries.

SUPERIOR FEATURES

Just check the advanced PocketCom features now possible through this new circuit breakthrough: 1) Incoming signals are amplified several million times compared to only 100,000 times on comparable conventional systems. 2) Even with a 60 decibel difference in signal strength, the unit's automatic gain control will bring up each incoming signal to a maximum uniform level. 3) A high squelch sensitivity (0.7 microvolts) permits noiseless operation without squelching weak signals. 4) Harmonic distortion is so low that it far exceeds EIA (Electronic Industries Association) standards whereas most comparable systems don't even meet EIA specification. 5) The receiver has better than one microvolt sensitivity.

The PocketCom measures approximately ¾" x 1½" x 5½" and easily fits into your shirt pocket. The unit can be used as a personal communications link for business or pleasure.

PocketCom should give you years of trouble-free service, however, should service ever be required, simply slip your 5 ounce Pocket-Com into its handy mailer and send it to Mega's prompt national service by mail center. It is just that easy.

EXTRA LONG BATTERY LIFE

The PocketCom has a light emitting diode low-battery indicator that tells you when your 'N' cell batteries require replacement. The integrated circuit requires such low power that the two batteries, with average use, will last weeks without running down.

EXECUTIVES POLICE MOTORISTS

SHOPPERS HIKERS FOREMEN

The PocketCom can be used as a pager, an intercom, a telephone or even a security device.

MULTIPLEX INTERCOM

Many businesses can use the PocketCom as a multiplex intercom. Each employee carries a unit tuned to a different channel. A stronger citizens band base station with 23 channels is used to page each PocketCom. The results: an inexpensive and flexible multiplex intercom system for large construction sites, factories, offices, or farms.

NATIONAL SERVICE

The PocketCom is manufactured exclusively for JS&A by Mega Corporation. JS&A is America's largest supplier of space age products and Mega Corporation is a leading manufacturer of innovative personal communication systems—further assurance that your modest investment is well protected. The

GIVE IT A REAL WORKOUT

Remember the first time you saw a pocket calculator? It probably seemed unbelievable. The PocketCom may also seem unbelievable so we give you the opportunity to personally examine one without obligation. Order only two units on a trial basis. Then really test them. Test the range, the sensitivity, the convenience. Test them under your everyday conditions and compare the PocketCom with larger units that sell for several hundred dollars.

After you are absolutely convinced that the PocketCom is indeed that advanced product breakthrough, order your additional units, crystals or accessories on a priority basis as one of our established customers. If, however, the PocketCom does not suit your particular requirements perfectly, then return your units within ten days after receipt for a prompt and courteous refund. You cannot lose. Here is your opportunity to test an advanced space-age product at absolutely no risk.

A COMPLETE PACKAGE

Each PocketCom comes complete with mercury batteries, high performance Channel 14 crystals for one channel, complete instructions, and a 90 day parts and labor warranty. To order by mail, simply mail your check for $39.95 per unit (or $79.90 for two) plus $2.50 per order for postage, insurance and handling to the address shown below. (Illinois residents add 5% sales tax). But don't delay.

Personal communications is the future of communications. Join the revolution. Order your PocketComs at no obligation today.

$39⁹⁵ NATIONAL INTRODUCTORY PRICE

JS&A NATIONAL SALES GROUP

DEPT. PS JS&A Plaza
Northbrook, Illinois 60062
CALL TOLL-FREE .. 800 325-6400
In Missouri call.... 800 323-6400
© JS&A Group, Inc. 1976

September, 1975

6. Paragraph Headings: To break up the copy into chunks, thereby making the copy look less imposing.

7. Logo: To display the name of the company selling the product.

8. Price: To let the reader know what the product or service costs. The price could be in large type or could be buried in the copy.

9. Response Device: To give the reader a way to respond to the ad, by using the coupon, toll-free number or ordering information, usually near the end of the ad.

10. Overall Layout: To provide the overall appearance for the ad, by using effective graphic design for the other elements.

After they clearly understood each of the elements that comprise a direct response ad, I then told the class that there is a singular purpose for all the elements in an ad—a purpose so important that it constitutes one of the essential concepts in my approach to copy.

When you were first attracted to the ad you might have looked at the photo at the top of the page or the other photos. You might have then read the headline, read the subheadline and then glanced down to the name of the company selling the product. You may have read the captions to both the pictures and the sketches and you may have noticed the toll-free number indicating that you could order the product on the phone.

When you looked at the ad overall, you may have noticed the layout, the paragraph headings scattered about the layout and the attractive graphic and typographic presentation.

There are plenty of elements that can draw your attention before you start reading the copy. But one of the most important axioms you will learn for becoming a great copywriter is my second axiom. Here it is:

Axiom 2

All the elements in an advertisement are primarily designed to do one thing and one thing only: get you to read the first sentence of the copy.

At this point, there was usually a confused look on the faces of my students. They thought that each of these elements had its own reason for existence. But I was saying, "No, they are there strictly for the sole purpose of getting you to read the first sentence."

I know what you're thinking. "What about the headline? Isn't it supposed to have a ben-

Each element should lead you to the first sentence.

efit, be 16 words long and what about . . ." Stop. Just accept my word at this point that each element has a single purpose and that is to get you to read the first sentence. Don't question me. Don't jump to any conclusions. Just remember this axiom.

This means if somebody asks you, "With the Sugarman approach to copywriting, what is the purpose of the subheadline in the ad?" don't answer, "A subheadline is designed to give you more information and to further explain the attention-getting headline."

Neither of the above reasons is as important as the fact that the subheadline is designed to get the reader to read the copy.

If somebody asked you for the main purpose of the logo in an advertisement, you could answer, "to establish the corporate integrity of the company selling the product," or you could answer, "to provide a degree of continuity." But the real answer is to get you to read the copy. Really.

If you don't believe it, have patience and I will prove it to you. But if you'll open your mind and just accept what I tell you, you will eventually realize that what I am saying is correct. Most importantly though, when you realize this and start writing with this in the back of your mind, you'll be amazed at the change in your results. But like I said, just take my word for it now and let me prove it to you later in this book.

Chapter 5 | The First Sentence

If the purpose of all the elements in an ad is therefore to get you to read the copy, then what we are really talking about is reading the first sentence, aren't we? What does this tell you about the first sentence? Pretty important, isn't it? And if the first sentence is pretty important, what do you hope that the person who looks at your ad does? Read it, of course. If the reader doesn't read your very first sentence, chances are that he or she won't read your second sentence.

Now if the first sentence is so important, what can you do to make it so compelling to read, so simple, and so interesting that your readers—every one of them—will read it in its entirety? The answer: Make it short.

If you look at many typical JS&A ads, you'll notice that all of my first sentences are so short they almost aren't sentences. Some typical ones might be as follows:

> Losing weight is not easy.
> It's you against a computer.
> It's easy.
> It had to happen.
> Hats off to IBM.

Each sentence is so short and easy to read that your reader starts to read your copy almost as if being sucked into it. Think about the analogy of a locomotive. When the locomotive starts to chug from a standing start, it really works hard. The amount of commitment and energy that the train must exert is monumental. But once the train starts to move, the next few feet become easier and the next few even easier. So it is with copy.

Magazines Use This Technique

Many magazines use a variation of this technique in their articles. They start an article not with a very short sentence but maybe with very large type. Once they have you sucked into reading the copy and you turn the page to read the rest of the article, you notice that the typeface has gotten smaller. But that's OK. The purpose of the large type was to get you into the article and it worked. Now it's up to the author to keep you reading and turning the pages.

In an advertisement, you've got a lot going against you unless the readers are genuinely interested in your product. And if they are, then you've got to really grab and keep them. So your first sentence should be very compelling by virtue of its short length and ease of reading. No long multi-syllable words. Keep it short, sweet and almost incomplete so that the reader has to read the next sentence.

If all the elements are designed to get you to read the first sentence in an ad, then what is the purpose of the first sentence? If you guessed, "convey a benefit or explain a feature," impossible. How could a short first sentence do anything more than get you to read it? The correct answer is, of course, "The purpose of the first sentence is to get you to read the second sentence." Nothing more, nothing less. You probably figured this one out already anyway.

The Purpose of the Next Sentence

Now if you're starting to get a feel for my approach to copywriting and I asked you what the purpose of the second sentence is and you answered, "to get you to read the third sentence," you would be absolutely correct. And for those of you who missed that last answer and I asked you what the purpose of the third sentence was and you answered, "to get you to read the fourth sentence," congratulations. I think you've got it.

Was there any mention of benefits? Or product description? Or unique features? Of course not. The only purpose of those first few sentences in an advertisement is to get you to read the following sentences. True, you may at one point have to start talking about product features or benefits, but if you lose sight of the fact that your sole purpose at the beginning of an ad is to hold that reader's attention at almost any cost, then you may lose your reader for lack of interest. Therefore we have the third axiom:

Axiom 3   *The sole purpose of the first sentence in an advertisement is to get you to read the second sentence.*

Just compare the situation in our ad example with a sales-person selling somebody face-to-face. If the first few minutes of the sales presentation put the prospective customer to sleep or if the customer stops hearing the presentation and walks away, that salesperson has lost everything. So in copywriting as in selling, if your reader is not riveted to every word you write in the first few sentences, then your chances of having that reader get to the real sales pitch are very remote.

My most successful ads have followed this format, with very few exceptions. What about making the sales pitch at the beginning of an ad? This is certainly possible, of course, but then it is often not very effective. I've tried putting the sales message at the beginning of an ad. I've tried using every trick in the book to prove my theory wrong and have failed at each attempt. Just remember that the sole purpose of all the elements of an ad is to get you to read the first sentence. Make that first sentence so easy to read that your reader is almost compelled to read it. If you grasp this, you've got an awfully good start and a great under-standing of copywriting and the persuasive process.

Chapter 6 | Creating the Perfect Buying Environment

Besides holding the reader's attention, there is another important function we are trying to accomplish in the first paragraphs of an advertisement and that is to create a buying environment. Let me cite an example.

Picture this. You're a salesperson and you need to sell a prospect. You've been given a choice of environments in which to meet the prospect, and you must pick one.

The product you are selling is very expensive and you'll need at least one hour to explain and properly sell the product. The choices you have are as follows:

1. At noon at a very fancy restaurant near the prospect's office.
2. After lunch in the board room at the offices of the prospect.
3. After work at the prospect's health club while working out with him.
4. In the evening with the prospect at his home while the prospect baby-sits for his three children.
5. Any of the four above might be an acceptable choice.

The correct answer is 5. Why? Because the correct answer to the question "Which is the best location?" is simply "in the best selling environment for what you have to sell."

If the product is a piece of exercise equipment, the health club might be perfect. If the product has something to do with parents and children, at home with the prospect and his children in the evening might be the perfect environment.

Now if the correct answer for the salesperson is "in the environment best suited for the selling activity," it is true in print advertising too. Yes, but let me cite another example before we discuss print advertising environments.

The Honolulu Experience

I was in Honolulu after a trip to the Far East. I usually stop at Honolulu to recover after traveling so long and so far and over so many time zones. As I was walking down one of the main streets in Waikiki, I stopped to look into an art gallery and saw a painting of scenes from outer space.

Since JS&A was known for selling space-age products, I thought that the painting would fit very nicely in my office. I walked into the gallery noticing how very elegant it looked and saw the paintings neatly displayed on the wall. The gallery looked like it sold expensive paintings. In short, I expected the prices to be high.

It didn't take too long before a well-dressed saleswoman noticed me, walked over and asked if I needed assistance. "Beautiful painting, isn't it?" she asked.

"Very nice," I nodded. "It really looks great."

At that point the lady said, "Please follow me," as she lifted the painting off the wall and walked towards the back of the large gallery. I followed.

We entered a large room, carpeted from floor to ceiling. In the middle of the room were three very comfortable easy chairs all facing the front of the room where the saleslady mounted the painting on the wall. She then went back to the entrance of the room, turned up the classical music being piped in through loud-speakers and dimmed the lights leaving two spotlights focused on the painting.

Painting Looked Incredible

I must admit that the painting looked incredible. The vibrant colors, the quality of the art, and the nice feeling I experienced from hearing the classical music put me in such a buying mood that I was ready to reach into my pocket and pull out my credit card and buy the $2,000 painting.

That lady and that gallery had put me in such a focused buy-ing mood by creating the perfect environment for selling me that painting that I almost bought it right there and then. By the way, I eventually sponsored the artist, Mark Rickerson, and sold his paintings and prints through JS&A. I personally ended up with 50 of his paintings.

Once you realize the importance of setting up a buying envi-ronment, you'll know that it must be done in the early stages of an advertisement. When you establish the reading momentum at the

*Your copy has
to put the
prospect into a
relaxed buying
environment.*

start of an ad, you also want to start establishing the buying environment as well. The saleslady first had to get me into the store and then slowly get me in that room to put me in the ideal buying mood. If this all sounds hard to do in print, it really isn't. You'll see examples later of how to establish the buying environment as you establish the momentum.

Since you are creating your own environment in a print ad, you have total control over its appearance. Common sense will dictate the rest.

For example, if I was selling products at a discount, I would use big type for my prices and lots of busy graphic elements. In short, I would make the ad look like a typical discount ad. And conversely, if I was selling something expensive, I would present myself in an environment that showed class and refinement—that exuded confidence and trust.

Unlike the salesperson who may or may not be able to create the ideal selling environment, you can create your own. And unlike the salesperson who sometimes can't control the environment, you can.

So for selling products through Battram Galleries, the collectibles company I formed, my graphic and copy approach was upscale and conservative—just what you'd expect from an expensive gallery. However, when I presented my Consumers Hero concept, a club that sold refurbished bargains, it had a totally different environment—one that was clearly bargain-oriented.

The JS&A ads all had a uniform, well-organized format that seemed to be the perfect environment for all my space-age electronic products. I rarely deviated from it, but when I did, it was to create a better environment for a specific product I was selling.

You wouldn't expect to buy an expensive painting from an Army surplus store and you wouldn't expect to find much of a bargain at Tiffany's.

You Control the Environment

As a writer of direct marketing, you have control over the environment. The environment you choose is created in both the graphic elements and the copy, but especially the copy—by the way you phrase your words, the choice of words and the level of integrity you convey.

Unlike a store where you spend thousands of dollars to create an environment, you can do it all simply in the copy of your ad.

The environment is critical in getting a prospective customer into the buying mood. And to create that environment, you attract the customer's attention (the headline, photos, logo, etc.) and then you've got to get the person to read the first sentence by making it so simple and so compelling that the reader cannot help but read it. And the next sentence and then the next.

And while the reader is reading, you are creating an environment just as surely as that art gallery was drawing me into that back room. So now we are ready for the fourth axiom.

Axiom 4

Your ad layout and the first few paragraphs of your ad must create the buying environment most conducive to the sale of your product or service.

Creating the ideal buying environment comes from experience and the specific knowledge you get from studying your product and potential customer. It comes from understanding the nature of your product or service. Greater understanding will come as you read this book. But for now, realize how important creating the buying environment is to eventually selling your product.

To understand how we get the reader not only to read, but to feel comfortable and be in a buying mood in that environment, let's take time out for a little lesson on personal sales ability in general, in the next chapter.

Chapter 7 | Resonating with the Reader

When I was only 20 years old, my father sent me to New York City to run the branch office of his printing equipment company, Consolidated International. He was having financial difficulties and I was happy to help him out since I wasn't getting as much out of college as I had hoped. I dropped out of college and while in New York, too young to sell his expensive equipment, I took an interest in salesmanship. I knew that he expected me to eventually help him sell his equipment, so I set out to prepare myself.

I went to bookstores and bought everything I could on selling. I read every book available at the public library—all to become an expert in salesmanship. And during that year in New York I would stroll down Broadway and visit small auction shops located right on Times Square.

Wonderful Sales Technique

These small auction shops would prey on unsuspecting observers by appealing to their greed. The shop's proprietor would auction off what appeared to be terrific bargains, hook one of the prospective bidders in the audience and create a buying frenzy that plenty of the onlookers would get sucked into. The bidders ended up buying junk that wasn't much of a bargain. The sales techniques were wonderful to watch and I spent hours just observing them and human nature.

Then I would go back to my small apartment and read more books on selling. It wasn't easy for a young, inexperienced 20-year-old to sell expensive and complicated printing equipment. I thought that if I could become an expert on selling in general and printing equipment in particular and then, through experience, pick up specific knowledge about selling the equipment, I could be an effective salesman for my dad.

Selling was something I was suited for. In the preference tests I took in high school, I had the highest score in a category called "persuasion" and another high score in "literary." My career in advertising could have been predicted even back in high school, for when you think about it, print advertising is nothing more than "literary persuasion."

Some of the really significant lessons I learned in New York were the steps in selling a prospect, which also apply to selling in print advertising. Let me review the procedure.

The first thing you do in selling is to set up the selling environment. Whether it be a private room in a gallery or a car dealer's showroom, you configure the physical environment to be your selling environment.

Next, you have to get the attention of the prospect. That certainly makes sense and is related to the headline of a print ad.

Once you have the prospect's attention, the next step is to introduce yourself and say something that will keep the attention of the prospect. This is similar to the subheadline and the photos and captions. Then comes the sales pitch or the copy in a print ad.

During this activity, the seller has two thoughts in mind. The first is that the buyer must like and develop confidence in the seller. The buyer must believe that the seller knows his product. Secondly, the seller must somehow relate the product to the buyer and the buyer's needs. That's clear. But the buyer and the seller must literally vibrate together. There must be a harmony struck in both the buyer and seller, or the persuasive sales message won't come through.

There are many methods for creating this harmony and two of the most important apply very directly to space advertising. First, you've got to get the prospective reader to start saying yes. Second, you've got to make statements that are both honest and believable. Let's cite an example. A car salesman says, "Nice day, Mr. Jones." Mr. Jones then answers, "Yes." (It is a nice day, the statement is truthful and the customer answers in the affirmative.)

"I see, Mr. Jones, that you keep your car very clean." "Yes, I do." (At this point, the salesman has Mr. Jones saying yes and

NOW THAT YOU LIKE OUR PRODUCT, HOW ABOUT **ORDERING** IT?

YEP!... YEP!... YEP!

Get the customer to nod in the affirmative and agree with you.

*Get your reader
to say "Yes."*

nodding his head.) "I see, Mr. Jones, that since you now own a Buick and we sell Buicks, you probably could use a new one?" "Yes." (The salesman asks a rather obvious question and Mr. Jones, nodding, replies in the affirmative.)

"May I show you one of our latest models with improvements over the model you currently own?" "Yes." (The salesman once again says the obvious to get a yes answer and the harmony continues.)

In short, you try to get the customer to nod his head in the affirmative and agree with you, or at the least, you make truthful statements which the prospect knows are correct and would concur with. Make sure that the prospect does not disagree with something you're saying. If for example the salesman said, "Could you use a new Buick?" and the customer said "No," the sale would have taken a bad turn right there and the harmony would have been lost. In a print ad, the reader would have stopped reading and turned the page.

Harmony Is the Key

The moment you get the reader to say "No" or even "I really don't believe what he is saying" or "I don't think that relates to me," you've lost the reader. But as long as the reader keeps saying yes or believes what you are saying is correct and continues to stay interested, you are going to be harmonizing with the reader and you and the reader will be walking down that path towards that beautiful room in the art gallery.

To show you a specific approach to this method, let's take an example from an ad I wrote for one of my seminar participants. Entitled "Food Crunch," it offered dehydrated survival food. On occasion, when one of my students wrote a good ad that did not succeed, I would help him or her by either suggesting minor copy changes or sometimes rewriting the entire ad myself if I felt I had a better overall concept. The first ad, by John Sauer, was written right after our major fuel crunch in 1973, when there were lines of cars at gas pumps that had little or no fuel to pump. The ad is shown on the next page with my ad above it. John chose the concept of insurance as the best approach in his ad. I

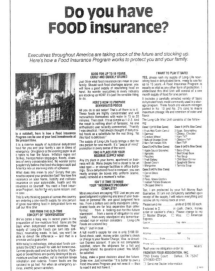

Which ad would you read first right after the fuel crunch?

felt that insurance put people to sleep. See if you agree with the copy statements in my ad as I tie in the then current feelings of helplessness during the fuel shortage with John's product.

We all take our food supply for granted. And for good reason. Americans have always had plenty. But we may be heading for one of the most serious periods in our history. Let me explain.

The ad then goes on to explain the writer's firsthand experience of arriving at a supermarket right after the news of the Kennedy assassination only to discover that the shelves were bare and that people in time of distress or calamity think first of their own survival.

Notice that the reader's attention was riveted. The headline, "Food Crunch," and subheadline, "We've all experienced the fuel shortage and most of us were unprepared. Will you be prepared for the food crunch?" caused us to read the first sentence. The first sentence was short and the typical American who could afford this offer would nod his or her head in the affirmative. The sentences were both interesting and true and caused the reader to start nodding his or her head.

So now we have three things we are trying to do at the beginning of an ad. First we want the reader to read the copy. Remember, that's the objective of all copy. Without the prospect reading the ad, you have nothing.

Then we create the type of environment through copy that causes the prospect to feel comfortable in exchanging his or her hard-earned money for your product or service. And finally, we want the prospect to harmonize with us—to agree with us—by feeling that indeed we are saying something that is truthful, interesting and informative and that the prospect can agree with. In short, we want agreement. We want that head to nod in the affirmative. We want harmony.

Easy Reach

If you think you're reaching all of your prospects, think again.

This is the ad that Cycle *magazine created as a sales tool to harmonize with JS&A and convince us to buy.*

Look what *Cycle* magazine did to create the perfect harmony with me when they tried to get me to buy media in their magazine. They created a knockoff of my ad format and sent it to me with a copy style that resembled mine. Of course it could have backfired if I was upset that they were copying me, but they also knew that I would quickly recognize the format and the effort they were making to land me as a customer and that I would respect their creativity. Indeed I harmonized with their effort and bought some space in their magazine.

Another illustration of this concept is in the ad I wrote trying to appeal to bargain hunters for a company called Consumers Hero. After a few sentences the copy read as follows:

Consumers are being robbed. Inflation is stealing our purchasing power. Our dollars are shrinking in value. The poor average consumer is plundered, robbed and stepped on.

If you were a consumer looking for bargains when inflation was skyrocketing, during the years when I wrote this, you would very likely be in harmony after that brief paragraph. I used words that the consumer could relate to. I spoke in the consumer's language.

I once had a top-producing salesman say to me, "Joe, I really admire you. I can sell anybody on a one-to-one basis. Put me up against the toughest customers and I'll melt them down and sell them. But you have the ability to do that on a scale that dwarfs mine. When you sell, you manage to duplicate yourself and sell millions of people all at the same time."

And that's what is so incredible about selling in print. You can duplicate yourself on billions of pages. You've got to be able to reproduce a selling job in print that will harmonize with the consumer, and then you've got the essence of a powerful tool that will bring you rewards for the rest of your life in all forms of communication whether they be in print or on TV or in any of the new electronic media of the future.

So our fifth axiom is simply:

Axiom 5

Get the reader to say yes and harmonize with your accurate and truthful statements while reading your copy.

Now you have the basis for another very important principle in writing effective copy.

By now you have learned several very important points about copywriting. First, you learned that you have, in your life, experienced general knowledge through your actions, circumstances and personality. You have also been given the tools to obtain specific knowledge, such as the ability to inquire, read and research. Then you learned that practice is a great teacher—that the more you write, the better you get. And finally you learned that copywriting is the mental process of transferring what is in your head onto a sheet of paper.

Every element must be so compelling that you find yourself falling down a slippery slide unable to stop until you reach the end.

Then we got into the pure Sugarman stuff. We learned what most people think elements like the headline and captions do for a typical ad. And then we learned what I believe their primary purpose is: to get the reader to read the first sentence.

And if you remember, we said that the sole purpose of the first sentence is to get prospects to read the second sentence and that the sole purpose of the second sentence is to get them to read the third and then the fourth—all while you are building a selling environment for the sale of your product.

We also compared the selling process in print to what a live and in-person salesperson does. You learned that ideally, as your reader starts reading your copy, you get the reader to start nodding in agreement with everything you say.

So now the reader is reading your first few sentences, is feeling comfortable in the environment you have created and is nodding in agreement. Now comes the critical part called the "slippery slide."

Picture a steep slide at a playground. Now picture somebody putting baby oil or grease along the entire length of the slide including the side rails. Picture yourself now climbing up the ladder, sitting at the top of the slide and then letting gravity force you down the slide.

As you start to slide down and build momentum, you try holding on to the sides to stop, but you can't stop. You continue to slide down the slide despite all your efforts to prevent your descent. This is the way your copy must flow.

Every element in an advertisement must cause that slippery slide effect. The headline must be so powerful and compelling that you must read the subheadline, and the subheadline must be so powerful that you are compelled to read the first sentence, and the first sentence must be so easy to read and so compelling that you must read the next sentence and so on, straight through the entire copy to the end.

The Force of "Reading Gravity"

I once received a letter from a reader of *Scientific American* magazine in response to one of our ads on thermostats. The lady who sent me the typewritten letter told me that she had no need for a thermostat, was not interested in the subject, rarely reads advertisements and when she does, she just scans through them. But, she went on, "I am a busy scientist. When I started reading your ad, I wasted five minutes of my valuable time reading the entire thing and I was so upset at the complete waste of my time, that I wanted to write you and complain." As a copywriter, I couldn't have gotten a more complimentary complaint letter.

If you can get the majority of the people who scan a magazine to read your ad, maybe you won't sell every one of them but you will sell a good percentage. Creating the slippery slide will cause people to "traffic" your ad—to go through the entire text of your ad and then decide if they want to buy.

'Traffic' is a good word in retail selling. Any shopping center that can draw increased traffic will have increased sales for its stores. But the traffic generated by these stores can only be compared to the people who actually read your copy. That's why some of the greatest magazines with the largest circulations do not guarantee the success of your advertisement. Traffic is strictly the number of people who get into your copy. When I say "get into," I mean falling down the slippery slide all the way through to the end of your copy.

Creating the slippery slide effect is not that difficult once the reader is well into your copy. In fact, it's been proven that if a reader reads over 25% of your ad, there is a great probability that he or she will read the entire ad. So once you've grabbed your reader at the start of your ad with your perfect environment and once they're reading your compelling first sentence, you've got them started down the slippery slide.

Slippery Slide Examples

Let's look at a few examples of the use of the slippery slide in some of the advertising I've written through the years. I referred to the thermostat ad above, so let's start with that. The copy starts out with the following headline, subheadline and first two paragraphs:

> **Headline:** Magic Baloney
>
> **Subheadline:** You'll love the way we hated the Magic Stat thermostat until an amazing thing happened.
>
> **Picture Caption:** It had no digital readout, an ugly case and a stupid name. It almost made us sick.
>
> **Copy:** You're probably expecting our typical sales pitch, but get ready for a shock. For instead of trying to tell you what a great product the Magic Stat thermostat is, we're going to tear it apart. Unmercifully.
>
> When we first saw the Magic Stat, we took one look at the name and went, "Yuck." We took one look at the plastic case and said, "How cheap looking." And when we looked for the digital readout, it had none. So before the salesman even showed us how it worked, we were totally turned off.

Now if you're reading the above ad, you're starting down the slippery slide unable to stop. You might find yourself reading the copy even though you have no intention of buying a thermostat by mail. You're curious. What's the gimmick?

The environment was set by the very clean layout. The tone of the ad was one of a flip, sarcastic and skeptical company exploring the possibility of selling a product that we were not very impressed with.

Of course the rest of the ad told of how we discovered a few nice points and then a few more and then some really great features and finally decided that this was one great product. At the end of the ad, we finished with:

Beauty is only skin deep and a name doesn't really mean that much. But we sure wish those guys at Magic Stat would have named their unit something more impressive. Maybe something like Twinkle Temp.

That single ad ran for over three years and not only generated large volume for us but propelled the Magic Stat people to become one of the major thermostat contenders nationwide. Finally, after three years of promoting their product, I received a call from the owner of the company thanking me for the wonderful sales and awareness we created for him. "Had it not been for JS&A, the company would have never even gotten off the ground."

"And by the way," he added, "we just sold our company for $20 million to Honeywell. From now on, you'll be dealing with their national sales manager."

It was this small incident that planted the seeds for the creation of BluBlocker Corporation—the sunglass company that I launched along with the help of my operations manager, Mary Stanke. After helping companies such as Magic Stat for the past several years, I thought it was time to launch my own product through my own company instead of everybody else's products through their companies. Our first BluBlocker ad appears later in this book in Chapter 33.

Another example of the slippery slide theory is in my ad for a company I started that sold bargains, called Consumers Hero.

Picture yourself scanning through a magazine and coming across the following copy:

> **Headline:** HOT
>
> **Subheadline:** A new consumer concept lets you buy stolen merchandise if you're willing to take a risk.
>
> **Highlighted copy block:** Impossible-to-trace Guarantee—We guarantee that our stolen products will look like brand new merchandise without any trace of previous brand identification or ownership.

Well, if you're like most readers, you had to start reading the copy. How could you help but not?

> **Copy:** We developed an exciting new consumer marketing concept. It's called "stealing." That's right, stealing!

Now if that sounds bad, look at the facts. Consumers are being robbed. Inflation is stealing our purchasing power. Our dollars are shrinking in value. The poor average consumer is plundered, robbed and stepped on.

So the poor consumer tries to strike back. First, he forms consumer groups. He lobbies in Washington. He fights price increases. He looks for value.

So we developed our new concept around value. Our idea was to steal from the rich companies and give to the poor consumer, save our environment and maybe, if we're lucky, make a buck.

I then went into the concept, which was our plan to take defective merchandise, repair it and then make it available to the consumers through a club that cost $5 to join. Newsletters were sent to members offering the products. One of the paragraphs near the end of the ad summed it up beautifully:

So that's our concept. We recycle "lousy rotten" garbage into super new products with five-year warranties. We steal from the rich manufacturers and give to the poor consumer. We work hard and make a glorious profit.

The above two ad examples are but a few of the many I've written through the years that illustrate the slippery slide theory. Once you start reading the headline, which forces you eventually down to the first sentence, you are in my slide. And then I take you all the way to the bottom of that slide so before you know it, you've read the entire ad. You've been in my store, you entered and didn't get out until you fully examined the merchandise I offered you. I took you into my private room and gave you a demonstration of my product in an environment that was so compelling, you couldn't help but buy. And I did it with integrity and honesty while getting you to nod your head as I sold you.

That's what the slippery slide is all about. Getting your reader to read all of the copy. So a major axiom of mine is simply:

Axiom 6   *Your readers should be so compelled to read your copy that they cannot stop reading until they read all of it as if sliding down a slippery slide.*

As we explained above, one of the most important elements in creating the slippery slide is the start of your ad copy. I often will start my copy with a story or even pick up a piece of news from a magazine that I feel would be of interest to my readers. The story is often offbeat, always interesting and a great short story.

A good example of this technique is the story about a trusted accountant who was caught embezzling money from his company. Here's the copy I wrote based on that article and the very unusual connection I made to the product I was selling:

Headline: Last Wish

Subheadline: He was a prisoner confined to a cell block. "Give him one last wish," pleaded his wife.

Copy: George Johnson is in a state penitentiary for a white-collar crime. His seven-year sentence gives him plenty of time to exercise.

Johnson, 36 years old, always took care of himself. He exercised regularly, ate good food and took vitamins. But he got greedy. As a company accountant he kept issuing bogus checks to "Cashin Electric Company" for electrical contracting work.

One day his boss noticed the large payments being made to the Cashin Electric Company and discovered that the outfit didn't exist. Johnson was actually typing out checks to "Cash," cashing them himself and then after the checks cleared the bank and were returned to his company, he carefully typed on the checks "in Electric Company" after the word Cash." Since he was a trusted accountant, who would suspect?

WIFE MORE SYMPATHETIC

His wife was more sympathetic than was the judge. She wanted to help her husband and suggested he pick an exercise product for his cell—something that was easy to store and could give him a complete workout. And the prison agreed. Johnson chose a Precor precision rower. Here's why.

I then described the Precor rower and how beneficial it was for your entire body, how it stored easily out of the way and why George selected the product for his primary exercise device.

Later in the ad I admitted the liberty I had taken with the story out of frustration. The copy ended with the following:

Before I tell you which rower Johnson selected, I have a confession to make. I love the Precor line of rowers so much that I probably committed a crime too. The story about Cashin Electric Company is true. Some trusted accountant was sent to prison. But his name wasn't Johnson and his wife never called JS&A to order a thing, let alone a rower.

But one night, while I was trying my hardest to figure out a new way to share my enthusiasm for the Precor rowers, I started getting a little silly and concocted this dumb story about Johnson and his interest in the rower. Copywriting is not easy and sometimes you go a little bonkers.

I then finished the ad with a selection of rowers and my usual close. In this case the offbeat article about Cashin Electric Company had nothing to do with the product I was offering but it created a very strong beginning for my slippery slide.

The news item could have nothing to do with your product or it could tie in perfectly. For example, I was reading *Forbes* magazine and in their "Forbes Informer" section, there was an article entitled "Growth Market." The copy read as follows:

> It looks like U.S. underwear manufacturers have overlooked a potential growth market. According to a survey of 1,000 adult Brits conducted by London-based Survey Research Associates, one in ten British men wears the same underpants two or three days running. One in a hundred wears the same pair all week. Half the women polled said they kept wearing underwear after it went gray with age.

I would cut out articles just like the one above and keep a collection of them. And then when appropriate, I would use one of them to begin an ad that somewhat related to the news item.

For example, I was in England appearing on QVC, the TV home shopping network. QVC has a branch office in England and I often appeared on TV selling my products there. While in the lounge waiting to go on the air, I met a man who showed me a new product he was presenting called "Scrub Balls." They were simply nine golfball-sized spheres that you put in your washing machine with your laundry. They sloshed around scrubbing the clothes to bring out more dirt and make the clothes cleaner and whiter. They also saved on detergent and made your clothes cleaner while using less water. If I were marketing that product in print, I might pull out that *Forbes* article and start my ad with something like the following:

> **Headline:** British Men Have Underwear Problem
> **Subheadline:** New survey shows that many British men do not change their underwear for up to three days. Some even as long as a week.

Copy: Holy Odor Eaters! Has Britain got a problem. It seems that the men in Britain don't change their underwear often and the survey mentioned above shows that many men change their underwear just once a week. But there's an important question I'd like to ask you.

How often do you change yours? If you're like most Americans, you change them every day. And as an American, you probably use more detergent than most Britains. But there is one more surprise that you may not realize either. Americans have a serious waste problem. Let me explain.

I would then go on to explain how we waste our resources by not efficiently washing our clothes and that there was this product I discovered in England called Scrub Balls and how efficiently it cleaned your clothes with less water and laundry detergent.

I could also use the same article to sell an electronic product simply by saying:

Now you probably wonder what dirty British underwear has to do with this new pocket-sized computer. I'm glad you asked. It has nothing to do with it except for one important fact which I will reveal shortly. But first let me explain an unimportant fact.

I would then go into the computer features, playing off British men, and I would use odor or smell to relate to some of the computer features. I would then come up with a computer feature at the end of the ad that would tie into the story.

Save Those Articles

I realize that it may seem a little far-fetched to sell a rower tied into an embezzlement story or a computer using that *Forbes* article on British underwear habits. But the point I am making is simply this: The use of an interesting article or bit of information, when tied into your product or service, often makes for a good start to the slippery slide. And when blended nicely with your product, it can work to cause a reader to read every bit of your copy. So save those offbeat articles you come across that tweak your interest

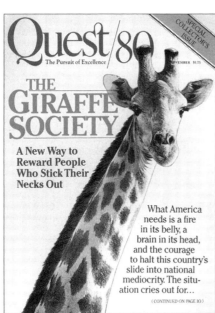

Quest magazine started their feature story on the cover to hook the readers and get them interested.

and might interest your readers—regardless of how ridiculous or offbeat they may be.

Some magazines create the slippery slide by simply starting out their stories with larger type to get you into the copy. Larger type is easier to read and so you tend to start reading the copy which may seem less imposing. *Quest/80* magazine (no longer around) started the copy of an article on the front cover and then continued it inside the magazine to get you into their slippery slide. Many articles written for magazines use similar graphic elements to get you into their stories. Of course, the key is to make the copy so compelling that once you start reading it, you can't put it down. And there are even more techniques to create the slippery slide which I will cover later in this book.

You're now in store for some fun. For in the next few chapters, I'm going to stretch your imagination and then continue to build the foundation we've been building in Section One of this book. So stay with me as we cover the timely topic of Assumed Constraints.

Chapter 9 | Assumed Constraints

Have you ever looked at a circus elephant anchored to the ground? If you have, you might notice that the elephant has a metal collar around its leg to which is attached a small chain. And the small chain is attached to a small wooden peg driven into the ground. Pretty good protection?

Pretty lousy, if you ask me. That 12,000-pound elephant could very easily pick up its foot and with one fell swoop, yank the peg out of the ground and walk away. But the elephant doesn't. Why? I'll explain.

When that elephant was still a baby, that same collar and chain and peg were used to hold the elephant in place. The restraint was sufficient to hold the baby elephant in place even if it wanted to break away. And break away is indeed what the baby elephant tried to do.

So every day while the baby was chained up, it would pull at the chain and pull and pull until finally a cut appeared on its leg exposing the sore sensitive layers of deep skin tissue. It hurt to pull like that and soon the baby elephant, realizing the effort was both futile and painful, stopped trying to escape.

Elephants Never Forget

As the baby elephant grew older, it never forgot that bad experience with the chain and the peg. And so whenever it was anchored down in a spot, it would think, "Hey, it's impossible to break away and besides, it hurts."

The large elephant had what I call an "assumed constraint." And all of us have the same problem to one degree or another. We all have the power to be great copywriters. But at one point in our lives, we may have written something and gotten a bad grade in English. Or we may have attempted to communicate something in writing to somebody else and had a bad experience as a result. As we've grown older, those hurt feelings, the feelings of inadequacy and the wrong guidance we may have received from teachers or friends are still in our subconscious and whether we want to admit it or not, they really do affect us.

If you understand the hurt and you understand some of the constraints we put upon ourselves, then you are better able to cope with breaking out of those assumed constraints and becoming anything you want to be and accomplishing anything you want to accomplish. Let me cite some examples.

One of the best is the following nine-point puzzle. I gave this puzzle to my students as an example of an assumed constraint. The rules to solve this puzzle are very simple. You must draw four straight lines and connect all the points without taking your pen off the page. In short, all the lines have to be connected. Please do the puzzle before reading on.

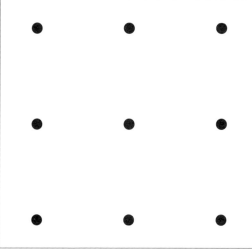

See if you can connect the dots in this puzzle with four straight lines without taking your pen off the paper.

Most people who try to solve the puzzle make one fatal error and it is simply that they don't realize the constraint they subconsciously put upon themselves. The solution is in Appendix A on page 263. Turn to it now for the answer.

As you can see, you were constrained by the box surrounding the points and did not go out of the box in order to find the solution. Often, to solve that very important problem, you've got to go out of the problem area itself to find the answer.

A good example of assumed constraints was my choice of mailing lists for my first direct mailing when I sold the first pocket calculator by mail. I had to select 10 mailing lists for my 50,000-piece mailing and I picked eight good lists that made a lot of sense to me.

I selected engineers, accountants and surveyors for example. I selected wealthy people at their home addresses. I chose the mail order buyers from a certain catalog that sold similar products. But when it came to the last two lists, my list broker suggested the presidents of corporations with $20 million in sales or more.

I thought the idea really didn't make sense. I thought that the presidents of these companies would be so busy that more than likely they wouldn't even open their own mail and that some secretary would throw my mailing in the garbage. But I went along with the list broker and to my surprise, those lists he suggested turned out to be the best ones, while the others really pulled poorly.

I can point to hundreds of assumed constraint examples that I personally experienced:

1. "You can't sell your airplane for over $190,000." I sold it for $240,000 in ten days.

2. "You can't sell a $600 pinball game through the mail." We sold over 3,000 of them.

3. "Consumers will rip you off if you let them buy using their credit card over a toll-free line without having them sign anything." We launched toll-free order taking in the U.S. and were very successful with very few problems before everybody else caught on.

4. "This calculator isn't selling at all at retail. It's the biggest bomb in calculator history. How are you going to sell it via mail order?" We sold over 30,000 of them at $59.95.

5. "Who would buy sunglasses through the mail? People need to try them on first and besides, people buy different styles." We sold over 10 million pairs of the same style.

Or how about the following business examples of other historical assumed constraints:

1. "There is no reason anyone would want a computer in their home." This was said by Ken Olsen, president, chairman and founder of Digital Equipment Corp., in 1977.

2. "Computers in the future may weigh no more than 1.5 tons." This was quoted by *Popular Mechanics* magazine forecasting the relentless march of science in 1949.

3. "The concept is interesting and well-formed, but in order to earn better than a 'C,' the idea must be feasible." This was said by a Yale University management professor in response to Fred Smith's paper proposing reliable overnight delivery service. Smith then went on to found FedEx.

If you'd like to read more examples of assumed constraints, look in Appendix A, which lists other historical quotes.

You Never Really Know

I can give you dozens of examples from history and from our company or from friends, but my point is simple. You never really know what will work or what won't. If you believe in your idea, do it. Step out of those assumed constraints.

This concept also applies to coming up with marketing solutions too. When thinking about a problem or looking for a solution, don't rule anything out. Sometimes that big idea will come to you if you step out of the traps that we very often fall into. Remember de Bono's concept of lateral thinking, which is somewhat the opposite of assumed constraints. Step away from the problem, think of some possible situations that have nothing to do with the problem and guess what? You'll be amazed at how often you find a solution.

As you proceed in this book, remember the baby elephant and the nine-point puzzle and break out of those assumed constraints.

Axiom 7   *When trying to solve problems, don't assume constraints that aren't really there.*

Chapter 10 | Seeds of Curiosity

We have already learned that 'traffic' is a key word to any retailer. A shopping center that increases traffic will generally see an increase in sales for its stores. And since the traffic generated by these stores can only be compared to getting a prospect into your copy, you increase traffic by increasing readership.

One way to increase readership is by applying a theory I call "seeds of curiosity." It goes like this. At the end of a paragraph, I will often put a very short sentence that offers some reason for the reader to read the next paragraph. I use sentences such as:

> But there's more.
> So read on.
> But I didn't stop there.
> Let me explain.
> Now here comes the good part.

These seeds of curiosity cause you to subconsciously continue reading even though you might be at a point in the copy where the copy slows down. This concept is used a lot on TV before the show host goes to a commercial. She may say, "When we come back, we'll see something that you've never seen on TV before. Stay tuned." Well, it should be done in print too. And here's why. (Notice how I just used it.)

In print, the ideal situation is to create such interesting and compelling copy that you don't need the seeds of curiosity, but often that is very difficult. And using these seeds of curiosity enhances most copy. But like every good thing, don't overdo it. Later in this book I will be showing examples of seeds of curiosity at work in many of my ads. Use them; they are very effective. But there's another example.

Seeds of curiosity can be used at the beginning of an ad where you mention some benefit or payoff that you are going to reveal somewhere in your copy. In short, the reader has to read the entire ad to find it. A good example of this technique was in our Consumers Hero ad mentioned in Chapter 8. In that ad, you had to read the entire copy before you got to the punch line.

A great example of both seeds of curiosity and traffic is what happened to me at my office. It's something that I've quite frankly never experienced again but it is very relevant to this subject.

A Very Unusual Call

I received a call one day from a very sensuous sounding young woman who called herself Ginger. She started the conversation with: "Mr. Sugarman, I love you."

I was a little taken aback and at first thought that this was a practical joke. "Thank you," I responded. "I love you too."

"No, I'm serious," continued the woman. "I've been reading your advertisements for the past five years and I love your mind, I love your thought process and I love your creative personality. I really believe that I can tell a great deal about you from what you write and I really believe in you and truly love you."

I was surprised and then flattered. Even before I received her call, I had gotten comments from people who claimed that my personality really came through in my copy. And I believed it.

If you are dishonest, it is sensed by the reader. If you are hiding something about a product you are describing, it comes through. If you're very creative, it too is picked up. And it is the combination of all of these impressions that creates the buying environment that we referred to in Chapter 6.

If you study the copy of others, you can sense what they are like from their copy. You'll be amazed at how the copy reflects the personality of the person writing it. Any copywriter working for a CEO of a company will try and reflect the personality of the CEO and not him- or herself. Since I'm the guy who writes all the copy, you can pretty well tell a lot about my personality. But back to Ginger.

An Invitation I Couldn't Refuse

Was Ginger just flattering me or did she have an emotional attachment to me personally without having met me—strictly from reading my copy? She continued.

"Mr. Sugarman, you are the only one who could help me. I need your help. Please, may I have an appointment to see you, privately? I promise you that you'll be very glad to see me."

When she arrived at my office I could see what she meant when she said that I'd be glad to see her. She was a beautiful blonde with long legs and a miniskirt so short I was embarrassed to have her sit down. "Mr. Sugarman, may I call you Joe?"

"Sure," I replied, looking away as she adjusted her skirt.

"Joe, I want to be very frank with you. I have admired your copywriting for years. I'm not even into electronics and gadgets but I enjoy so much what you do in print that quite frankly I have a real emotional attachment to you. I know this sounds silly but when I got in trouble, I couldn't think of anybody else who could help me but you. I really need you."

She paused for a moment as if to hold back tears. She then continued.

"I run a beauty shop in a shopping center. I know that when the shopping center is full, I get a percentage of that traffic and they buy my cosmetics. I also know that when the shopping center is empty, I get a smaller number of people who come to my store. It's almost directly proportional to the traffic in the shopping center.

"So Joe, when I decided to offer my cosmetics in a direct mailing, I thought that if I sent out 50,000 mailing pieces, I would get a certain percentage of response and I would make a profit. All I needed was half a percent return rate to make a nice profit.

"I then invested all the money I had to get this 50,000-piece mailing out. I borrowed from my friends. When I launched the mailing, the results were so bad I couldn't believe it. I ended up with one-tenth of what I needed to break even. I need you to look over my mailing piece and just tell me what went wrong with it. And Joe, if you could help me get it to work, I'd be extremely grateful."

What Was Her Angle?

Was I being propositioned in return for my help? I wondered. Was this all a ploy or a guilt trip to get me to write her next mailing piece? I was a happily married man with two children and quite busy running my own business. And quite frankly, I didn't like the idea of somebody trying to use guilt or sex or anything else to entice me to write copy or do a mailing piece. Still somewhat reserved, I said, "Show me the mailing piece."

Ginger reached for her purse, which was on the floor, and as she reached, she exposed even more of her legs. I was convinced she was in my office to seduce me. No question about it now. I was convinced that she was determined to entice me into writing copy for her. But I wondered how far she would go. I was soon to find out.

She pulled out her mailing piece and handed it to me. I examined it for a few minutes, read the copy and studied the entire package. I also asked her which mailing list she used. "From the entire local area served by the beauty shop," she said.

I looked at the mailing and saw many problems. She was using a mail-in offer yet her mailing list was not oriented toward mail order buyers—just the retail community—so it was no wonder her mailing didn't work. Even the copy in the letter was very poorly written. It was a horrible presentation. It wasn't that it looked bad, but it violated many of the principles I discuss in this book and some that apply to direct mail. I told her the presentation was not very good and that I wasn't surprised that the piece did so badly.

You already know the principles on traffic. You already know from previous examples that unless the recipients read all of her copy, the mailing most likely won't work. Of course, she also used the wrong mailing list and that didn't help either.

I Explained the Problems

After I explained to Ginger the problems with her mailing piece and mailing list, I brought out another very important fact about direct response advertising. "You can't spend that kind of money without testing. That's one of your problems too. You just mailed to too big a list. You could have picked just 5,000 names and not 50,000 names for your mailing. And then you would have known if the mailing was successful without risking too much money."

I finished talking and there was a short pause. As she looked straight into my eyes, she said, "Can you help me? I mean really help me? Like write the copy for the mailing piece, help me pick the proper list and guide me as my mentor?"

Since I was a little turned off by Ginger's use of sex and guilt to get me to do her piece, I responded, "Ginger, I really don't have the time. Plus, I have established a seminar in the north woods of Wisconsin where I take 20 people and teach them as a group. I just don't have the time to help you on an individual basis."

A Shock I Never Expected

What Ginger whispered to
prise. In fact, there have been ?
have been at a complete loss f?
on copywriting and not about ...
doors of successful direct marketing ex...
ceived by beautiful cosmetic executives as the answ...
dreams. "Aw shucks," you're probably saying. "Why doesn't he
finish the damn story and tell us what happened."

OK, I will. But not here. I want you to continue uninter-
rupted with my thought process on copywriting, so I have
devoted Appendix B on page 265 to the rest of the story—an
episode that actually took place in my office and that could be
part of a very steamy novel.

Once you understand the concept of traffic in retailing and
how it relates to direct marketing, then you should realize how
important the slippery slide concept is in getting the reader to
read the entire text of your ad. And one of the most powerful
techniques to keep your slippery slide greased is the use of seeds
of curiosity. Your readers must get into your copy. They must
read your headline and be so compelled to read further that they
read your subheadline. Then they must be so moved that they
read your first sentence. And the rest of the copy must be so compelling that by the time your prospects read 50% of your ad, they
are helplessly caught in a slippery slide and can't escape.

Once you understand the slippery slide and the seeds of
curiosity, you will have two of the most powerful copywriting
tools you can use.

Axiom 8

*Keep the copy interesting and the reader interested through
the power of curiosity.*

Chapter 11 | Copy as Emotion

Up to now we have covered some general principles of copywriting. You learned that all the elements of an advertisement are designed to get prospects to read the first sentence and we showed you how to get them to start reading your copy by creating a very simple first sentence. And then we told you how important it is to get the second sentence read and the third and so forth. We mentioned nothing about benefits or features of a product because the sole purpose of the copy was to first get people to read the copy. The benefits come later.

And then we covered the environment you create at the beginning of your copy. We explained the importance of resonating with your reader by getting the reader to say yes, believe you or agree with your assumptions.

We expressed the importance of the reader slipping through your copy as if on a slippery slide—reading the copy so they can traffic your ad—and we gave the example of Ginger and her failed mailing. And we just showed you how seeds of curiosity work to keep the slippery slide fully greased.

Most of My Concept You've Learned

Armed with the above principles, you have a major portion of the overall philosophy of my copywriting concept. There are only a few more points to learn to have the complete foundation upon which you can build your skills and write great copy.

I can still remember the first seminar when I taught these same philosophies. At the end of the course, a Texas farmer named Frank Schultz locked himself in a room at the nearby Holiday Inn motel and, inspired by the seminar, wrote his first ad for the grapefruit he wanted to sell nationally in a print campaign in major magazines.

His very first space ad was so powerful that it sold more fruit than he could pick and ship. He received letters from other prominent copywriters congratulating him on his simple yet beautiful ad. We'll study that ad later, but if knowledge of the principles I teach can make a Texas farmer a great copywriter, it can do the same for you.

Emotion in Advertising

This chapter is about emotion in advertising. And there are just three points to remember about the subject.

Emotion Principle 1: Every word has an emotion associated with it and tells a story.

Emotion Principle 2: Every good ad is an emotional outpouring of words, feelings and impressions.

Emotion Principle 3: You sell on emotion, but you justify a purchase with logic.

Let's take the last point first. Why do you think people buy the Mercedes-Benz automobile in America? Is it because of the rack and pinion steering or the antilock braking system or the safety features? Other cars have the same features, so why spend a fortune to buy one when, for a fraction of the cost of a Mercedes, you can get an American or Japanese car or even a Volvo that has many of the exact same features?

The answer: We buy on emotion and justify with logic. I know that when I first bought a Mercedes and my friends saw it, I told them that the reason I bought it was because of a series of technical features that I found very impressive. The real reason I bought the car was not for the technical features at all. I wanted to own a prestigious car and belong to the crowd that drove a Mercedes. But when I had to explain the reason for my purchase, I ended up using logic—something that I really believed was correct when I used it.

Mercedes Advertising

Look at a Mercedes ad. Since the Mercedes advertising agency knows the real motivation behind the purchase of their cars, they focus on the reasons people use to justify their purchase. All their ads talk about the terrific drive you get or the technical features that make the car a breed apart. In reality, feature by feature, there is nothing so revolutionary that it can't be duplicated in a less expensive car. The car is sold by virtue of its emotional appeal and then justified in its advertising by an appeal to logic.

Look at the emotion of a message conveyed in the form of a song. The music is like the vibration or that special harmony that you work at creating in an advertising message. If the music appeals to the audience and their soul, they are really set up to receive the sales message—or in the case of a song, the words, which incidentally also have an attached emotion. A song is similar to an advertisement.

Take a song and say the words without the music and it may sound rather funny. Steve Allen back in the '50s on *The Tonight Show* would recite the words of a number one hit song and get lots of laughs reciting, "Ooh pappa doo pappa doo pappa woo. I love you. Ooh pappa doo da ditty." Without the music, the words sounded absolutely ridiculous.

Logic Often Doesn't Work

In writing copy for an advertisement, often you get your reader in an emotional frame of mind as a result of the environment you have created, and logic becomes less important. For example, I've always used the phrase near the end of my ads, "If you aren't absolutely satisfied, return your product within 30 days *for a prompt and courteous refund.*" Who ever heard of a refund being courteous? It doesn't matter. The emotion or the feel of that phrase really says that we are a very respectful and understanding company that will return your money very promptly. With very few words, I conveyed the feeling of being a concerned company that acts promptly. And even though the phrase makes no logical sense, it has been picked up by several direct marketers and used in their catalogs and print ads.

Often, a phrase or sentence or even a premise does not have to be correct logically. As long as it conveys the message emotionally, it not only does the job, but does it more effectively than the logical message.

A good example of this was an ad I wrote for a device that had a breakthrough digital calculator display. The new display showed both alphabetical and numeric characters. And because it had such a large memory, you could use it to hold the phone numbers of your friends along with their names.

At the time I had two competitors who got hold of the product first and came out with advertisements—both of which failed. There were several reasons they failed, but one of the main reasons was the way they pitched the product—on a logical level. They tried to explain what the term 'alphanumeric' meant in a display and how much memory the unit had. The ad was filled with facts and logic and because it was such a new break-through product, you would think it would sell just based on logic. It didn't.

On a lark, I decided to sell a similar product myself in my catalog. Canon Corporation had approached me and told me that if I took their product, they would give me an exclusive for sev-eral months as long as I advertised it nationally.

I first tested the ad in my catalog and came up with the head-line "Pocket Yellow Pages" with the subheadline being "Let your fingers do the walking with America's first pocket yellow pages." Now listen to the emotional version of the copy.

> You're stuck. You're at a phone booth trying to find a phone num-ber, and people are waiting. You feel the pressure.
>
> To the startled eyes of those around you, you pull out your calcu-lator, press a few buttons, and presto—the phone number appears on the display of your calculator. A dream? Absolutely not.

The Emotional Approach

The ad was a terrific success. We eventually placed the ad in dozens of magazines and while the other competitors dropped out, we succeeded handsomely. But look at the emotional approach I used. There is nothing about the product's technical advantages, nothing about the powerful memory of the unit. I just knew the nature of the product and the person buying this prod-uct. Each product has an inherent nature, and understanding that inherent nature will help you sell it. (I explained this partially when I talked about the Midex burglar alarm and the insurance salesman in Chapter 2, "Specific Knowledge," and will explain it in more detail later.) I realized that the product would appeal to the gadget-motivated person who would want to show it off to his or her friends. The ad copy reflects this specific knowledge.

Later on in the ad I justified the purchase with the facts and the technology but not too deeply. The real motivation for people to buy this product was the emotional appeal of the sales message.

I was invited once to speak at New York University to a class on direct marketing. As I addressed all the students on copywriting,

I told them that if I was handed a product, showed it to the class and told the class to write an ad on the product, I would venture to say that everyone in the class would write a better ad than I would. I said, "Your grammar would be correct, your spelling would be perfect and mine would be just horrible."

What Comes after the First Draft Is What Counts

But it is what I do after that first draft that makes my copy successful compared to the rest of the class. I then went on to explain the editing process and its importance. But the reason, I explained, for my ad appearing so poorly written in my first draft is because it is simply an emotional outpouring of my thoughts on the product and how I feel it should be sold. It is a free release of my emotions.

And as you write copy, keep this in mind. It makes absolutely no difference what your first draft looks like. If you can get all your feelings and emotions about the subject out on paper and work from there, you will have mastered a very important technique.

The final point on the emotion of copy relates to words themselves. If you realize that each word has an emotion attached to it—almost like a short story unto itself—then you will also have a very good understanding of what emotion means in the copywriting process.

Look at a dictionary not as a collection of words but as a collection of short stories. Webster once was quoted as saying that if you took every one of his possessions away and left him with just his words, he'd get all his possessions back. The power of words is enormous.

Words Have Strong Emotions Attached

What emotions do you feel when I mention the following words: Cleveland, rip-off, consumer, farmer, lawyer, Soviet? Cleveland may have evoked a little laughter as a place you might not consider moving to unless you live in Cleveland, and if you do live there, please accept my apologies. Cleveland is a very nice city. But every country has a famous city that everybody makes fun of. The Russian comedian Yakov Smirnoff once said that in Russia they also have one city that the Russian comedians make fun of. He says it too is Cleveland.

And then what do words like 'consumer' and 'rip-off' make you feel? The word 'farmer' may not only remind you of what he does for a living but also bring to mind words like 'honesty', 'integrity', 'earthy', 'hard-working'. Think of all the feelings the word 'farmer' conjures up, not only from your experience but from what you feel emotionally. The word 'Soviet' sounds more sinister to me than 'Russian'. What thoughts come to mind with the word 'lawyer'?

When you analyze these words and see how you can use them to create a message that has emotional impact, then you have mastered an important lesson in writing copy.

Here's some copy I wrote that points out the emotional differences in copy. Which sounds better?

Example 1: The old woman in the motel.
Example 2: The little old lady in the cottage.

I was writing an ad on some rubbing oil I had discovered in Hawaii and describing how I had discovered it. Example 1 was in my first draft but example 2 sounded much better.

I'm not suggesting that you materially change the facts of a situation to suit an emotional feeling. In the above case, the motel office was in a small cottage, and the word 'cottage' gave the copy a better emotional feel. What do you think? Do you "feel" the difference?

Sometimes changing a single word will increase response in an ad. John Caples, the legendary direct marketer, changed the word 'repair' to the word 'fix' and saw a 20% increase in response.

Don't feel that you have to have a total command of the emotional impact of words to be a great copywriter. It takes testing and common sense more than anything else. And knowing the emotional feel of words is like your general knowledge—it comes with time. It is enough for now that you realize the importance of the emotional values in every word. As time goes on, you will feel this influence play a bigger and bigger role in your successful copywriting.

Chapter 12 | Selling the Concept, Not the Product

Let's discuss one of the most important and basic copywriting principles I teach. In fact, if you can understand and learn this single point, you will have mastered a major lesson in writing good advertising copy.

Axiom 9

Never sell a product or service. Always sell a concept.

What do I mean by 'concept'? There are many words that mean the same thing. One day, for example, the hot buzzword in advertising might be 'positioning'. A product is positioned or placed in such a way as to appeal to the consumer.

Other terms commonly used are 'Big Idea', or 'USP' (unique selling proposition), maybe even 'gimmick'. Whatever it's called, it means basically the same thing. You sell the sizzle and not the steak—the concept and not the product.

The only exception to this rule is when the product is so unique or new that the product itself becomes the concept. Take the digital watch for example. When the watches first came out, I could hardly keep them in stock. When I first announced them, my main thrust was to explain the various features, which were all new, and then just take orders.

But as the digital watches became plentiful and everybody understood what they did and how they worked, each ad had to differentiate the features of the watch through a unique concept. For example, the world's thinnest digital watch or one with a built-in alarm or one with the most expensive band, or the one with the finest quality, or even one that required a laser beam in its manufacturing process—all were different concepts. Concepts started selling watches; the product was no longer the concept.

Another example is the Pocket CB. It had its concept right there in the headline. There were walkie-talkies and there were mobile CB units, but we had the first Pocket CB. And it was the name itself that expressed the concept.

In fact, I remember receiving a personal call from Marlon

Brando. He wanted more information on the Pocket CB and was only about five miles away in the Chicago suburb of Libertyville where his sister had a farm. "Pick one up for free, if you'd like," I said. "I think our staff would really appreciate meeting you." But Brando wanted his privacy and never showed up.

Or take the example of the Pocket Yellow Pages I referred to in the previous chapter. Doesn't that name express everything you really need to know about the product in a simple concept? In that ad I didn't sell the product, but rather the concept of standing in a phone booth and pulling out an electronic directory to the surprise and delight of those around you.

Another example was a smoke detector I was selling. Instead of selling it as a smoke detector, the headline screamed, "Nose"—a product that just sat on your ceiling and sniffed the air. It sold quite well.

Combining Products into Concepts

Sometimes the concept naturally comes from the product and other times the concept can be created. I remember once running several products in my catalog without much copy and discovering two that sold quite well. Rather than run them as separate products in full-page ads, I decided to run them together in one full-page ad as a concept.

The two products were a miniature travel alarm and a chess computer. But rather than develop a concept for each, I wrote the headline "Winners" and told how both products were the top-selling products in our recent catalog. The headline put both products under a single concept and made them both winners while drawing attention to our catalog.

Sales continued briskly with the chess computer in 1978 when I received a call from the company in Hong Kong from whom we were importing the product. "Joe," said my friend Peter Auge, the man in Hong Kong supplying me with the computer, "I think I can get Anatoli Karpov, the Soviet chess champion, to endorse our chess computer. I'm friends with him through a contact in Russia and it might make the chess computer sell better."

Indeed it would, I thought, but let's come up with a concept using Karpov—not as a person who will endorse the product but as somebody whom we can challenge to play our unit. And indeed, that's what we did. Our first major ad with Karpov's name appeared with the headline "Soviet Challenge."

> **Subheadline:** Can an American chess computer beat the Soviet chess champion? A confrontation between American space-age technology and a Soviet psychological weapon.
>
> **Copy:** The Soviet Union regards chess as a psychological weapon, not just a game. It is a symbol of Communism's cultural struggle with the West.
>
> So when Russian Anatoli Karpov competed against the Russian defector Victor Korchnoi, he had the entire Soviet Union's resources at his disposal, including a hypnotist and neuro-psychologist.
>
> Karpov won. And with it the world's undisputed chess championship. Karpov, however, has never confronted American space-age technology and in particular JS&A's new chess computer.

Of course the copy continued to talk about the challenge we were making against Karpov. That was the concept. We weren't selling chess computers. We were selling the challenge against the Russian champion and as a consequence selling chess computers. It was taking a very staid product and giving the entire promotion a more emotional appeal.

Then the ad went on to explain how the unit worked, its features and ended with the challenge to Karpov.

The ad had some pretty effective copy. And I've reproduced it in Appendix E at the end of the book. Read it. It's a lot of fun.

Soviet Intrigue

I was sitting in my office as the ad was breaking throughout the United States when I received an urgent telegram from overseas. Opening it up, I saw right away it was from Karpov. "I am going to sue you for using me in your advertising without permission." Signed: Anatoli Karpov.

I was told that I had permission to use his name by my friend Peter, who said, in fact, that he would be sending me the endorsement contract and that I should go ahead and run the ad. So I did, thinking all was OK.

What to do. Simple. I could just see my next headline: "Soviet Union Sues JS&A" or maybe "Little JS&A Attacked by Soviets." What a great concept. But before I could sit down and write it, my friend Peter called and advised me that he had gotten a copy of the telegram too and that everything had been worked out with Karpov's agent and there was nothing to worry about. Karpov would endorse the chess computer and I could continue my ad campaign.

I then sat down and wrote the third ad in the series, entitled "Karpov Accepts," which talked about the challenge made to Karpov and how he then decided that for whatever reason, he didn't want to play the chess computer as part of the challenge. Instead he could just endorse it and hope that many Americans would learn to improve their chess game on it.

Concept Selling Does Well

All three ads did very well and over 20,000 chess computers were sold. And all three had different concepts associated with them. Meanwhile, my competition was out there in force trying to sell their chess computers but not succeeding because they were selling chess computers and not Soviet Challenges and Karpov Accepts—all concept advertising.

If your advertising just sells the product, be careful. You need a concept. If you've come up with a unique concept, fantastic. You'll do much better.

Price Can Also Affect Concept

Sometimes simply changing the price of a product can dramatically alter its concept. For example, when we were offering our Pocket CB at $39.95 it came across as a serious electronic product similar to a full-sized CB radio. When we dropped the price to $29.95 it became more of a sophisticated walkie-talkie. And finally when we dropped the price to $19.95, the product was perceived as a toy—all this despite the fact that the copy in the ad was pretty much the same.

Finding the concept is often not easy. It takes all the skills of a conceptual thinker to come up with the right idea and the right position. One of my favorite advertisements that really captured the essence of this chapter was an ad I once read from the Leo Burnett ad agency. It was a full-page ad that appeared in *Advertising Age* magazine and is reproduced on the next page.

Tcudorp

The first job of an ad agency is to look at your product in every imaginable way: frontwards, backwards, sideways, upside down, inside out. Because somewhere, right there in the product itself, lies the drama that will sell it to people who want it.

There may be 10,000 ways to bring that inherent drama to the stage. And given a world in which "me-too" products multiply like mayflies, the drama may seem that much harder to find.

It is.

But every good product has it.

And every good agency finds it.

(Please note: The "t" in tcudorp is silent.)

It's so true. Every product has that unique selling proposition that makes it stand out from the rest. And it is indeed up to you, the copywriter, to realize this fact and discover each product's uniqueness. If you do, the simple positioning of a product and the developing of a concept can be so powerful that it can make the difference between a huge success and a loser.

In the next chapter, you'll discover how to come up with that great idea as we study the incubation process.

Chapter 13 | The Incubation Process

It's fine to read about the real secrets of copywriting but let's get serious. One of these days you're going to have to implement what you've learned and start writing copy. What are some of the mental steps required to write copy in general and how do you go about writing effective copy?

Let's establish a few things that you have learned already in this book and then take everything a step further. As you recall, I referred to general knowledge—the knowledge you have picked up simply by living—and specific knowledge—the knowledge you learned while studying the specific product you want to write copy about.

Assume you are now an expert on a particular product and you are ready to start writing. The first thing I would do is go over all the material you have on your subject and give a great deal of thought to what you have just read and studied. Do plenty of thinking about what you want to write. You may jot some headlines down and some of the copy points you would like to bring out. You might list those points which best describe the nature of the product you are selling and you might like to list some of the strong reasons that your product would appeal to your customers. Put all your thoughts down on paper. But keep in mind, you have not yet started to write the copy. This is just preparation.

Or don't put a thing on paper and just think through everything you know about the challenge you have to solve through copy.

You might even visualize the end result of your work. Maybe it's imagining that a stack of mail has arrived showing what a great response you received. Maybe it's your boss coming up to you and patting you on the back for a job well done. Once

I'M SORRY, MR. SUGARMAN CANNOT BE DISTURBED - HE'S INCUBATING RIGHT NOW.

Take a break from your work and do something pleasurable while your brain incubates.

you've done all that, do something that may seem strange to you at first. Stop.

That's right, stop. Go on and do something else. Forget about the project. Do something pleasurable—a stroll in the park, a walk down the street or lunch with a good friend. Whatever you do, let it be a total diversion from what you are currently working on, and please don't even think of the copy project.

Whether you realize it or not, you are actually working on the ad constantly even though you've put it out of your mind. Your subconscious mind is actually processing everything you've learned—all of that data that you have accumulated in general and all of the information in particular. And your mind is then taking all of that data and running it through everything you know about copywriting and communications, mentally preparing the first version of your ad copy.

It is taking this information and working through the millions of permutations possible to come up with the best solution to your marketing problem. And you're doing absolutely nothing about it. You're just out having a good time while your brain is working like crazy. And ironically, if you start thinking about your project again, it interrupts this process and the results won't be as good. This entire subconscious activity is called the incubation process, and the time you are giving to it is called the incubation period.

Your subconscious is processing millions of bits of data like a computer in your brain running a very important program in the background. Then, while you're taking a walk or standing in a shower or even daydreaming, suddenly that big idea will flash across your mind. Eureka. Then go to your desk and start writing down some of that good stuff your mind has created and organized for you.

Your Mind Is Always Working

Sure, you might think you can eliminate the incubation period. You never do. Even when the pressure of deadlines prevents me from taking the luxury of time to incubate, I'm still incubating but at a much more rapid speed. The results may not be as good, however. The time pressure only increases the incubation process and speeds up the assimilation of data in your brain. If you have the luxury, your copywriting and what you produce will improve if you balance the pressure of deadlines with time away from the project. This could also mean working on one project, then going to another and then coming back to the first one. This is another way of allowing you the luxury of having your subconscious mind work on a project while you do something else.

The incubation process actually works best with pressure. If you have no pressure, your brain will not work as fast or as efficiently. So it is a balance of various pressures that produces the optimum results.

What causes pressure? We already know that time causes pressure but there are other factors as well. Ego for example. If you have a big ego, it creates a certain amount of pressure. This pressure can be very positive in the incubation process. For example, your boss expects you to produce some knockout copy and your ego won't let you disappoint her. You've added to the incubation pressure. Your creative orientation plays a role too. For example, if you are naturally creative, you have a big advantage over someone who is not. And finally, the environment plays a role. If you are in a creative environment which encourages those incubation activities required in the creative process, it will help the incubation process along.

Just Allow It to Happen

Now don't show this chapter to your boss and say, "See, Joe Sugarman tells me to take a pleasurable walk in the park on company time and enjoy myself while my brain incubates." That's nonsense and not the purpose of this chapter. In this chapter, I just want you to realize that there is a constant process going on in the background of your brain. And with the proper balance, you can create blockbuster copy by allowing the incubation process to function.

The biggest mistake a manager can make in a mail order company is to have the creative department in the same building as any other department in the company. Imagine the operations people walking in to see the creative people incubating—staring into space or taking a long break with one of their peers. "Those privileged bastards in creative really get away with murder" would be a typical comment. But the creative department needs that atmosphere in order to function to its optimum.

If management imposed the same rules on the creative

department as on the rest of the staff who have to function on a conscious level during their jobs, the end result would be a sure drop in good creative work. It's important to keep the creative staff separate from the rest of a company because the copywriter needs a little more freedom to incubate and create.

When it comes time to sit down and knock out that copy, discipline comes into play. You've got to let that copy come pouring out of your brain, forgetting about spelling and grammar. Remember, your mind takes the data you've accumulated and runs it through everything you know about copywriting, communications and life in general. Well, hold back the stuff on spelling and grammar just long enough to let the copy flow out freely.

Left Brain vs. Right Brain

If you're knowledgeable about writing and creative thinking, you know that there has been much said about the different hemispheres of our brains controlling different types of thinking. The right brain does the intuitive or emotional thinking and the left brain does the logical. Which side of the brain should write the copy? The right brain of course. Let the copy flow out of that right brain and let it pour out unencumbered by any left-brain restraints.

The pouring out of that copy or idea is the culmination of the incubation process. It is the end result of all the mental activity that has been running in the background. And so, the axiom that I suggest you remember is as follows:

Axiom 10

The incubation process is the power of your subconscious mind to use all your knowledge and experiences to solve a specific problem, and its efficiency is dictated by time, creative orientation, environment and ego.

If you've gone through the incubation process and then put your thoughts on paper, you've accomplished half the challenge of writing good copy. Next comes the fun part—the editing process. We'll have to wait for that process in later chapters of this book. Now that you are mentally prepared to tackle the copywriting process, it's time to decide how much copy you should actually write.

Chapter 14 | How Much Copy Should You Write?

Incubate, slippery slide, seeds of curiosity—all may be neat concepts, but often at my seminars the question would come up: Do people read all the copy in your ads? Students of direct marketing learn that there is no such thing as copy that is too long. And there is some truth to this.

The key is simply this: Copy is never too long if the reader takes the action you request. Therefore, it can't be dull, it must be compelling, it must relate to the reader and, finally, it's got to be about something the reader is interested in.

What we're talking about here is the slippery slide concept. The copy must be so compelling that it will be read from the beginning to the end. Everything else is secondary. If you don't write compelling copy, you'll never get the reader to read the part of the copy that sells your product.

Will people read long copy? Let me answer the question in a different way by having you go through a little experiment. On the following lines I want you to fill in the blanks of a headline for an article as I direct you.

Headline:

_____ (Your Last Name) family chosen as heirs of multi-million-dollar fortune.

Family who lives on _____ (Your Street) in _____ (Your City) was willed millions of dollars by an anonymous person.

If you saw that headline in your local newspaper, would you read the first sentence? Of course you would. Let's say the copy read as follows:

Wow, what a score! How would you like to inherit millions of dollars from somebody you don't even know?

Well, that's what happened to _____ (Your Full Name), who has yet to be found but who might have fallen into one of the greatest fortunes ever received from somebody who remains unknown.

Of course you would read the entire 3,000-word article. After all, the article is talking about you. You are involved, you relate to what is being written in a very intense way and it's both informative and interesting, to you in particular.

And that's my point about long copy. If the copy does all the things I've just described, the reader will be intensely interested in it and will read it all—maybe not with the intensity of somebody who just won millions of dollars, but with an intensity that could come very close if your copy is effective.

Intense Interest

I'm writing this book on a Macintosh computer. A short time ago while I was mastering my word processing program and had an intense interest in this computer, I would read anything on the Macintosh. And I would read an entire article or advertisement if it was on the subject I was interested in. Later, as I mastered what I had to learn, the information was not as interesting to me and I did not seek it out with the same intensity.

BE WITH YOU IN A MINUTE, HONEY. I'M ALMOST FINISHED READING THIS JS&A AD IN MY MAGAZINE.

If the copy is interesting, the reader will read it all.

This is also true about products. When digital watches first appeared, my customers were very intense about buying them. And they bought them in droves. They read every word of my copy. It was informative, helpful, it involved them and they read the ads with interest. When the market for digital watches deteriorated and the fad was over, my customers were not as intense about the product category and went on to other things. Therefore readership dropped.

Copy will be read if it is interesting to the reader. I can remember when I would visit the car showrooms in the '50s looking at new cars with their huge tail fins and sleek new designs. Ads would talk about rack and pinion steering and I often wondered what that meant. All that the copy would do is go into the emotional feel of driving the car, which is good emotional copy but didn't really tell me enough. And when something doesn't tell you enough, it will cause you to go to the showroom and ask questions, which is maybe what the car companies want you to do.

But often the salesmen didn't know much either. Rack and pinion steering was foreign even to them.

I learned a lesson from those visits to car showrooms. You can't tell the prospect enough about a subject he or she is truly interested in. And so it is with copywriting. People will read with a high degree of intensity if you are talking about something they are genuinely or passionately interested in.

Long Enough but Short Enough

Back in the days when copywriters were mostly men, there was an old adage about copy length: "Copy is like a woman's skirt. It should be long enough to cover the essentials but short enough to make it interesting."

Let's use the same example of the salesperson visiting a prospect that we used earlier in this book on page 35. But this time, the salesperson appears for the appointment and the prospect explains that he can't meet for 45 minutes because he is in the middle of a budget session. Could the salesperson make the presentation in 15 minutes? What would you do?

A good salesperson would make a new appointment. If the sales presentation takes an hour, then it should be an hour long. Not more and not 15 minutes. And so it is with copy. Depending on how long your sales pitch is, the copy should cover the amount of time you need to create the selling environment, develop interest in the product, relate to the prospect's needs and make the sale.

The copy has to be long enough to tell the entire story or make the entire sales pitch. No longer and no shorter. Of course there are certain practical limits, but even these can be broken. When Gary Halbert, one of the great mail order copywriters, was looking for a girlfriend, he ran a full-page 3,000-word personal ad in a local Los Angeles newspaper. He was deluged with potential dates.

And when Richard DelGaudio wanted a personal assistant to help him run his fund-raising company, he ran a 4,000-word want ad that pulled in more qualified respondents than he was able to interview.

The Long-Copy Approach

There really is no limit to how long copy should be if you get results. For example, if a good salesperson made his or her pitch in 10 minutes and sold a prospect on purchasing a $19.95 household gadget and another salesperson selling a million-dollar high-speed printing press took several months to consummate a sale, then who would be the better salesperson? There is, of course, no answer. Both could be great or both could be lousy. Why then should there be such controversy over copy length? If, as I hope you believe by now, selling in print is very similar to selling in person, then shouldn't the same rules apply?

So let's take a moment and look at two factors that increase the need for a lot of copy.

Price Point: The higher the price point, the more copy required to justify the price or create the need. This is a general rule unless the price point is perceived to be a tremendous value (then less copy may be required) or the lower price point appears to lack credibility (then more copy is required). More copy will allow you to increase the value of a product and add many more dollars to your retail price. In short, by educating the consumer you can demand more money for your product.

Unusual Item: The more unusual the product, the more you need to relate that product to the user and the more you've got to focus on creating the buying environment and explaining the product's new features. At retail, generally, this type of item will not sell. Mail order is the perfect method to use when you have the right amount of copy.

In conclusion, there are two basic reasons for using the long-copy approach. The first is to allow you to create an environment that will place your prospect in the proper buying mood, and the second is to give you the time necessary to tell the full story of your product.

Short Copy Works Too

Robert Scott of Scottcade Ltd., an English mail order company, came to my seminar and told me that his approach broke all of my rules. His catalog copy was very short, yet he still sold a lot of merchandise.

But his catalog really appeared to follow my rules. First, he created his environment through photography. The products were placed in elegant settings using fine photography. Second, his prices were very low compared to other companies or retailers. Since he was offering his products at such low prices and since his environment was so effective in placing the customer in a buying mood, a lot of what normally would have been done in copy was being done visually and through the price points of his products. Then too, his medium was a catalog, and in catalogs long copy is often not required. The catalog creates the environment, thus saving you the time of creating it with copy.

I am not trying to sell you on using long copy. I use short copy at times and sometimes very short indeed. But the short copy I use is usually all that is required and the price points are low enough that the short copy does the job. In fact, I am not for long or short. I'm for causing the prospect to exchange his or her hard-earned money for your product or service, and quite frankly, copy length has always been just one of several considerations in producing an advertisement.

So the axiom to remember from this chapter is simply:

Axiom 11   *Copy should be long enough to cause the reader to take the action you request.*

Do people read all that copy? Some do. And there are enough of them who do to have earned me and several other copywriters a nice living.

Chapter 15 | The Art of Personal Communication

If you have read the chapters of this book in sequence, you are building a good foundation to understand and learn copywriting.

This chapter builds upon the knowledge that took me several years of copywriting to really understand and learn. Learning it wasn't difficult, but understanding why it was so important took a little longer.

One of the things that ads should do is harmonize with the reader or viewer. Advertising is the ultimate form of communication in that its purpose is to cause an action to be taken by consumers—usually to exchange their hard-earned money for a product or service. But for some reason, many advertisers are missing an important key in this form of communication—namely, it should be personal.

Every advertisement should be a personal message from the advertiser to the prospect.

As a good example of personal communications, let's first cover direct mail. In direct mail, personal communication is easy to understand. After all, you are writing a letter to a single individual.

But in creating the letter that goes with a mailing, too many copywriters write their letters as if they were hiding behind a podium, speaking through a microphone and addressing a large audience. For example:

> We at ABC Company wish to invite all of you to visit our exhibit again at the upcoming trade show. Our staff will be there to meet you and demonstrate our new and novel button machine.

The personal way of saying it might be:

> Hi. You might remember me from the last trade show. Well, I'd like to invite you to the next one where I will be looking forward to meeting you again to demonstrate our new and novel button machine.

You see the difference? The second version is more personal and direct. It is me talking to you—not me talking to a large crowd. It is as if I, as an individual, were writing that letter to another individual.

Now, in direct mail this makes sense. Why not make your letters more personal and direct—more like one person talking to another in a direct and eyeball-to-eyeball sort of folksy way? Of course, folksy might not be the best way in certain circumstances. That's OK. As long as you use words like 'I', 'you' and 'me', you create the feel of a personal form of communication.

Emotional Process in Communication

Remember I said earlier that copywriting is an emotional outpouring of an idea onto paper. And I said that copywriting is very much an emotional process. Look at the following two letters from the same company and see how much more emotional one sounds than the other.

> Dear Customer: We here at Consolidated International would like to thank you for your recent order. We realize that you could have given your business to many of the other companies in our industry, but the fact that you chose Consolidated International is really appreciated by our entire staff. Thank you very much. Sincerely, Mr. John Smith.

Now compare it to the following:

> Dear Mr. Jones: I just wanted to thank you personally for your recent order, which I've just received. I took your order and even showed it to the president of our company. I realize that you had a number of other choices, but I really appreciate the fact that you chose my company. Sincerely, John Lee.

Both letters would have served the same purpose. But the second letter was warmer, more personal and you felt that Mr. Lee was talking to you directly. Indeed, he was happy to get your order—so happy that he went to his president and showed it to him. It was a genuine expression of thanks and a direct message—all with genuine emotion.

On the other hand, the letter from Mr. Smith could have been a form letter that the company sends to all its customers, thereby losing the personal feeling that Mr. Lee's letter had. It lacked the warmth and personal touch. The difference should be obvious. Read both letters again, and this time feel the difference. Put yourself in the place of Mr. Jones and imagine how he would have felt if he had received both letters.

Letters Should Be Personal

Good examples of a personal letter were the letters I used to send out to a membership program in my Consumers Hero club. They may have been totally off the wall, but they served my purposes well.

The membership program was created in response to our advertisement for our discount club in which we refurbished new but defective products and then sold them, at discount prices, through a club we established.

Part of the club program was our regular monthly bulletin. It listed all the buys for that month and along with it came a very folksy letter talking about the club.

The image I conveyed was not that of a very large, impersonal corporation filling the needs of its membership but that of a bunch of hard-working people, of all ethnic backgrounds, working together in harmony to make the company a success.

The company had to be portrayed as being small. That was essential for the concept. After all, that was part of the image— a little consumer-oriented company fighting the big U.S. corporations and the effects of inflation.

And one of the techniques we used to keep the image of a small company was to use old envelopes from companies that had gone out of business. We simply explained that the envelopes were no longer good and it was our way of saving money as well as the environment and passing the savings on to the consumer.

So in one month, members might get an envelope from Ski Lift International, a defunct company, and the next month they might get a letter from CMT Machine Tool Company, another defunct company, but the contents of the envelope were always from Consumers Hero.

As membership cards, we sent out Batman credit cards. (There is a whole story on that card, but that's for some other book I plan to write.) And one of the qualities we tried to convey was absolute total honesty. We were so honest that the reader would actually be embarrassed for us. The typical letter is on the following page.

Three JS&A Plaza, Northbrook, Ill. 60062   (312) 564-9000

Dear Member:

Enclosed are the latest bulletins on our Consumers Hero program.

Two new companies now join our group. The first is Panasonic and the second is McGraw Edison--both highly respected and well established companies.

We want to thank many of you for the very nice letters we receive about our efforts. We appreciate receiving those very much.

The other day, we received the following letter from a Mr. R. F. in Glastonburg, Ct. It read, "I am thoroughly disenchanted in your Consumers Hero gimmick. I sent in $5 in the hope that your offer would be worthwhile. To date I have received only one bulletin which offered rebuilt items for more than I would pay at most discount stores. If any item was less it was just plain junk. You did not live up to your promises. Therefore I am returning your silly Batman card and please return my $5."

I'm truly sorry that Mr. R. F. feels this way about our company. We are growing and we will be offering many more products from many more different companies but in the meantime we must work very hard to attract all these new offers that are finally starting to come our way. Please bear with us as we are trying our best. We try to insist that these manufacturers keep their prices as low as possible and we will continue to put pressure on them to make sure the bargains are truly great bargains. We think most of them are and although we disagree with Mr. R. F. we respect his opinion.

We are pleased to announce the addition of Dennis Delaney who joins our staff to assist us in stuffing envelopes. Dennis is a student at our local high school and is on the football team and has worked on the school paper. His hobbies are skin diving, waterskiing and photography.

It's rather difficult keeping our staff together. Betty Jane Williams has decided to move to Los Angeles with her boyfriend. She will be missed as she always added a bit of sunshine whenever she showed up for work.

In the next mailing we hope to add a few more bulletins from some new companies so thank you all very much for your patience and understanding. We even appreciate Mr. R. F.'s letter even if his letter was not very complimentary. We promise to continue to do our best.

Sincerely,

CONSUMERS HERO

Your Heros

Your Heros

Your Heros:
Cindy Donner   John Handmeister   Dennis Merrins   Burt Mertz
Allan Milnik   Doug Ramis   Toni Venturini   Dorothy Vinkowski
Dennis Delaney

The very down-to-earth and personal letter sent to Consumers Hero members.

Even though the letters were from the staff as opposed to an individual, they still conveyed a personal feel to the reader. And weren't they fun to read? We often got comments that the letters alone were worth the price of the membership.

In print ads, the need to be personal becomes less apparent. After all, you are talking to the masses, aren't you? But the fact remains that you are indeed talking to a single individual—that person reading your ad. And he or she is listening to a single individual—the person who wrote the ad. So it is essential that you write your copy as if you are writing to that single individual. Your copy should be very personal. From me to you. Period.

Use of a Byline

An effective way to do this in print is to use a byline. Use your name or the name of somebody in your organization such as the president—like the news organizations do in a magazine or newspaper article. This allows you to use words like 'I' and 'me' and 'we' and 'you'. Let's look at the example of the ad I first ran for BluBlocker sunglasses that launched a multi-million dollar company.

> **Headline:** Vision Breakthrough
> **Subheadline:** When I put on the pair of glasses what I saw I could not believe. Nor will you.
> **Byline:** By Joseph Sugarman
> **Copy:** I am about to tell you a true story. If you believe me, you will be well rewarded. If you don't believe me, I will make it worth your while to change your mind. Let me explain.

Read that personal copy. It's as if I were talking to that person directly. I used the words 'I' and 'you' and 'me'—all very personal words used in a one-to-one conversation. Let's examine the first paragraph of copy from a few other ads that were written in this personal tone.

> This may surprise you. In fact, if my hunches are correct simply reading this article may change your idea of aging for the rest of your life. Here's why.

Or how about the following:

> If I were to buy a ticket in the Illinois State Lottery, my chances of winning would be a million to one. But if I were to bet that you, as a reader of this publication, have high blood pressure and don't even know it, my chances of being correct would be eight to one.

The above paragraphs show how very personal you can get in copy and still convey a very powerful thought or develop the environment and slippery slide you need to cause your reader to continue reading and then respond.

When I started writing, I kept a low profile and never used my name in any advertising communications. But as I became more proficient and saw the effect a personal message could create in direct mail, I started using my byline in print on a regular basis. In my catalog, I could speak in the first person about all the products because on the first page of the catalog, I introduced myself in a letter to my customers.

Even Magazines Have Personalities

I remember reading a story about the image conveyed by the magazine itself. *Forbes* magazine has a strong personality. Steve Forbes now runs the publication and his editorials appear in every issue. A reader feels more personally involved with the publication. On the other hand, *Business Week* appears more like a corporate publication even though it has many bylines. A businesswoman once commented that she could put her arms around *Forbes* and hug the magazine but would only feel comfortable shaking *Business Week*'s hand. So it is with copywriting.

You want to create a very personal image so that people will emotionally respond to you, feel close and feel very comfortable taking their hard-earned money and buying your product or service.

Axiom 12

Every communication should be a personal one, from the writer to the recipient, regardless of the medium used.

So as you start to write copy to reach and motivate an individual, think in terms of writing in the first person with a personal message.

You are now ready to write that first ad. Everything you've read has prepared you for this moment and everything that you are going to learn later in this book will only polish what you already know. True, you're also going to get a whole bunch of new insights too. But right now you're ready for the big plunge. In the next chapter, we discuss writing your first ad using my techniques and thought processes.

Chapter 16 | The Copy Sequence

You are now really ready to write that first successful ad. You already know how important it is to know your subject. You already know the purpose of all the elements in an advertisement—to get the prospect to read the first sentence. And you know all the axioms to get the reader to read beyond the first sentence and all the way to your last word.

Copy must also flow. And its flow must make sense. It must be in an understandable order where each thought flows logically to the next.

I've had many people tell me that when a question comes into their minds as they read my ads, I answer it in the next sentence. They often claim that it's almost uncanny. But that's the skill that makes the good direct-response copywriter the envy of any one-on-one salesperson.

Leading the Reader

Since we copywriters do not have the benefit of having the prospect in front of us to ask the questions, we must craft our ads in such a manner that they literally lead our prospect (by the flow of the copy) to ask the question we want to answer. Sounds hard, doesn't it? It really isn't.

Start by writing the headline. Will it grab the reader? Then write the subheadline. Will it compel the reader to read further? Then write the caption to go under an imaginary picture. Is all this strong enough to get people to read the first sentence? And then write the first sentence.

Once you start using my thought process, you'll find a discipline and a direction that you might not have experienced in writing copy before.

You might even write a paragraph in the copy to stand out in boldface type similar to the Consumers Hero ad that reads:

Impossible-to-trace Guarantee—We guarantee that our stolen products will look like brand new merchandise without any trace of previous brand identification or ownership.

At my seminar, I would call on various students and ask them to read their headline. The class would then critique their headline to determine if it would get us all to read the subheadline. It was a good process with 18 students from all walks of life coming up with some of the most creative approaches on a variety of subjects.

One day, my eight-year-old daughter April was sitting in one of the chairs in the class. She was taking notes, listening intently and, in short, acting exactly like one of the students. I would always allow my children free access to the entire seminar process and they had never been a nuisance. In fact, the students liked this family touch.

April Becomes Real Nuisance

After I had assigned an ad-writing exercise and asked for volunteers to read their ads, April started waving her hand wildly. I called on a man from New Zealand—Archie Mason—who was in the wool business. Later, when I asked for another volunteer, April once again waved her hand wildly but I called on another student—Fred Simon, president of Omaha Steaks. Finally, April came up to me in front of the class and whispered, "Dad, let me read my ad. It's a good one. It follows your principles."

I was annoyed. "Later, April. Can't you see I'm trying to teach the class?"

Finally at break time, April came up to me and handed me her ad. I read it. It indeed was a good example of anticipating what a consumer would ask and then answering it. It was very simple—after all, an eight-year-old had written it—but it contained a question-and-answer format that was very logical and covered a topic of interest that her eight-year-old peers would enjoy reading. Her product was a guinea pig. The ad read:

> **Headline:** The Best Pet
> **Subheadline:** Do you want a pet that doesn't shed?
> **Copy:** Think about it. You can get a pet that doesn't shed, doesn't run around the house, and is easy to take care of.
> You have probably guessed it's a rabbit, bird, fish or a turtle. Well, you're wrong. It's a guinea pig.
> You probably want to know how do you take care of the guinea pig? Where should I keep it? What does it eat?

> It's all simple. If you don't have a guinea pig cage, then get a box high enough so it won't get out and large enough so it can run around.
>
> Feed it guinea pig pellets and feed it a couple fresh greens. Put plastic at the bottom and newspaper on top then at least an inch high of shavings. Put a bowl in for food and a water bottle for water.
>
> That's all you need to know. To order, call [phone number] and order today.

April's ad made an important point which I have reminded each class of since. Good copy can be written at any age and by anybody. Simply understanding the principles and applying them to something you intuitively know is all it takes.

Logical Progression of Flowchart

In class I would ask my students to write a headline and a subheadline. I would then ask for the first sentence. Then the next sentence and then the next until each student had composed a complete ad.

The ads had to flow on paper and then, once they were on paper, the editing process was of paramount importance. One of the tips I gave during this process was to create a block diagram of a logical way the copy should flow and the questions that might logically be asked.

In order to develop a sense for this, you break your ad into small abbreviated copy blocks similar to those in a corporate flowchart. But this flowchart goes in one direction only—down.

I made a block diagram of the ad I did for the Bally pinball game. I showed that at the start of the ad, I wanted to get my reader into the copy and then I wanted to set the environment for the product. So, I started the ad with the fun times that this product represented. The ad started like this:

> It's you against a computer. And the action and excitement from Fireball, your own computerized pinball machine, is nothing short of spectacular.
>
> Fireball's computer replaces many of the mechanical, scoring, conventional electronics and sensing devices of a standard pinball machine. It's a dramatic change in pinball devices and the start of a new consumer electronics revolution.

INTEREST
EXCITE-
MENT

DRAMA

WHY
DIFFERENT

HOW TO
PLAY

UNIQUE
FEATURES

JUSTIFY
PURCHASE

LASTING
PLAY
VALUE

SERVICE

ASK FOR
ORDER

The flowchart for copy sequence goes in one direction— down.

With the first paragraph I create *interest and excitement* for this product. With the second paragraph I start to weave the *drama* of the product and the differences between Fireball and conventional pinball games.

Then I go into the next block of copy and explain why and how the game is *different, how to play it* and some of the *unique features* made possible by the computerized electronics.

Logically, a reader who had read this far would want to know a little more about how the game was constructed, the quality of the product and the many new features. Therefore, the next block of copy has this information.

OK, you are really interested in purchasing this game. But you say to yourself, "How can I justify it? I'd love to get this Fireball game. Emotionally I'm hooked, but how can I justify purchasing it?"

So the next block should *justify the purchase.* I used cost comparisons with what you pay for a TV set, pool table or your stereo system. I plant the seed about its practicality when guests pop in and how Fireball will be the hit of any party or family gathering. It's here that I'm giving the prospect the logic he needs to make that emotional purchase. I even suggest that a business might purchase one as a way to entertain employees at work and claim it as an investment tax credit and depreciation expense— all tax-saving measures. I knew I had to provide all the logic possible for this $650 purchase.

By now the customer is saying to himself, "OK, I want to get the unit and I can justify the purchase, but what if I use it, get tired of it and it sits in the corner like that exercise device that's gathering dust?"

So I go into the fact that it has *lasting play value.* And I describe several reasons why he won't get tired of it.

The customer is now thinking to himself, "Hmm. I like the product, I can justify it and I can see that it will have lasting play value, but what if I buy this big pinball game and suddenly the computer poops out?" I then raise the *service* question in the ad copy and answer it. The point of each of these blocks of copy is that they are logically placed as if to anticipate the next question a prospect is going to ask—all in an environment that you have created and all flowing logically to the last part of the ad when you *ask for the order.*

Flowing in a Logical Sequence

When you work with copy long enough, the flow is automatic. You don't need to do flowcharts, as you can instinctively sense the next question and answer it. And that is the special skill that a good direct-response copywriter has over a one-on-one salesperson. We sense the questions, answer them—and we do it on a mass scale.

You still might find it helpful to create a block diagram of your ad after you've written it to see if it flows properly and raises the right question at the right time. How do you want to sequence your questions in your copy? What kind of environment do you want to weave through the early part of the text? What are some of the questions you would surely be asked about the product if you were a salesperson and you were selling the product face-to-face?

It's really all common sense. Looking at your copy as it flows out onto a computer screen or onto a piece of paper is the mechanical part of this process but not the important part. It's the common sense you use to anticipate the sequence of what will be asked next and how your copy should flow that really counts at this stage of the copywriting process. This brings up my next axiom.

Axiom 13

The ideas presented in your copy should flow in a logical fashion, anticipating your prospect's questions and answering them as if the questions were asked face-to-face.

By now you understand the basic concepts of good direct-marketing copywriting. You understand the importance of becoming an expert on the product you are going to write about. You know that the more you learn about a product or service, the greater the chances you'll come up with that unique copy angle or product position or big idea.

But there are some other tips I can give you that will help generate that concept you want to develop. First, state the problem. It might be as simple as "I want to sell this pinball game." Then, once you have stated the problem, restate it in a different way: "I would like to introduce my prospect to the unique aspects of this pinball game." Then restate it again: "I want to make the pinball machine easy to buy and seem like fun."

It's that last restatement that makes the pinball game seem to come alive and is closer to the copy approach I've actually used. During problem restatements (and you could list dozens of them), all the knowledge that you've learned about the product seems to come together to give a new perspective.

Prepare That Big Idea

Once you've restated your problem and you have the statement that you like best, sit down and list your big ideas or concepts. List several concepts. Then pick the one or two that make the most sense.

Visualize your concept and see how it might be incorporated into the ad. Think again about your problem restatement and whether your concept seems to be consistent with it. Then stop. It's time to incubate.

After you've slept on it for a while, start writing. First write your headline—an attention-getting blockbuster of a headline short enough to grab the reader's attention. Then write the sub-headline—so compelling and curiosity-building that your prospect must read the first sentence. And finally, write the first sentence of the copy—short, to the point and strong enough to carry you into the next sentence—and then it's down the slippery slide.

Block-diagram your ad. What do the first few paragraphs do for the ad? What is the emotional appeal? Are you anticipating those questions and answering them to the satisfaction of your prospect? Are you frank and honest in those answers?

Try Patterning Your Ad

Another approach is called "patterning." Simply pick an ad written by somebody you admire and whose product or service is similar to yours and use their ad as a pattern or style from which to write. If they use a long headline, make your headline long. If they use a lot of captions, then you create a number of captions. Capture the feel of the ad, but be careful. Do not copy the person's layout too closely so that people reading the ad might think at first glance it was from the company you were copying. This exercise is only to give you a format or guide from which to write. If you copy the layout too closely, you are violating the rights of the person who wrote the ad.

The main points in this chapter are the basic steps and the thought processes you go through as you construct your ad. The key point is that you don't have the prospect in front of you, so you have to anticipate the questions the prospect will ask in almost the same order the prospect will ask them.

This flow is important. But there is also a critical part of the copywriting process that really separates the best copywriters from the worst. It's called the editing process and we cover it in the next chapter.

Chapter 17 | The Editing Process

This chapter holds one of the most valuable secrets to effective and persuasive copy, for it is in the editing process that you turn that raw emotional outpouring of thoughts and ideas into a polished, harmonious, resonant tuning fork which will vibrate perfectly with your prospect.

It's like the story of a diamond. When a diamond is found it looks like a piece of coal or carbon. Take that black, ugly stone and polish it and it soon becomes the world's most beautiful gemstone.

Remember that lecture I referred to earlier in Chapter 11 that I gave at New York University? I mentioned to the students that if everybody in the class completed a writing assignment, my first draft would probably be the worst in the class. Poor grammar, atrocious spelling and disjointed sentence structure might be the way an English teacher would describe it.

But it is what I do after that first draft that makes the difference. It's the difference between just plain copy and a polished advertising message—from copy that doesn't move prospects to one that moves prospects so strongly that they reach into their collective pockets and exchange their hard-earned money for your product or service. It's the difference between earning a salary as a copywriter and earning millions of dollars as an effective copywriter/entrepreneur.

The Secret to Editing

Is there a secret to editing? Once again, it is a mental process that almost parallels that of the copywriting act itself. It requires lots of practice, although you will find it easier to do than writing the copy itself. In fact, it is a lot more fun. Look at the act of writing the first draft as giving birth. It may be a painful, long process or it can go quite quickly with little pain. Then compare the editing process to raising the child—the caring and nurturing required to ensure a healthy, happy child.

You wouldn't want your child to go out into the world in

funny clothes, unable to communicate or relate with others, would you? You therefore have to mold and nurture that child as you prepare to present him or her to the rest of the world.

Editing is a nurturing process. And just as there is no perfect way to nurture your child, there are many different approaches to editing copy that are certainly acceptable. I strive for one result when I edit and this can be summed up in the following axiom:

Axiom 14

In the editing process, you refine your copy to express exactly what you want to express with the fewest words.

Now this sounds rather simple, doesn't it? But it is the true essence of the editing process. You want to maintain the same emotional feel, the same thought process, the same vibration that you had in mind when you wrote the copy. It's just that you want to do it in the fewest words.

This may mean that you rearrange the words you wrote to make the thought more direct. Or it may mean cutting out words that have little contribution to the overall feel of the ad. It may mean substituting new words that express your thoughts better. And it may even mean adding words to clarify a thought. But the goal in writing ad copy is to express the thoughts you want to convey in the most powerful way but with the fewest words.

I remember the feeling I had writing my previous book, *Success Forces*. Since it was a book format and I was not under the same constraints as when I wrote my advertising copy, it was an easy process. In fact, it is a lot easier writing anything other than direct response advertising copy. You have the freedom to use as many words as you wish to express a thought or feeling. And you have no space restrictions.

Copy Has Space Restrictions

But with advertising copy you do have space restrictions. Your copy has a very focused purpose—to motivate your prospects to exchange their hard-earned money for your product or service. And everything you do or write must lead to this one goal.

Let me give you one example from an ad that I wrote. We'll look at my first draft of the initial two paragraphs, which contained 66 words, and then the final draft, which contained 43 words. We'll then study the two versions and certain lessons will emerge. The ad was for a bathroom scale, and here's the first draft:

Losing weight is not easy. Ask anyone.

And, if you've tried it, you know that part of a good weight reduction program is your bathroom scale. A bathroom scale is like a report card. It's a feedback mechanism that tells you how well you've done. In fact, one of the few pleasures of losing weight is stepping on your bathroom scale and seeing the positive results.

Now let's take the same ad and condense it to reduce the word count while still maintaining the same meaning and emotional feel.

Losing weight is not easy. Ask anyone.

One of the few pleasures of losing weight is stepping on your bathroom scale and seeing positive results. Your bathroom scale is like a report card—a feedback mechanism that tells you how well you've done.

If you removed the first paragraph from this exercise and just concentrated on the second paragraph, there would be a reduction from 59 words to 36. With nearly 40% fewer words, the meaning and emotional appeal of the second version is exactly the same as the first or even better.

Apply this percentage to a full-page ad with 1,000 words and you can see the difference the editing process can make. In fact, at this point, let's look at the advantages.

Advantages of Fewer Words

With less copy, your ad will look less imposing to the prospect and he or she will be more likely to read it. The second advantage is that you are making the slippery slide even more slippery by making it shorter. Your prospect will get to the bottom of the slide much faster, yet still get the full impact of your sales message.

The example above was given to my seminar class and they spent about 20 minutes coming up with their own edited versions of the ad. Many of them were excellent and some were even shorter than my version. Of course, the copy was taken out of context, they didn't have the rest of the ad and couldn't see far enough into the ad to see what my environment, goal and emotional appeal for the product were, so this might not be the perfect example. But it brought out many of the principles of good editing. The following are a few of the principles they learned:

Some Principles of Editing

1. Look for any 'that' words. For example, in my first draft I used the words, "And, if you've tried it, you know that. . . ." The words up to and including 'that' can very often be eliminated. In this example, I could eliminate eight words.

2. Edit for rhythm. Make sure that you vary the length of sentences so they don't sound monotonous. I discuss rhythm later in this book, in Chapter 18.

3. Consider combining sentences. Note that in the edited version, I combined the two sentences that read, "A bathroom scale is like a report card. It's a feedback mechanism that tells you how well you've done." I condensed it into "Your bathroom scale is like a report card—a feedback mechanism that tells you how well you've done." I saved only one word by doing this, but it made sense to combine the sentences and eliminating even one word is a good move.

4. Eliminate unnecessary words. Look at the word 'the' in the phrase "and seeing the positive results." The word 'the' can easily be eliminated without changing the meaning so that the final sentence will read, "and seeing positive results."

5. Rearrange thoughts so they flow better. Note that in the first draft, the flow of the copy pointed out that the scale was a report card and the second thought was that part of the pleasure of a weight loss program was stepping on a scale and seeing the positive results. By reversing these two thoughts, I made the ad more emotional by focusing on the pleasure of using a scale when losing weight and then I explained why. This sounds a lot better and more logical from a flow standpoint than the first draft.

Take As Long As You Need

Sometimes editing is like raising and nurturing your child and you need to take a lot of time. You may end up doing ten drafts before you get to the final draft. Other times it may flow right out of your mind with hardly a correction.

When Frank Schultz, the grapefruit marketer, attended my seminar and wrote his famous grapefruit ad, it was so close to perfect that it didn't need much editing at all. When Joe Karbo, who wrote *The Lazy Man's Way to Riches,* attended my seminar, he told the class that after his ad was written, other than two words that needed correction, the ad was perfect. On the other hand, other seminar participants who had a great deal of copywriting experience spent many hours editing their ads.

And the same holds true for me. I've written ad copy that flowed right out of my brain through my pen, or later my computer, and never had to be edited much. On the other hand, most of the time I would have to go through several drafts before I was satisfied. And then there is the experience factor. The more you write, the less editing you have to do. The easier the flow out of your brain, the better you are at expressing the emotional feel of copy and the excitement that each word represents.

The novice copywriter will usually need the editing process to craft and polish an ad, whereas the experienced copywriter has many of the editing mechanisms programmed in his or her brain. The copy seems to flow out through a filter that comes only from experience.

On the other hand, the need for editing is sometimes unpredictable regardless of your experience. You could produce copy that needs plenty of editing or you could end up with excellent copy that never needs much at all.

You want to remove the unnecessary words and still have the ad make sense.

Read the Periodicals

I'm always amazed at the lack of editing I see in many of the periodicals I read. Phrases like "Finally, it is important to note that . . ." can be totally eliminated and not affect the flow or understanding of what follows. Another example: "Fortunately or unfortunately as the case may be . . ." is not really required to make the information that follows clearer. Many of the articles written in periodicals contain these unnecessary preliminaries that fill up space but mean very little. In writing effective copy you can't afford to be too wordy.

If you'd like a little practice, take a look at the examples that follow and edit them yourself, or read any periodical and edit the copy by seeing how many extraneous words can be eliminated. Or write a draft and practice this critical skill.

Example 1:

"About the only redeeming feature of this product is that we don't have huge quantities to sell. The importer is afraid to order too many for fear that nobody in their right mind would buy it let alone sell it. So we only have a few hundred to sell as part of this test program."

Example 2:

"I was sitting in an office in New York City talking to a very successful friend and businessman whom we'll call Stuart. I told Stuart that I had to make a very critical decision in my business. I needed some guidance and advice."

When I started writing a great deal of copy in the '70s, I would use a legal pad and ballpoint pen and write my draft in longhand. I would then give it to my secretary, who would type it out for me in rough draft form, usually double spaced.

I would then make my editing corrections and hand it back to my secretary for her to retype. And this process would continue for several drafts until it was in a final form for the typesetter.

Computers Are a Great Help

When computers with word processing programs first came on the scene, I resisted using them. I was used to writing the copy in longhand and to switch to a computer and keyboard seemed difficult. But I made the transition sometime in the early '80s on an Apple II computer and I haven't looked back since.

Writing copy on a computer makes the editing process very easy. Word processing allows you to pick words or entire sentences and drag them to another place in the copy. Sophisticated spell-checkers whiz through copy and correct your spelling even as you type. Thesauruses, grammar-checkers and all sorts of editing aids are built into every decent word processing program. Today, I never have to give a draft to a secretary. I type it in draft form first on the computer and then do all my editing, often before I even print my copy. The computer has done more for my copywriting and editing than any other single factor and it is making a difference for copywriters everywhere.

Another technique that will help you in the editing process is time. If you can put aside your copy after you edit it and look at it the next day or even in a few days, you will often discover things that you never saw before. If time is critical, put the copy down for a short while and get back to it. The key is to allow time for your subconscious mind to digest what you've done and pick out the areas that need work.

Many other rules for editing can be found in English textbooks and style books. There are also other books on writing that cover this subject very nicely. In fact, it was a book I read in college that really opened my mind to the importance of editing in the copywriting process. I am currently trying to get the rights to that book and may offer it as one of my future books on marketing.

Finally, after you think you have that perfect final draft—a draft so well edited that you can't possibly make one more correction—give it to somebody who is a professional editor or English major and have them edit it to correct the English and grammar that you missed. This does not mean that you have to accept all of their changes. Sure, you want to correct the spelling and the dangling modifiers and any other terrible grammar that may negatively impress your prospects. But then simply weigh each one of the changes and if you feel that any interfere with the style of your writing and your original version does not violate grammar or spelling rules, then ignore them. The point is, don't be intimidated if you don't feel comfortable with somebody else's suggestions to change your writing.

The Use of Commas

A good example is the use of commas. There are two schools of thought—one which uses a lot of commas and the other that does not. I do not believe in too many commas as they take up space. And as a copywriter you don't have much space to work with. So I use commas where the rules of grammar are clear that they are needed for clarification. I don't use commas in places where I am not violating any grammar rules or where they are considered optional. For example, when three items are grouped together, such as 'apples, oranges and tomatoes', I don't use a serial comma after 'oranges'.

I would have both my sister Judy, who is a high school teacher, and Mary Stanke, my associate at JS&A, proof all my copy. I didn't accept all their changes but I certainly paid a lot of attention to them.

It is important that you do make your copy as free from error as possible. If you don't, it reflects badly on the integrity of your offer. It raises doubts in the minds of your readers. They may think, "If this guy can't get his grammar straight, how do I know he runs his business right?"

A good example of how a prospect thinks is reflected in a letter I received from an irate reader of one of the airline magazines in which we ran the ad for our Consumers Hero club. We received the following:

> Dear Sir: Despite the intended conversational tone of the attached advertisement, no license within consumer-oriented ad writing permits the type of glaring poor grammar usage circled in paragraph five of your copy. "We better not" may occur in sloppy, colloquial speech, but it is not acceptable in writing. The phrase should read, "we'd better not", of course.
>
> I cannot believe that your ad agency would permit such poor proofing in an ad which finds its way into the hands of a sharp consumer such as the type which pays the kind of money required to purchase an airline ticket today, and thus is inflicted with this bad grammar in a captive audience magazine like the attached.

The above individual took the time to write us about a simple grammar error. How many others saw it and didn't respond? And whenever we do make a mistake, our readers do usually find it.

One editing error was actually quite funny. In copy describing a blood pressure unit, I wrote, "blood pressure can be very dangerous" instead of "high blood pressure can be very dangerous." Nobody picked it up. Sometimes I'm amazed at what the public misses and what they complain about, but the fact remains that in the editing process you really do want to be as thorough as possible.

What I have conveyed in this chapter is simply how important the editing process is, the value of editing in terms of the final copy, and some of the logic I use in the editing process.

Now you're ready for some interesting, subtle and sophisticated insights into copywriting. By now you understand the entire copywriting process, can write an ad and edit it. In Section Two, I give you some of the significant insights I've gained during years of experience.

Section Two

Now comes the fun part. In the following chapters you'll find not only insights and tips on how to write copy but also revelations of what has worked exceptionally well during my 30-year career as a copywriter.

This section contains only six chapters. But packed into these chapters is the heart of this book—the basis for the copy I write and many of my copywriting secrets. It's an education that cost me millions to learn and you're going to learn it for the simple price of this book.

In my seminar promotional outline, I listed several topics that would be presented, one of which was "The 57 Points Every Ad Should Cover." And very often, my seminar participants, in anticipation of coming to the seminar, would sit down and in advance list some points to see if they could guess what I taught in the course.

Typically, they knew maybe six or seven of the points. And typically, they were amazed at what they didn't know. You've already learned the first 10 of these points, the graphic elements of an ad, in Chapter 4. You're now about to discover the rest—23 copy elements and 24 psychological triggers to buying. And from the other chapters in this section you will further build the base you need in order to write incredibly effective copy.

So study this section completely and continue to build your solid copywriting foundation.

Chapter 18 | Powerful Copy Elements Explained

Remember our discussion about graphic elements in Chapter 4? We explained that each of these elements was designed to get prospects to do only one thing—read the first sentence. And we explained how important the first sentence was in your copy.

And if we know that all those graphic elements are designed to get you to read the first sentence and eventually all of the copy, then the next thing we should address is the nature of the copy elements in an advertisement.

In this chapter, I will cover all the copy elements and their relationship to the advertisement—23 concepts that you should review for each ad you write.

1. Typeface: This element is really important. If you're a graphic designer, you know that each typeface has its own personality, emotion and legibility. And that's the point of this subject. You've got to determine the combination of personality and legibility that will make your ad easy to read and inviting. Since we are talking about copy here, we are talking about only one style of type called "serif" type. Serif type has those little curlicues whereas the other style of type called "sans serif" (French for 'without curlicues') doesn't. The type used for the text of this book is serif type. Why? Because in legibility tests, serif type produced greater comprehension than sans serif type and by a 5 to 1 margin. I didn't discover this until well into my writing career, but now all my ads are printed in serif type. This was one test I wish I had known about earlier.

Another important factor is the legibility of all your typefaces in other parts of your ad such as the headline, subheadline and various headings. Fancy type might look elegant to the type designer, but if it can't be read it has no value. It's like talking to a foreigner and finding the words difficult to understand. The most important role a typeface has is to allow the greatest comprehension possible, and the second role, less important by far, is to convey the image of a company.

2. First Sentence: This we discussed in Chapter 4 as the purpose of all the graphic elements of an ad—to get the prospect to read that all-important first sentence. Keep your first sentence short, easy to read and compelling enough to cause the reader to read the next sentence.

3. Second Sentence: This sentence is almost as important as the first. You've got to maintain interest, so you must also create another sentence with a compelling reason to cause your reader to want to continue. You must continue this momentum throughout the first and second paragraphs. Put aside any facts, benefits or product features. Your only goal is to get the momentum going and create that buying environment.

4. Paragraph Headings: In Chapter 4, paragraph headings are mentioned as one of the graphic elements in a print ad. They are supposed to make the copy look less intimidating, and thus encourage the reader to read all the copy. But paragraph headings are also a copy element that needs to be addressed in this chapter as well.

Paragraph headings could introduce material in the paragraph that follows or they could have absolutely nothing to do with the copy underneath or the copy in the entire ad for that matter. Remember, they are designed to break up the copy and make it look less intimidating. They have little to do with selling or presenting your product. They simply make the copy look more inviting so your reader will start the reading process.

When a reader looks at copy that appears like one continuous paragraph, subconsciously it looks a lot more difficult to read than copy that is broken up into neat little chunks headed by various paragraph headings.

Use paragraph headings to break up copy in the middle of columns but not at the very end or beginning. Avoid placing paragraph headings right next to each other in two adjoining columns.

As I just mentioned, your paragraph headings could say anything. I once ran an ad for a radar speed indicator, and as a test I used the most outrageous paragraph headings you could think of. They included "Scrambled Eggs," "Working and Playing" and "Success and Good Things." Even though the headings had absolutely nothing to do with the ad copy, they drew absolutely no attention. Nobody ever asked me what the headings meant or commented that they were not consistent with the copy. But had I misspelled a word in the body of the ad, I would have heard plenty about it.

The primary purpose of paragraph headings is to get the reader to read the copy by making the copy look less intimidating.

A secondary purpose might be to arouse curiosity. Maybe my "Scrambled Eggs" paragraph heading did just that, i.e., created curiosity and caused somebody to start reading the copy to find out what scrambled eggs had to do with the product I was offering. Although I've never tested to see if this was the case, my experience with paragraph headings tells me that curiosity does play a minor role but that the main purpose is to make the copy less intimidating.

5. Product Explanation: Sounds simple. Sounds basic. But you'll be amazed at how many ads leave out the simple step of explaining what the product does. A rule of thumb here is to explain a complicated product in a very simple way and explain a simple product in a very complex way.

For example, I once sold a smoke detector. At the time it was a very common household product whose function was clearly understood by the consumer. In short, the product was simple. In the ad I wrote for an expensive brand, I told a story about the inside workings of my smoke detector. I described the gold contacts (which every other smoke detector had) and even explained how the comparator circuit functioned to determine if there was smoke in the room. Even though this smoke detector was $10 more than the market price, it was a big success. The ad illustrates a way to present a simple product in a complicated way. You should sell a simple product that is clearly understood by the consumer in a more complicated way and a more complicated product in a very simple way.

When I first explained the computer to my customers, it was always a very simple explanation of what it could do for them. My ad was not about the technology inside (although some reference was made to the inside) but focused on the simplicity of the product and its use. At this time, consumers were just getting into computers. They were new, seemed complicated to use and indeed many were. By explaining computers in very simple and basic terms without getting too complicated, I was able to ease them into a purchase.

Later, as consumers understood more and the products became a commodity, explaining them in greater detail proved more effective.

In addition to the above concept, you should always check your copy to make sure you have explained all of the features. Ask yourself, "Did I explain the product sufficiently to my prospect?" You might ask a number of people to read your copy to see if they understand the product and its features. Look at the questions they raise and see if you've addressed them fully in your copy.

6. New Features: Highlight those features which make your product or service new, unique or novel. This might appear to be the same as the copy element "Product Explanation" that we've just discussed, but it is different. Here you are revealing not just the features of the product, but the features that distinguish it from anything else on the market.

7. Technical Explanation: Regardless of the product or service, each ad can be enhanced with a technical explanation. We all like to buy something from an expert—somebody we like, respect and trust. Buying is indeed a process of trust. The buyer's thought process might be, "I trust that you really know your subject and fully understand the product category and have described your product to me properly and will give me something of value that I want in return for my hard-earned money."

I DON'T UNDERSTAND ANY OF THIS TECHNICAL STUFF .... BUT, HEY, IF THEY UNDERSTAND IT, THE PRODUCT MUST BE **SUPER!**

A technical explanation will build confidence in the prospect.

Trust is always enhanced when the seller has become an expert at what he or she is selling. Let's say the seller says, "I have studied everything I could on competitive products and know everything there is about the product I am selling, so I know that what I am offering you is the best product at the best value." You would naturally have a great deal of confidence that this seller's product is indeed good.

You might also be impressed if the seller, in describing the product, used words that you didn't understand. Why? Because it would appear that the seller really was an expert about the product. This is not deception. A seller must become an expert on the product in order to talk about it in technical language.

In a mail order ad, technical explanations can add a great deal of credibility, but before you write them, make sure you indeed become an expert. If not, the consumer will see right through the ploy.

A good example of this technique is expressed in the following caption I wrote for a picture of the integrated circuit in a watch:

> A pin points to the new decoder/driver integrated circuit which takes the input from the oscillator countdown integrated circuit and computes the time while driving the display. This single space-age device replaces thousands of solid-state circuits and provides the utmost reliability—all unique to Sensor.

Very few people would be able to understand the technical commentary. In fact, when I sent the ad to the manufacturer for approval, he called my attention to the caption under the picture and said, "What you wrote there is correct but who is going to understand it? Why did you even use it?"

Providing a technical explanation which the reader may not understand shows that we really did our research and if we say it's good, it must be good. It builds confidence in the buyer that he or she is indeed dealing with an expert. Incidentally, the watch was one of our best-selling products.

Another example of a technical explanation appeared in the outline of a seminar. Jimmy Calano of CareerTrack came up to me after I explained the reasons for a technical explanation and said, "Joe, do you realize that the outline of one of my seminars is, in fact, a technical explanation? By using technical terms that not too many people understand until they come to the seminar, they sense that we know what we are talking about."

Yet another example is an ad written by Frank Schultz after attending my seminar. His product was grapefruit and he was explaining how he graded them:

> Even after picking there are other careful inspections each fruit must pass before I'll accept it. I size the fruit. And I grade it for beauty. Sometimes the fruit will be wind scarred. I won't accept

it. Or sometimes it will have a bulge on the stem that we call "sheep nose." I won't accept it. You can see I really mean it when I say I accept only perfect Royal Ruby Reds.

In many of my ads, catalogs, direct mailings and infomercials I convey thorough knowledge not only of what I am selling but of the entire universe of products available. I convey the thought process I went through in picking the product I chose and why it is better than anything similar at a particular price point. And the consumer appreciates the effort I took, feels more confident in the purchase and consequently is motivated to reach into his or her pocket and exchange hard-earned money for my product or service.

8. Anticipate Objections: This is a very important element to consider when writing copy. If you feel that your prospect might raise some objection when you are describing a product, then raise the objection yourself. Remember, you're not in front of the consumer and you have to sense what the next question might be. If you sense that there might be an objection and you ignore it, it's like ignoring that consumer. You won't get away with it. The consumer is too sharp and will not buy.

A good example of anticipating objections is in that ad we saw earlier in Chapter 16 for that expensive electronic pinball game from Bally Manufacturing. The average consumer would raise the question about service. We resolved it in our ad.

Another example of raising an objection is in my ad offering a thermostat for the home. If you remember from Chapter 8, I looked at the product and saw that it was really ugly. It didn't have a good design at all. In fact, it would turn me off if I were a consumer. So I raised the objection at the very beginning of the ad, calling it the worst-looking product I'd ever seen. I later justified the product by calling attention to its spectacular features, but only after I had raised the objection myself.

Often products that require installation concern consumers. It is then that you have to raise the question about installation yourself and not hide from the facts.

9. Resolve Objections: Just as you have to recognize objections, it is your opportunity and duty to resolve the objections too. You must be honest and provide alternative solutions or dispel the objections completely. With the pinball game, we talked about the modular circuit boards that you simply snap out and exchange if service is required. More on this later in copy element 14, "Service." In the case of the thermostat, we explained that beneath that ugly skin was an incredible advance in technology. Finally, when it comes to installation, we are very open and honest and explain exactly what the consumer can expect during the installation process.

10. Gender: Who is the consumer? Male, female or both male and female? Are they female golf players, lady pilots or professional women? Make sure there are no sexual or sexist comments that would offend any group and know your target audience so that you can communicate in their terms.

I once ran an ad for gold chains in my catalog. It was in the form of a story about a salesman named Bob Ross who tried to convince me to sell gold chains in my catalog. I resisted until he showed me a picture of his cousin whom he offered to have model the chains in one of my ads. I quickly accepted the product after seeing a picture of Bob's cousin. The ad copy was considered by many to be one of my most creative approaches to selling a product. The chains had nothing to do with the core products we had been selling—electronic gadgets—however, I did get a few letters as a result. A woman in Egg Harbor City, New Jersey, wrote:

> Dear Sir: Your friend, Mr. Bob Ross, may regard himself as a successful salesman, but unfortunately he comes across in your ad as a consummate asshole.

The letter then went on to point out the achievements of women in many technical fields, the military, air traffic control, sports and leisure, racing and several other professions in which women now play a very active role. She finally concluded:

> Perhaps a long, hard look at the person or department responsible for the ad on page 37 is in order. Apparently he has to "come a long way, baby" to catch up to the Twentieth Century. Cordially wishing you immediate bankruptcy, I remain,

And with that she signed her name. It was a two-page single-spaced letter which included a copy of our mailing label. Was I really insensitive to women? Did I demean them in my ad copy? I've reproduced the ad in Chapter 34 and it is called "Gold Space Chains." See if you agree.

It is also important that you recognize the differences between men and women in terms of what is important to them. Women are generally into color, fashion, family, home and relationships. Men are more likely into sports, military combat, machines, earning money and supporting their family. Sure, they overlap tremendously today. Women are assuming the roles that men once had exclusively and men are doing things today that years earlier would have been considered feminine. Being aware of the differences (and sometimes the lack of differences) is the most important point here. And this awareness can help you harmonize with your target audience by understanding how to communicate with them and knowing what might offend them.

11. Clarity: Your copy should be clear, simple, short and to the point. Avoid big words that confuse those who don't know them and which often establish the writer as a pompous snob—unless, of course, you're trying to appeal to pompous snobs. Keep it simple. The clearer the copy and the more concise, the easier it will be for people to read and get on the slippery slide and stay there. The only exception to this rule is when you give a technical explanation, as described earlier in copy element 7 in this chapter.

12. Clichés: Avoid the obvious ones: "Here's the product the world has been waiting for," or "It's too good to be true." If you feel inclined to use a cliché, don't. Clichés seem to be used when you have nothing really significant or good to say and must fill up space. How do you know if you are writing a cliché? If it sounds like you're writing typical advertising copy some agency may have written 20 years ago, that's one clue.

Have I used them? You bet. My first several ads were replete with them. Back when I wrote them, I didn't know better.

For example, in my 1972 ad for a desktop calculator, I stated, "It's the breakthrough the world has been waiting for!" Bad, isn't it? I wrote it then but would never write anything as trite today. The lead sentence for the first pocket calculator I introduced in the U.S. in 1971 read, "It's the most exciting new breakthrough in electronics since the transistor radio!" Ironically, at the time, it may have actually been more truth than cliché.

13. Rhythm: Just as a song has a rhythm, so does copy. Humor writers know this well. If you can write good humor, you've already got the rhythm thing down pat. In fact, the most difficult copy to write is humor. Why humor? Because you have to know how to build up to a punch line and then deliver it. You have to know how not to be too obvious in your delivery and you've got to understand the art of timing. So what does this rhythm sound or feel like in advertising copy?

It has no distinct pattern: a short sentence, then a long sentence followed by a medium sentence followed by a short sentence and then another short sentence and then one really long sentence. Got it? In short, a mixture of sentence lengths which, when read together, gives a sense of variety and rhythm.

Think about how copy would sound if all the sentences were very short or very long or all had a distinct predictable pattern. Pretty boring. And that's the point of copy rhythm. Vary your sentences; vary their length to give your copy a rhythm.

Another rhythm technique is the use of what is called a "triad." Very often when I list examples or attributes of something, I use just three of them. For example take the sentence, "I went shopping for a hammer, a screwdriver and a pair of pliers." In copy you list three items in a series with the last item preceded by the word 'and', and you create a nice rhythm within that sentence. In fact, when you read some of the ads in Section Three of this book, you will see how many of them have triads throughout.

14. Service: If you are selling an expensive product or one that is not easily returned for service, you must address the question of service and convey the ease of that service to the consumer. Often the mention of a brand name manufacturer is all that is needed to establish ease of service. But if there is a remote possibility that the consumer would still ask about service, then you must address this issue in your ad.

In selling our Bally pinball game by mail, we knew that a buyer might have concerns about the matter of service. What if the pinball game broke and required repair? It was large and expensive and the inconvenience of a broken game would be in the back of our customers' minds. We addressed that in the ad. The following is the subheading and paragraph we used to alleviate any customer concerns:

A FRANK DISCUSSION OF SERVICE

Fireball is a solid-state computer with its electronics condensed on integrated circuits—all hermetically sealed and all pre-tested for a lifetime of service. Fireball is also self-diagnostic. Let us say something goes wrong with the system. Simply press the test button on the back panel of your machine and the exact problem is displayed on your scoreboard in digits. Check the instruction booklet and simply remove the designated plug-in circuit board, light bulb or part and send it to the service department closest to you for a brand new replacement. Even your TV or stereo isn't that easy to repair.

A full paragraph was used to cover the issue of service. And we sold thousands of pinball machines to people who ordinarily might not have purchased a unit because of their concern about service.

Another good example of how important service is to help sell a product took place during the height of the digital watch boom in the mid '70s. The industry was expanding very rapidly but there were problems with the reliability of these space-age timepieces. Unlike mechanical watches, these new electronic timepieces had batteries, used sophisticated chips and circuitry and had a high defective rate.

I recognized this as a problem that had to be addressed in our copy. And since I look at problems as opportunities, I wondered, "Where is the opportunity in this serious and rapidly growing problem?" I then came up with the following copy to establish the quality of the product we were offering and our commitment to back it.

The Sensor 770 has an unprecedented five-year parts and labor unconditional warranty. Each watch goes through weeks of aging, testing and quality control before assembly and final inspection. Service should never be required, but if it should anytime during the five-year warranty period, we will pick up your Sensor at your door and send you a loaner watch while yours is being repaired— all at our expense.

Then later in a summary of the offer, we again played up the part on service.

We have selected the Sensor as the most advanced American-made, solid-state timepiece ever produced. And we put our company and its full resources behind that selection. JS&A will unconditionally guarantee the Sensor—even the battery—for five years. We'll even send you a loaner watch to use while your watch is being repaired should it ever require repair.

We alleviated any concern about service in the copy of the ad. If the issue of service was raised in the minds of our prospects, it was now resolved. By showing such a strong commitment to service, we had overcome a major objection that we realized, in advance, could be a problem, and turned it into an opportunity.

Indeed when a customer's watch did not work, the customer would call us on our toll-free number and we would immediately send out a package containing a UPS call tag that allowed UPS to pick up the defective watch free of charge, a loaner watch and a postage-free envelope for the consumer to return the loaner after receiving the repaired watch.

This gave our company the opportunity to prove to our customers how consumer-oriented we were. Our customers were literally amazed at the way we followed up with our service program. And after they received their repaired watch, they even got a call from us to make sure everything was OK.

But that's not the point of this example. If service is a consideration in the subconscious mind of the consumer and you address it up front, you will melt any resistance to buying your product. The Sensor watch was one of our best-selling watches and the mailing list of watch customers became one of our strongest mailing lists for future offers.

Service in the selling process has been a critical factor in the success of a personal friend, Joe Girard, who is in *The Guinness Book of World Records* for having sold more cars in a single year than anybody in history. Joe's books on salesmanship are worth reading for their many insights, but the one factor that made Joe such an effective salesman (aside from the fact that he was a very personable guy) was the way he handled service. His customers' service problems became his. And each time he sold a car, Joe became that buyer's personal service representative. And Joe performed. Then when buyers returned for another car, they only wanted Joe. It wasn't price that made Joe's success, although that was important; it was his attitude toward service.

15. Physical Facts: In copy you must mention all the physical facts about a product or you risk reducing your response.

I'm talking about weight, dimensions, size, limits, speed, etc. Sometimes you might think that a certain dimension isn't really important or the weight may not be necessary. But it's not true. Give readers any excuse not to buy and they won't buy.

I remember running ads for products and then personally taking the orders on our toll-free lines. I did this because it was on the phone lines that I got many of my insights into the buying process. Here were my customers, motivated enough to reach into their pockets and pull out their hard-earned money for a product they trusted me to sell them. What a wonderful opportunity to peek into this process and hear the really subliminal reactions people made when they responded.

It was during my time on the phone lines that I learned that if you don't give all the facts, it gives your customer the excuse not to order. It may be a weight or dimension that you thought was irrelevant, but if you don't mention it, people will call and ask for it. And how many more customers didn't bother to call and check on it? Of course, they didn't order either.

I remember an ad for a scale pictured on the floor. I didn't give the actual weight of the scale itself. "Who would care?" I thought. But my prospects did care and frequently asked. We eventually included the weight of the scale in the ad. I remember showing an object that was being held in my hand. I gave the exact dimensions but failed to give the weight because the weight was not really relevant. I got a lot of calls from people wanting to know the weight before deciding whether to buy.

The point: List the physical dimensions even in cases where you think they are not that important.

16. Trial Period: You must offer a trial period for any product that the consumer cannot touch or feel at the time of purchase, as is the case with mail order items. The only time you can make an exception to this rule is when the value is so strong and the product so familiar that the consumer is willing to take the risk. If I were selling a box of 24 rolls of toilet paper at a bargain price delivered to your home and it was a brand that you already used, then you wouldn't need a trial period.

Make sure your trial period is at least one month, or even better, two months. Tests have proven that the longer the trial period, the less chance the product will be returned and the more confidence the consumer will have in dealing with you and purchasing the item.

Let's say you receive a product that has a one-week trial period. You've got one week to make up your mind. You feel the pressure, so you examine the product and try to make the decision as quickly as possible. If you are unsure after the week is up, what do you do? You say, "I'm not sure, so I'm not going to take the chance," and you return it.

But let's say you have two months to make up your mind. No pressure there, right? You even have a pretty good feeling about the company offering the product. The company must be confident that you're going to like the product because they are giving you a two-month trial period.

So you put the product aside. You use it freely, not worried about having to make a decision, and then before you know it the two months are up and you've not even thought about returning it. Just knowing you could have returned it was enough to make you feel comfortable holding on to the purchase.

17. Price Comparison: Whenever possible, offering a price comparison to another product establishes value in the mind of the purchaser. This points out one of the really important considerations that motivate consumers to buy—namely that they are getting real value.

An example of a price comparison was my ad for the Sensor watch. I stated:

> The $275 Pulsar uses the LED technology which requires pressing a button each time you want to review the time. Even the $500 solar-powered Synchronar watch, in our opinion, can't compare with the Sensor and its 5-year warranty. And no solid-state watch can compare to Sensor's quality, accuracy, ruggedness and exceptional value.

If you are selling an expensive item or something that is a good value when compared to another product, you should always consider a price comparison as a means of establishing the value of your product. If your product is the most expensive product being offered, then you want to suggest that it has more or better features. If your product is less expensive, then you want to focus on better value and use a price comparison.

But there's a word of caution. Your comparison must be totally accurate and be 100% fair or you could be sued by the company whose product you are comparing.

18. Testimonials: A testimonial is a good way to add credibility if it is from a very credible person or organization. This approach can be used not only in the copy but in the headline or photo. See if your ad copy could use a celebrity for a testimonial, but make sure the testimonial makes sense for the product.

When I was selling a space-age Midex security system, it made sense to have Wally Schirra, the famous astronaut, endorse my product. He did, and the product sold very well. If I were selling basketball shoes, Michael Jordan would be a natural.

Make sure that the celebrity matches with the product and adds credibility. The use of a celebrity that doesn't make sense for your product or doesn't add credibility could backfire, have the wrong effect and kill sales if the offer is not believable.

You can also use what I call a "reverse testimonial." That is where you don't use a spokesperson but you refer to your competitor's. For example, when I was selling the Olympus micro recorder, I stated the following:

> **Headline:** Endorsement Battle
>
> **Subheadline:** A famous golf star endorses the Lanier. Our unit is endorsed by our president. You'll save $100 as a result.
>
> **Copy:** Judge for yourself. That new Olympus micro recorder shown above sells for $150. Its closest competition is a $250 recorder called the Lanier endorsed by a famous golf star.
>
> **FANCY ENDORSEMENT**
>
> The famous golf star is a pilot who personally flies his own Citation jet. The Olympus recorder is endorsed by JS&A's president who pilots a more cost-efficient single engine Beachcraft Bonanza. The golf star does not endorse the Lanier unit for free. After all, a good portion of his income is derived from endorsing products.
>
> Our president, on the other hand, does not get paid for endorsing products—just for selling them. And his Bonanza is not as expensive to fly as the golf star's Citation. In fact, our president also drives a Volkswagen Rabbit.

I then continued to show how inefficiently the Lanier was sold (through a direct selling organization) and how efficiently the Olympus was sold (via direct marketing and through JS&A). The conclusion: savings of $100 for an even better product—all because we didn't have our product endorsed by an expensive spokesperson.

Another form of testimonial is from the man on the street—used primarily on TV. I've used them extensively in my BluBlocker infomercials. And finally, another one could come from those people who use your product and send you an unsolicited testimonial. Whatever testimonial you do use, make sure it is authentic and honest. The public will see right through a lie and the FTC won't be far behind.

19. Price: Another important copy point to consider is price. Should the price be obvious? Should it be large? Small? These are important considerations and must be examined.

If you're selling a product or service at a very good price, then make the price larger. After all, you want people to see that benefit very clearly. If the product is expensive and it's not the price that will sell it, you want to underplay it. Don't hide it; just underplay it.

As I write my ad I have always anticipated the questions my prospects will ask. There is one exception. I never know when they are going to wonder about the price of the product. I have always felt that the point at which your reader will want to find out about the price could happen anytime during the reading process. It could happen before they read the ad. It could happen halfway through or it could happen near the end. You must, as an effective copywriter, answer the question that is being raised by the reader when the question is being raised.

By putting the price in a logical position in the copy—whether it be in the coupon, which is the ideal place, or in the copy highlighted with a bold typeface—you are answering the question that the reader asks without knowing when the reader is ready to ask the question. The reader simply scans the ad and if the price is in bold or in the coupon, the price will pop out and answer the question.

20. Offer Summary: It's a really good idea to summarize what you are offering the consumer somewhere near the end of your ad. "So here's my offer. Order two pots with Teflon coating and you'll receive the two pots plus our handy cookbook and video for the price of only $19.95." You'll be surprised at how many ads miss this important point.

21. Avoid Saying Too Much: This is probably the biggest mistake my students make. They say too much. There are really two issues here. The first issue is one of editing. It is normal to say as much as you can about a subject and then refine the copy to a point where it flows smoothly. This usually means editing and reducing the copy length until it has rhythm and flows. This could take time and involves a few steps.

First, say to yourself as you go through the editing process, "Is there a simpler way of saying this?" Very often you can cut your copy down 50 to even 80% and still say the same thing. It's the difference between a salesperson who talks too much and one who is to the point and succinct. Wouldn't you rather be sold by the one who is to the point?

There is another issue involved with not saying too much, and later in this book in Chapter 20 I explain how not saying too much will actually enhance and even stimulate the selling process. Chapter 17 on editing also has ideas which will help you reduce your copy.

22. Ease of Ordering: Make it easy to order. Use a toll-free number, a coupon, a tear-off reply card or any vehicle that is easy to understand and use. My recommendation: Use a coupon with dotted lines. In tests, it usually generates more response because the dotted lines clearly convey at a glance that you can order the product from the ad.

23. Ask for the Order: Always ask for the order near the end of your ad. Believe it or not, this is often forgotten by many copywriters. At the end of an ad, I state the following or something similar: "I urge you to buy this at no obligation, today." Have you ever met a salesperson who has already sold you and you are waiting for the salesperson to ask you for the order but he or she never does? It's happened to me. And it is one of the problems with a lot of inexperienced salespeople. You've got to ask for the order, and if you're doing it right, it should be at the very end of the ad where you've finished selling your prospect, summarized the offer and your prospect is ready to buy.

These 23 copy elements are points you want to consider when you are writing copy. Use this chapter as a checklist when you get started. Consider all of these points when you write an ad. Can some of them be eliminated? Possibly. But simply by using them as a checklist, you might discover a few deficiencies in your ad copy which can be corrected with my suggestions and might result in enhancing your response.

One of the other benefits of the list is to give you an insight into the relative importance of the various copy elements. Some, like the Paragraph Headings, have little purpose other than to make the copy less imposing. Others, like Resolve Objections, can make a dramatic difference in the credibility of your copy.

Use the convenient copy elements checklist located in Appendix C in the back of this book and make a copy to keep right next to your computer or desk when you are writing an ad.

But the really interesting part of my checklist is in the next chapter where you'll learn about the psychological triggers that need to be considered when you write an ad. You first learned about the 10 graphic elements and their purpose (to get you to read the first sentence of the copy) in Chapter 4. You have just learned 23 copy concepts and how they are to be used. Now learn the 24 psychological triggers—the underlying motivational messages that good direct-response copy should convey, often in subtle but very effective ways. When I was teaching my seminar course, this was the part my students enjoyed the most. So read on.

This is probably going to be the most interesting of the 57 points you want to consider when writing a direct response print ad or any kind of selling message.

The first part of the 57-point checklist involves the 10 graphic elements of an ad—those elements designed to get you to read the first sentence. The previous chapter covered points to consider when writing the actual copy. But now get ready for the psychology that should be considered when writing your advertising message—concepts that took me years of failure, experience and gradual insight to understand and implement.

You may understand and relate to some of these concepts right away. Some you may not fully understand without experiencing them yourself. And finally, some will require a fairly detailed explanation.

If you've found this book informative so far, you will find this chapter fascinating. So let's start.

1. Feeling of Involvement or Ownership

I was once told this story by a master salesman who worked at a TV and appliance store. He was the most successful salesman this store ever had. He consistently beat out all the other salesmen. He had some very good sales techniques, but that wasn't what impressed me. It was the way he decided in advance who his best prospects might be.

What he would do was stand in the aisles watching customers walk into the store. He would observe them. If they walked up to a TV set and started turning the knobs, he knew that he had a 50% chance of selling them. If they didn't turn the knobs, he had a 10% chance of selling them.

In direct response advertising, you don't have the opportunity of sitting in your prospects' mailboxes or in their living rooms observing them as they read your sales presentation. You are not there to see any knobs being turned. But you can get them to turn the knobs by giving them a feeling of involvement with or ownership of the product you are selling.

In all my ads I try to make the prospects imagine they are holding or using my product. For example, in one of my earlier calculator ads, I might have said, "Hold the Litronix 2000 in your hand. See how easily the keys snap to the touch. See how small and how light the unit is." I create through imagination the reader's experience of turning the knobs.

In short, I take the mind on a mental journey to capture the involvement of the reader. I make the reader believe that he or she could indeed be holding the calculator and experiencing the very same things that I've described. It's mental energy creating a picture for the prospect, whose mind is like a vacuum waiting to be filled.

In your copywriting, let your readers take a stroll down a path with you or let them smell the fragrance through your nose or let them experience some of the emotions you are feeling by forming a mental picture from your description.

If I were writing an advertisement for the Corvette sports car, I might say, "Take a ride in the new Corvette. Feel the breeze blowing through your hair as you drive through the warm evening. Watch heads turn. Punch the accelerator to the floor and feel the burst of power that pins you into the back of your contour seat. Look at the beautiful display of electronic technology right on your dashboard. Feel the power and excitement of America's super sports car."

I would still explain all the special features of the car—the logic upon which to justify its purchase—but I would really play up that feeling of involvement and ownership.

This technique is used in many different ways. In direct response, it is often referred to as an involvement device—something that involves the consumer in the buying process. Sometimes it may seem silly. Have you ever received those solicitations that say, "Put the 'yes' disk into the 'yes' slot and we will send you a trial subscription to our new magazine"? I often wonder who invented that seemingly simpleminded and juvenile concept. Yet, as direct marketers will tell you, this type of involvement device often doubles and triples response rates. It's not simpleminded at all but rather a very effective direct-response involvement technique.

The reader becomes involved in the solicitation. Similarly, your reader is either taking action or imagining taking action through the power of the words you write.

The Involvement of TV

TV is a great example of involvement. You see, hear and can almost touch the product. It is no wonder that TV advertising is one of the most effective ways to sell.

My own daughter, when she was four years old, clearly demonstrated how you can get involved in the sales message. There was a Peanuts Valentine's Day TV special and my daughter Jill was sitting and watching the show with her seven-year-old sister, April. My wife, who was watching as well, told me this fascinating story.

> Charlie Brown was passing out Valentine cards in a classroom and was reading off names of the recipients, "Sarah, Mary, Sally . . . Jill. Where's Jill?" said Charlie Brown. My daughter immediately raised her hand and said, "Here." She was so involved in watching the show that she thought she was a part of it.

I use involvement devices quite often. An involvement device that ties in with what you are selling can be very effective. Let me give you a perfect example from an ad that I wrote. The results really surprised me.

The product I was offering was the Franklin Spelling Computer—a device that helped correct your spelling. It was a novelty when it first appeared and it sold quite well. Although I wasn't the first to sell it, I had a model that was a little more sophisticated than the first version.

I examined the product and felt it was priced too high. But the manufacturer would be pretty upset with me if I were to drop the price. So I tried an involvement device as a method of lowering the price.

First, I wrote an ad that described the product but with an unusual premise. The ad that I wrote had several misspelled words. If you found the misspelled words, circled them and sent the ad with the misspelled words circled, you would get $2 off the price of the computer for each misspelled word you circled.

My concept was simple. If you didn't find all the misspelled words, you paid more for the computer, but then again, the computer was worth more to you than to somebody who found all the mistakes.

I ran the first ad in *The Wall Street Journal* and the response poured in. I also received a few phone calls from people I hadn't heard from in years. "Joe, I want you to know, I spent the last hour and a half trying to find all the words and I don't even intend on buying your damn computer. I normally don't read the entire *Wall Street Journal* for that length of time."

I Even Made More Money

And the response was surprising. I anticipated that the readers would find all the misspelled words. In fact, even the word 'mispelled' was misspelled. When the response was finally tallied, to my amazement, people only caught, on average, half of the words and I earned a lot more money than I had expected from the ad. And, of course, those who really needed the computer got real value.

The feeling of ownership is a concept that is pretty close to the feeling of involvement, but here you are making readers feel that they already own the product and you're letting them use their imaginations as you take them through the steps of what it would be like if they already owned it. An example might be, "When you receive your exercise device, work out on it. Adjust the weights. See how easy it is to store under your bed. . . ." In short, you are making them feel that they have already bought the product.

Advertising copy that involves the reader can be quite effective—especially if the involvement device is part of the advertising. Whenever you write an ad, keep this very important concept in mind. It can make direct response copy far more effective.

2. Honesty

If I had to pick the single most important point of the 57 points, I would pick honesty. Your advertising must be honest. This doesn't mean that if you are dishonest in your message, you won't achieve a successful result. Give the consumer a price that's too hard to believe or a product that doesn't live up to its claims and you might be able to get away with it once, maybe even twice, but not for the long haul.

But this section on honesty is not about whether you can get away with being dishonest and for how long. It's about honesty as a psychological selling tool. First, let's start out with a very important premise.

Consumers are very smart—smarter than you think and smarter collectively than any single one of us. With all the experience I have in marketing products and with all the product knowledge I've gained over the past 35 years, you can take my word for it, the consumer is quite sharp.

The consumer can also tell whether people are truthful in what they are trying to communicate. And the more truthful you are in your advertising, the more effectively your message will be accepted by your prospects.

Try to lie in your copy and you are only deceiving yourself. Your copy will say what you think you wanted it to say, but it will also say what you thought you covered up. Even a reader who hurries over your copy can feel the difference.

When I wrote a JS&A ad, I would include many of the negative features of my products. I would point out the flaws up front. And of course, I would explain why the flaws really didn't amount to much and why the consumer should still buy my product. Consumers were so impressed with this approach and had such trust in our message that they would eagerly buy what we offered.

And it seemed that the more truthful and frank my ads were, the more the consumer responded. I soon realized that truthfulness was one of the best advertising lessons I had ever learned.

Consumers really appreciate the truth. And since they are smarter than you or I, you can't fake the truth. They'll pick out a phony statement every time.

I learned to make every communication to my customers truthful, whether it be on national television or in my print ads. And the more truthful I am, the more responsive my customers.

3. Integrity

Not too far from honesty is integrity. An advertisement is a personal message from an organization or an individual and is a direct reflection of the writer's personality and integrity. You can convey this integrity by the truthfulness of your message, the look of your ad, the image that you convey and even the typefaces that you use.

Integrity can be reflected by the choices you make in the layout of your ad. Is it clean and neat? Or is it shouting out at you with color bars running in different directions and headlines screaming and words underlined and pictures exaggerated? You get the idea. The integrity of the person delivering the message is always amazingly clear to the recipient. And this integrity is often reflected by the appearance of the advertisement and the copy you write. Show good integrity and your advertising message will be well received. Don't show it and join the ranks of those who are rarely successful.

4. Credibility

If you convey honesty and integrity in your message, chances are you've gone a long way toward establishing your credibility. However, credibility is not just honesty and integrity. Credibility is being believable. In an ad for a product whose price is exceptionally low, you've got to convey that the offer you are making, as great as it may seem, is indeed a valid offer.

Let's say you are offering something for $10 that everybody else is selling for $40. Your job is establishing credibility for your price. You might explain that you are buying a very large volume from the Far East and that you were able to buy the remaining stock from a major manufacturer for a very low price. In short, you've got to establish the credibility of your company and your offer.

Credibility also means truthfulness. Does the consumer really believe you? Rash statements, clichés and some exaggerations will remove any credibility your offer may have had.

One of the most important factors that could affect credibility is not resolving all the objections that are raised in your readers' minds, such as hiding something or avoiding an obvious fault of the product or service. You need to raise all objections and resolve them.

Products that require installation or assembly are good examples. If it is obvious that a product doesn't just pop out of the box ready to use, you must explain that it does require assembly. You might say something like, "To make it easy, we provide you with the tools. In our tests, it only took five minutes for somebody with very little mechanical skill to put it together." Once again, it is the anticipation of objections and their resolution that means so much to the credibility of an ad.

You are in essence sensing the next question the consumer may ask and answering it in a straightforward, honest and credible way. The integrity of your product, your offer and yourself are all on the line, and unless you convey the highest credibility in your ad, your prospects will not feel comfortable buying from you.

When I appear on QVC—the TV home shopping channel— it is easy to sell a difficult product that normally would require a lot of credibility. The reason: QVC already has a lot of credibility with their customers. If a product is being offered on QVC, it must be good. It must have the quality that customers have come to expect, and chances are the product will be bought by somebody who has bought product before from QVC and already feels that the company is a very credible concern. In short, I've piggy-backed my product onto QVC's credibility, and the combination of QVC's credibility and my product's credibility is pretty powerful.

The effect of credibility also extends to the magazines or newspapers in which you advertise. If you advertise your product in *The Wall Street Journal*, you are piggy-backing onto their credibility and their constant vigilance, making sure their readers aren't being taken advantage of. On the other hand, place that same ad in *The National Enquirer* and you then take on the lack of credibility that this publication has established in the mind of the reader. Again, credibility is affected by the environment in which you place your advertisement.

You can enhance credibility through the use of a brand name product. For example, if I'm offering an electronic product by the name of Yorx with the exact same features as one whose brand name is Sony, which one has more credibility? The Sony would probably sell better if both were at the same price.

Adding an appropriate celebrity endorser is another effective way to enhance credibility. The name of a company can, too. For example, there was a company by the name of The Tool Shack selling computers. This company's name actually detracted from the credibility of the product they were selling. We once ran the same ad in *The Wall Street Journal* to test the effect of our JS&A name against a lesser known name—Consumers Hero. In the test, the JS&A ad far outpulled the other ad. Only the name of the company was different. Sometimes a city or state can add credibility. That's why some companies located in smaller cities have offices in London, Paris or New York. The various ways of adding credibility should be an important consideration in crafting your advertising.

5. Value and Proof of Value

Even if you are a multi-millionaire, you want to know that you are not being taken advantage of, and even more importantly, that you are getting value for your financial investment.

In an ad, you want to convey, through examples or by comparison, that what the customer is buying is a good value. A typical example in one of my ads is where I compare my prices to products with similar features and point out that I'm providing a better value.

By positioning your product and comparing it with others or by proving the value of something even though the value may not be apparent, you are providing the logic with which the prospect can justify the purchase.

Simply educating the reader to the intrinsic value of your product is equivalent to lowering its price. In short, there is a value associated with the education you are providing your reader.

The buying transaction is an emotional experience that uses logic to justify the buying decision. You buy a Mercedes automobile emotionally but you then justify its purchase logically with its technology, safety and resale value. So justifying its value is something that the consumer wants to do before making an emotional purchase.

And with such intense competition in the world, there is a question in the mind of the consumer: "Am I buying the product at the best price?" Once again, you must resolve that question or you are not communicating effectively with your prospect.

6. Justify the Purchase

One of the questions people may think about while reading an ad is "Can I really justify this purchase?" Once again, it is a question that is raised and then must be resolved. If you don't resolve it, then you won't answer all the prospect's questions and this will give the prospect the excuse to "think about it" and, of course, never buy.

Somewhere in your ad, you should resolve any objection by providing some justification to the purchaser. Sometimes it's just saying, "You deserve it." And other times you might have to justify it in terms of savings (the price is a one-time-only value), health reasons (protects your eyes), recognition (the men in your life will love the way you look in it) or dozens of other reasons based on the wants and needs of your prospect.

I've often had people tell me, "Joe, when I read your ads, I feel guilty if I don't buy the product." That's quite a compliment and probably due to the way I justify a purchase in the mind of the consumer.

The higher the price point, the more need there is to justify the purchase. The lower the price point or the more value the price represents, the less you have to justify the purchase. In fact, the lower the price, the more greed plays a role.

7. Greed

Greed in the form of attraction to bargains is a very strong motivating factor. I don't know how many times I've bought things even though I didn't need them simply because they were a bargain.

Don't hesitate to recognize greed as a very strong factor in either low-priced merchandise or expensive products offered at low prices. Too low a price may diminish your credibility unless you justify the low price. Many people are willing to risk dealing with an unknown vendor and pay less just to get something more for their money. Providing the consumer with more than what is normally received for the price is a way of appealing to the consumer's greed.

In one of my earlier ads in *The Wall Street Journal,* I offered a calculator for $49.95 and the manufacturer got really upset with me. "That product should have sold for $69.95 and now I have dealers all over the country calling me and complaining," screamed the manufacturer.

"Don't worry," I said. "I'll correct it." So I ran a small ad in *The Wall Street Journal* announcing my error, raising the price from $49.95 to $69.95 and giving consumers just a few days to respond at the old price. Even though the size of the ad was considerably smaller, it outpulled the previous one as people rushed to buy the calculator within those few days at the $49.95 bargain price.

Greed is not a technique that can be employed all the time. But it should be recognized as an effective element that plays on everybody's weakness.

When you lower the price of a product, you usually end up with more unit sales. Keep lowering the price, and you'll continue to generate more unit sales than before if the price drop is big enough. Go too low and you'll have to add a little justification for the lower price as it will start raising credibility issues with your prospects.

Greed is really not a very positive human trait. But it exists and it is a force to consider when communicating with your prospects.

8. Establish Authority

There's always something that you can say about your company to establish your authority, size, position or intention. The consumer loves to do business with experts in a particular area. That's why the trend is away from department stores that sell general merchandise to category stores that sell a specific line of products. These stores have more expertise, knowledge and authority in a specific category.

For example, for years I would call JS&A "America's

largest single source of space-age products." What I was really doing was establishing the authority of JS&A as a major supplier of space-age products. The words "single source" really meant that we shipped our products out of a single location. We may not have shipped more space-age products than Sears or Radio Shack, but we shipped more out of a single location and we specialized only in space-age products.

Establishing your authority is something that should be done in each ad regardless of how big or how little you are. For example, "America's largest supplier of specialized products for the chimney sweep industry." (One of my seminar participants was actually in the chimney sweep industry.) Or even if you are the smallest, you can always say, "The hardest-working bunch of guys in the advertising business." If you really examine your company, you will find something that you can say that establishes your authority and expertise in what you are selling.

Then, after you establish your authority, there is going to be the temptation to stop using the phrase that established your authority. I know that when we had run our phrase for almost six years I wondered if we really needed it. But there were always those first-time readers who caught the ad and needed that reassurance that they were dealing with an authoritative company in the field in which they were contemplating a purchase. That phrase gave them the confidence.

Sometimes it is easy to establish authority by virtue of the name of the company. "American Symbolic Corporation" was a company I set up once and which sounded like it was a very big operation. "Jack and Ed's Video" doesn't sound very big at all. Computer Discount Warehouse gives you a pretty good idea of their authority. It has name recognition, plus it tells you what it is through its name.

People Respect Authority

People naturally respect a knowledgeable authority. Let's say you want to buy a computer. You might first check with the expert in your neighborhood who is known as the neighborhood computer genius. Let's call him Danny. He has established his authority and you feel quite comfortable going to Danny to get advice. He'll then tell you what he thinks you should buy and from whom.

And chances are, he'll recommend some retail outlet that has established itself with some level of authority. It might be the cheapest computer company or maybe the company that provides the best service. You'll seek out the type of authority you need.

Sometimes the authority does not even have to be stated but can be felt by the copy, the layout or the message of an ad. Establish your authority in the field of the product or service you are selling and you'll find that it will make a big difference in your copy's effectiveness.

Let me give you a personal example of something that really illustrates the point. As I was about to walk into a local business supply store in Las Vegas, a young lady came running up to me and said, "Please, could you help me?"

I was a little surprised by the suddenness of her approach and, in fact, first thought that there was some kind of emergency. "Sure, what's the problem?"

Almost with tears in her eyes, she answered, "I'm about to buy a computer and I've picked out the one I like the most, but I need somebody to tell me if I've made the right choice. If you know about computers, could you come in the store with me and give me your opinion?"

I agreed and went into the store with her. The girl explained that she was attending college at UNLV (the University of Nevada at Las Vegas) and since this was her first computer, she needed reassurance from somebody who knew computers that this was a good and wise purchase. She told me how most of the people in the store really didn't know that much about computers. I looked over the computer and, having pretty good knowledge about home computers, told her that she had indeed made a wise choice and that the computer was also a good value. I pointed out some of the technical features that would help her in her schoolwork, and although she didn't have any idea of what I was talking about, she felt that she was making the right choice because I said so.

Nobody Wants to Make a Mistake

Relieved, she thanked me, and then was off to buy her new computer. As she was walking away, she looked over her shoulder and said, "I've worked hard for my money and I didn't want to make a stupid mistake."

Before you bought a computer, you may have first called somebody who was a partial expert on computers to ask for an opinion. You too wanted reassurance and confidence about the purchase you were making—that the money you were about to exchange for a computer was going to be spent wisely. The same holds true when you buy anything of value. You just want reassurance. If, however, you can trust the sales organization as the experts, then you won't need any outside expert opinion as the young student needed in the example above.

Even after you buy something, you often seek confirmation that your purchase was a good one. The late direct marketing consultant Paul Bringe once wrote: "One of the first things we do after making a sizable purchase is to seek assurance from others that our decision was a good one. We tell our family, our neighbors, our friends and our business associates and wait for their approval."

One of the surprises I had while taking orders on our phone lines at JS&A was the number of customers who stated something like, "I bet that's one of your best-selling products." In many cases, it wasn't. But in every case, whenever I mentioned that the product they had just purchased was indeed a very popular product, there was always a comment like, "I just knew that it was." People need reassurance that they have made the right purchase.

9. Satisfaction Conviction

When you saw this heading, you might have thought we are talking about the trial period. Indeed, a trial period could be defined as a form of satisfaction conviction. "If you aren't totally satisfied with my product within one month, you may send it back for a full refund." But that isn't what we mean here. Sure, every direct response offer should have a trial period. After all, the consumer needs to touch and feel a product to make a decision about whether to keep it. So the trial period provides the buyer with a level of confidence. The consumer can change his or her mind if it is not exactly what he or she is looking for.

But a satisfaction conviction is more than a trial period. It basically conveys a message from you to your prospect that says, "Hey, I'm so convinced you will like this product that I'm going to do something for your benefit to prove how incredible my offer is."

If your potential customer, after reading what you are going to do, says something like, "They must really believe in their product," or "How can they do it?" or "Are they going to get ripped off by customers who will take advantage of their generosity?" then you know you've got a great example of a satisfaction conviction.

Let me give you an example. When I first offered BluBlocker sunglasses, I said in my TV advertising, "If you're unhappy with BluBlockers, I'll let you return them anytime you want. There is no trial period." A lot of people thought to themselves, "That must be a good product or otherwise they wouldn't make that offer." Or they may have said, "Boy, are they going to get ripped off." In either case, I conveyed a conviction that my customer was going to be so satisfied that I was willing to do something that is rarely done.

In one ad, I stated, "If you aren't happy with your purchase, just call me up and I'll personally arrange to have it picked up at my expense and refund you every penny of your purchase price including the time you took to return the product."

Testing a Satisfaction Conviction

Once I was able to test the power of a satisfaction conviction. In an ad I wrote for the company called Consumers Hero, I was offering subscriptions to a discount bulletin showing refurbished products at very low prices. But rather than just mail the bulletin to prospects, I formed a club and offered a subscription to the bulletin. I tested various elements in the 700-word ad. I changed the headline and tested it and improved response by 20%. I changed the price and saw little change in total response. The lower the price, however, the more orders I received. But when I changed just the satisfaction conviction, the response rate doubled.

In one ad, I said, "If you don't buy anything during your two-year subscription, I'll refund the unused portion of your subscription."

In the second ad I stated, "But what if you never buy from us and your two-year membership expires? Fine. Send us just your membership card and we'll fully refund your five dollars plus send you interest on your money."

In the first ad, you see a basic, simple trial-period type offer. In the second version, however, you see an offer that goes well beyond the trial period and can be classified as a satisfaction conviction.

In the test, the response doubled even though the satisfaction conviction was at the very end of the ad. This meant that people read the entire ad and then, at the very end when that important buying decision had to be made, the satisfaction conviction removed any remaining resistance to buying into the concept.

If you have gotten the reader into the slippery slide and all the way to the end of an ad, it's that last part of the ad where you've got an awful lot to do. Think about it. You've got to explain the offer to the prospect, why it's a good offer and why he or she should buy the product, and then you've got to do something dramatic to push him or her over the edge—all within the very last part of your sales message. It's like a salesperson asking for the order and then also saying, "And if you buy this from me now, I will do something that few salespeople would do to ensure your satisfaction."

The right satisfaction conviction is important too. The ideal satisfaction conviction should raise an objection and resolve it, as I've indicated in the previous chapter, but in resolving it, go beyond what people expect.

It was effective in my Consumers Hero ad because it tied perfectly into resolving any last-minute resistance. First it raised the objection—"What if I don't buy from your bulletin over a two-year period?" And then I resolved it with a satisfaction conviction—something that went beyond what people expected.

But be careful to use a satisfaction conviction that makes sense for the offer. You wouldn't want to raise an objection and then satisfy it with the wrong resolution. Make sure any objection is indeed satisfied by the correct resolution. In short, it's got to make sense.

The satisfaction conviction is a critical part of the sales message and few realize its importance. Yet, if you can create a powerful satisfaction conviction, this simple device will do a great deal for the success of your offers.

10. Nature of Product

This is one of the really important keys in determining how to sell a product. First, you have to realize that every product has its own unique personality, its own unique nature, and it's up to you to figure it out.

How do you present the drama of that product? Every product has one very powerful way of presenting itself that will express the true advantages and emotion that the product has to offer and motivate the largest number of people to buy it.

Remember the Midex burglar alarm that I sold for many years through full-page ads in national magazines? What was the nature of that product and how could I motivate people to buy it? I explained that in Chapter 2.

I used the security system as an example of the nature of products. This was an unusual product because it had a unique personality. The product category itself had its own profile. By realizing the nature of every product and playing to its strengths, you will end up with a very powerful and emotionally dramatic presentation.

Think about other examples. What is the nature of a toy? It's a fun game. So you bring out the enjoyment. What is the nature of a blood pressure unit? It's a serious medical device that you use to check your blood pressure. Note the word 'serious'. What is the nature of a burglar alarm? It's a serious product that should be easy to install, work when it is supposed to and provide protection to concerned homeowners. Very often, common sense is all you need to understand and appreciate the nature of a product.

Realize that you must understand the nature of the product you are selling or you won't effectively sell it.

11. Current Fads

There are always a number of fads taking place at the same time. One might be a clothing fad, another might be an unusual expression made popular by a TV show or commercial, or a fad might be a popular trend.

There are also fads in direct response. On TV right now, the hottest products are exercise devices. There was a time when real estate shows were popular. Be aware of the current fads so you can determine the hottest product categories and also the new language of our time. You want to recognize them and harmonize with them.

A good example of recognizing fads and knowing what to do with them comes from an experience I had with Richard Guilfoyle, a direct marketer from Boston. He had a strong sense of history and prided himself on creating replicas of historic American objects—Paul Revere's lantern, a statue of George Washington at Valley Forge, a salt and pepper set from the time of the Revolutionary War. In 1975 his company was doing quite well.

And no wonder, the country was about to celebrate its bicentennial anniversary, and this class of merchandise was being recognized as a way of celebrating the birth of our nation 200 years ago. Sales were brisk. Richard was capitalizing on this current fad for American Revolutionary period products.

Then the bottom of his business fell out. Sales plummeted and he couldn't figure out why. And it all happened just prior to July 4th, 1976—the date of the bicentennial celebration.

When he attended my seminar, he was really quite disappointed with his business. What happened? I suggested that maybe it was because people were associating his merchandise with the anniversary of the United States. Since that date had already passed, his sales reflected this perception.

But Richard insisted that this wasn't the case. "My products have true historic significance and have nothing to do with the bicentennial." Could I simply look at his copy and help him improve it?

After looking over his copy, which was actually quite good, I saw clearly what the problem was. He had not recognized that consumers perceived his products as part of the excitement of the bicentennial and not as a part of American history that they could save and own.

He then showed me a few ads he had prepared as a result of attending my seminar. One of them was for a necklace consisting of a small replica of a Paul Revere lantern that had a diamond in the center representing the candle. It was a beautiful piece of jewelry.

I read the copy and said, "You have a winner here. This ad will do well—not because of the historic nature of the necklace but because of the beautiful piece of jewelry that it is. You're now selling jewelry, Richard, not good old Americana."

Sure enough, the ad was a huge success and he soon realized how a powerful fad can grow and fade.

Fads Generate Publicity

I used fads as a way of generating publicity when I was doing public relations for a few of my clients. One owned a ski resort and was trying to increase the awareness of snowmobiles at his resort. At the time, during the mid to late '60s, the women's lib movement was new, strong and vocal. I suggested that the resort owner ban women snowmobile drivers and issue a press release proudly announcing the fact. He did and the publicity went national. He rescinded his ban and snowmobile sales grew dramatically from the national publicity and attention.

At the same time, one of my accounts—Jerry Herman, owner of the Spot pizza restaurant near Northwestern University in Evanston, Illinois—wanted national publicity too. Women were in the middle of an unusual fad—throwing their bras away and going braless. I suggested to Jerry that he design a bra-shaped pizza and he too got national publicity. While these publicity stunts might seem a bit silly in retrospect, back then they were effective because they tied into a fad of the times.

Later I used fads as a way of selling products. When it was uncovered in 1973 that Nixon was using phone-tapping equipment to record all his phone conversations, there was enormous publicity about it. I immediately put together a JS&A offer of a system whereby anybody could tap their phones and ran the ad in *The Wall Street Journal* under the headline "Tap Your Phone."

That ad was a mistake. The FBI showed up at my door, *The Wall Street Journal* threatened never to run my ads anymore and even worse, I didn't sell many of the systems and lost money on the ad.

Catch One at the Right Time

On the other hand, I caught another fad at just the right time. Remember the Pocket CB that I described earlier in Chapter 2? By calling my walkie-talkie a Pocket CB because it broadcast on the CB frequencies, I was able to capture a major chunk of the walkie-talkie and CB market.

The minute there is a lot of publicity about something and it has the potential of turning into a fad, consider the possibility that it's a good signal for you to exploit the opportunity.

A fad can die just as quickly as it can grow. So you must capture the moment early enough and get out right after the fad peaks. The people who came out with radar detectors when they became a fad did exceptionally well. A few of them attended my seminar and wrote great ads and built their companies into very successful entities.

One of the companies selling radar detectors—Cincinnati Microwave—sent three of their top people to my seminar before it really took off and became a $140 million company with over $40 million in profits.

But be careful. I can tell you stories (I should say nightmares) that show how dangerous fads can be to your financial health. During the Watergate scandal, I once introduced "The Watergate Game—a game of intrigue and deception for the whole family." But no store would carry it because of the controversy and I lost my shirt. I once created the Batman credit card to capture the Batman fad of the '60s and printed 250,000 of them only to be denied a license to sell them.

But as you can see, knowing how to recognize a fad and capitalize on it can be a very powerful tool if your timing is right. This brings us very nicely to the next topic.

12. Timing

How many times have you been too early with an idea or too late? I've heard complaints from many of my students who have failed because their timing just wasn't right.

Timing certainly has a lot to do with fads. You want to be involved at the beginning of a fad and not enter in the middle or the end. That's smart timing. But there are products that have just been introduced too early or too late, and that relates to timing too. When do you introduce a new product? Is America ready for it? And how do you know?

The answer really is quite simple: Nobody knows. That's why every product that I sell, I always test first. The consumer will always tell me if I'm too early or too late or right on target.

When crime increased, it was good common sense to offer burglar alarms. When the O.J. Simpson case unraveled, there were plenty of opportunities to capitalize on it and the media sure did.

President Carter went on television in 1980 and reprimanded Americans, accusing us of running up too much debt. "Stop using your credit cards," was his suggestion. And millions of Americans did just that. Direct-response rates plummeted overnight. Tests that we had previously run and which showed great promise were coming up as losses. Our timing obviously was bad but through no fault of ours. Knowing the cause of the problem helped us keep our sanity.

It's just as important to know when the timing is bad. We came out with a product called the Bone Fone, a portable radio worn around the neck. It was perfect timing until a product called the Walkman came out and killed our new product. Timing. It can kill a product or make it.

I once ran a media test on an electronic blood pressure unit we were thinking of putting in our catalog. I thought it would do well and when the results were presented to me, I was amazed at how well it had done. Armed with a great deal of confidence, I placed a major national advertising campaign in all the magazines we normally advertised in—spending almost $300,000 at the time. But even before the ads started to run I discovered that the report I thought was so good was actually produced in error. The product did not do well in the test and in fact did quite poorly.

Since I had already placed the advertising, I braced myself for the bad response. But my timing proved to be coincidentally right on target. About the same time as the ads started to run, the American Heart Association started running a major advertising campaign suggesting that Americans take their blood pressure regularly. Our sales jumped and what was destined to become one of our biggest losses turned into a nice profit. And we even won the Life Extension Award from the Life Extension Association for our work in alerting the public to the need for measuring their blood pressure regularly.

13. Desire to Belong

The desire to belong is a strong motivational factor in marketing but it is often not appreciated. Think about it.

Why do people own a Mercedes? Why do they smoke Marlboro cigarettes? Why do certain fads catch on? It could be that these people buy a specific product because they subconsciously want to belong to the group that already owns or uses that specific product.

In the case of Marlboros, the smokers subconsciously want to join that group of smokers who have responded to the rugged western image the cigarette's ad agency has created.

The people who buy a Mercedes often want to belong to that special group of Mercedes owners. Do you think it's because of the special braking or suspension system? Forget it. They're going out and spending megabucks to buy something that's maybe slightly better than many of the other automobiles. The other cars can take you to the same places at the same speed and yet these people—all very intelligent—will go out and spend plenty more to buy a Mercedes.

And the list goes on. You name a product that has an established image and I'll show you a consumer who, somewhere in his or her subconscious value system, wants to belong to the group of people who own that product. Fashion, automobiles, cigarettes, gadgets, whatever the category—the consumer who buys a specific brand has been motivated to buy that brand by virtue of the desire to belong to the group of people who already own that brand.

When Volvo discovered that its customer base had one of the highest educational levels of any of the car manufacturers, they publicized this fact. They then noticed that when the same survey was conducted a few years later, the percentage jumped even higher. The increase was caused, in my judgment, by the association that other highly educated new buyers wanted to make with the Volvo owners—they wanted to belong to that group.

I've had my students say to me, "Well, what about hermits? Don't tell me they have the desire to belong."

And my answer was that they want to belong to the group of people who are hermits. To belong to the group means you don't necessarily have to be with anyone or be very social. And maybe the key word here is 'identify'. The Mercedes owner wants to be identified with the class or group of people who also own a Mercedes.

Owning a Rolls-Royce in California in the '70s was the ultimate status symbol. I couldn't believe how impressed people were with other people who owned one. Being a midwest boy and not growing up on the car-conscious West Coast, it was culture shock to realize how much a Rolls meant to somebody from the West Coast. Yet when you look at the car, it is one of the most conservative and old-fashioned-looking automobiles on the road today.

The desire to belong to and identify with a group of people who own a specific product is one of the most powerful psychological motivators to be aware of in marketing and copywriting. But one of the best examples I can give was a personal experience, which leads me to my next psychological point.

14. Desire to Collect

There must be a natural instinct in the human race to collect as I learned from my marketing experience.

If you are selling a collectible, it's pretty easy to understand that this urge exists and therefore, as a direct marketer, you need to capitalize on it. But often overlooked is the fact that it can be used to sell any other product too. Let's take the watch buyer. An enthusiastic watch buyer is your perfect prospect for another watch.

When I was selling watches in print, I would send mailings to those customers who had previously ordered from me and offer them other watches. I received a great response. My best list for watches consisted of my existing watch owners. Now you would think that if you had a watch, what would you need another one for? Wrong. Many people actually collect them. They'll have several watches, several pairs of sunglasses, several pairs of jeans, a library of videos or compact disks. The list is endless.

I'm always amazed at the number of dolls collected by QVC viewers. Some of the viewers are older women, long past childhood, yet among QVC's most avid collectors. And they have dozens of dolls.

You'd be amazed at what people collect.

Small car models are also sold on QVC. They are some of the most popular products. And not to be outdone, there must be thousands of viewers who own many BluBlocker sunglasses—often in several different styles.

The point is, when selling, whether in print or on TV, recognize that there is a very large segment of the population who, for whatever reason, has an emotional need to collect a series of similar products. These products bring great joy and satisfaction and in some cases utility.

And think about those who collect the real cars. Many who can afford them have collections that range up to hundreds of full-sized automobiles. What kind of emotional need are they fulfilling?

One of the ways that direct marketers optimize on the collecting instinct is by sending, free of charge with their very first shipment, some sort of device to hold the collection.

I can remember ordering a series of silver airplane tails with various airline logos embossed on them from the Franklin Mint. I started collecting them to see how the Franklin Mint conducted its program rather than from any interest in collecting airplane tails.

I received a beautiful chest with cutouts for each of the silver tails. And they came once a month and each month I put one more tail in the chest. I looked at my collection each time I put in a new tail and felt the pride of knowing that my tail collection was growing. Finally, I had enough to fill the chest so that when guests came over, I could display my entire tail collection. I finally sobered up and stopped collecting. It was costing me a small fortune, and after all, the only reason I had started was for the research. And the collection was kind of silly to begin with. The airlines were either merging, going out of business or changing their names so fast that even the Franklin Mint couldn't keep up.

But it was this experience that convinced me that there were lots of opportunities for selling to collectors.

15. Curiosity

If I had to pick the one major psychological reason which makes direct marketing so successful today, it would be curiosity. At retail, a customer can touch and experience the product first-hand and then decide. A mail order customer can't do that. The product might look good and do exactly what the customer expects it to do, yet there is always that level of curiosity that makes the product attractive to the prospect. "What is that product really like?" might be the typical thought of a prospect.

When I sold BluBlocker sunglasses on TV, I deliberately created an enormous amount of curiosity. I had my subjects—ordinary people we would find on the streets—try on a pair of BluBlocker sunglasses. I would then videotape their reactions. Some of the reactions were great and when I presented them on TV, the viewers were wondering, "What was it like to look through these glasses—that pair of sunglasses with the orange lenses that was making everybody go wild?"

I didn't take the TV camera and look through a pair. That would have destroyed the curiosity and would not have given the true picture of what the sunglasses would do for you. (Your brain adjusts to the color shift when you look through the lens, whereas the TV camera does not.) Instead, I enhanced curiosity by not showing the view. The only way you could look through them was to buy a pair. And buy the public did—almost 8 million pairs from a series of commercials that ran for six years.

Curiosity also works well with books. You can tease prospects by telling them what they will find out by reading your books. In fact, the strongest motivating factor in selling books is curiosity, followed only by notoriety and credibility.

Because a prospect can't touch or experience the product, curiosity is the strongest motivating factor in mail order. Immediate gratification is the strongest factor in retail. So if I recognize that fact and can deliver your product promptly—let's say with FedEx—I'm capitalizing on the curiosity in mail order and coming close to the retail advantage.

I've sold products relying completely on the factor of curiosity. In 1973 I offered a pocket calculator without ever showing a picture of it. By creating such compelling curiosity about that product, I sold thousands of them. Sure the price was good and the product was great, but without showing the product or even mentioning the brand name, I was still able to make the selling message very compelling.

How do you use curiosity in selling your products? First realize that when you sell books, curiosity is the key motivating factor and you should use it as your prime selling tool. But realize also that there are many other products that lend themselves to holding back part of the story in order to arouse curiosity and create a demand.

Show too much, tell too much and you run the risk of killing whatever advantage you had using mail order as a medium.

A friend of mine, Steve Dworman, who publishes an infomercial trade newsletter, was fascinated by my success using curiosity as the main selling tool in my BluBlocker commercial. He thought to himself, "Could the same technique be used to sell something that was impossible to sell on TV in a direct response commercial? Like perfume?" So he organized the shooting of a commercial using curiosity as its main motivating factor.

In the commercial, everybody was raving about the perfume but there was no way the TV sets allowed viewers to sniff it unless they bought Steve's product. The commercial generated enough curiosity to work.

How many times have you said too much, shown too much or failed to use the power of curiosity? It is one of the leading motivating factors in all direct response marketing.

16. Sense of Urgency

You might have already figured this one out. You've sold the prospect. The prospect believes in your product and is ready to buy. But like many of your customers, this one says, "Well, let me think about it."

It is a proven fact that when this happens, chances are the prospect won't buy. And the reasons are really very logical. First, in time that excellent sales message you wrote will most likely be forgotten. Second, if you're lucky and it isn't forgotten, it won't have the same impact it had when it was first read. That old saying, "out of sight, out of mind," holds true in a case like this.

Therefore, to avoid the delaying tactic, you've got to provide prospects with an incentive or reason to buy now. In fact, if you do your job right, the customer has to feel guilty if he or she doesn't buy right now. But how do you do it?

First, here's what you don't want to do. The prospect has spent a lot of time with your ad and you've convinced him or her to buy. The one thing you don't want to do is blow your integrity at the very end of the ad by making a statement that is not true. A statement like, "If you don't respond within the next few days, we'll be sold out," or some other deceit will turn off the prospect. So be careful. Whatever you say at the end should be the truth and should be crafted to maintain the same integrity expressed throughout your ad.

Now, what can you do to provide a sense of urgency? Some ads reek with a sense of urgency and nothing has to be said. For example, I once ran a retraction for an ad which said that the price listed for a calculator was the wrong price and that the new price was $20 higher, but you had a few days to purchase the product at the old price before the new price went into effect. That approach was an integral part of the concept and provided a sense of urgency that was obvious and very much real.

You can also convey a sense of urgency by offering limited editions. "We only have 1,000 sets and this will be our last advertisement" can be persuasive and motivate the buyer to act right away.

You might have a great ad with a good sense of urgency but a fatal error might still kill your ad's effectiveness. What is that fatal error? Omitting important information that the buyer needs in order to make that buying decision. Then the buyer has the excuse, "There's a question I have but I'm too busy to call and find out the answer," or a similar excuse. In short, even a great sense of urgency can be wasted if you leave out some critical information in your ad copy.

You can use the sense of urgency in many different ways—low supplies, closeout opportunity, price rise, product shortages, limited-time price opportunity or limited-edition opportunity. How about "Buy now so you can start enjoying the benefits of my product tomorrow." Or even "Buy one during the next three days and you'll get a second one free."

Another way to provide a sense of urgency is through your shipping methods. "We'll ship your purchase via FedEx if you order by (a certain date)." Or "Since you are one of our customers, you can buy this wonderful product prior to our national introduction if you order by (a certain date)."

We used to run all our new product introductions with the phrase, "National Introductory Price." This didn't mean that much but it raised the possibility that the price was the introductory price and later might go up. In actuality, the prices of calculators and electronics always went down, so we eventually dropped that phrase.

The number of possibilities is limited only by your imagination. The sense-of-urgency statements always go at the end of your advertising. And if there are two critical locations in your advertising, they are the very beginning and the very end. And it is at the end where the sense of urgency and several other important concepts meet and must be considered and blended seamlessly together.

17. Instant Gratification

This is a big advantage at retail. Think about it. At retail, you pick something up, hold it, touch it and look it over completely. You can make your decision to buy and then you can take it home with you where you can enjoy and use it immediately. You don't have that advantage in mail order.

So to compensate, you should convey to your customer either the advantages in ordering from you via mail or the assurance that you ship promptly and that the customer will have his or her purchase within a few days.

The effort by direct marketers to provide that instant gratification—shipping promptly—has made mail order one of the fastest methods of distribution in the United States and has thus taken a great deal away from the retail industry. I can call a computer mail order company and order a piece of software on Monday morning and use it by Monday evening. That's so much easier than running to the store, parking, finding the right department and then having to deal with the salesclerk. It's no wonder mail order has taken a dramatic bite out of many of the traditional retail categories.

The mail order computer industry created giants such as Dell and Gateway 2000 that specialize in next-day delivery.

And so if you have a product and want to capitalize on the main advantage that a retailer has, find a way to ship your merchandise out quicker, deliver it faster and provide better service than any retailer could ever offer.

18. Exclusivity, Rarity or Uniqueness

These are very strong motivating factors for the right product or the right situation.

The concept is to basically let the prospect feel that he is special if he buys a particular product—that he will belong to the very small group that can be envied for owning this very limited item.

The emotional appeal of this approach is quite strong. Everybody likes to feel special. Most people would like to belong to a rare group that owns a product that few people can own and enjoy.

By limiting the number they produce, some marketing companies have come up with a very strong appeal for consumers. The Franklin Mint—a multi-million-dollar business—was built on the premise of the limited edition, first with coins and then later with everything from plates and cups to model cars and dolls. Anything you could collect and they could limit was fair game for the Mint.

The thought behind the limited edition is also to provide value. As people build various collections of things, the objects grow in value if others start collecting the same goods too. Soon, the collections come to the attention of the mass market and that attracts more collectors. Then the value of the collections really starts to grow.

Those collectibles which have a limited circulation or a limited number in circulation grow in value even more. And there's always the story of somebody discovering an old heirloom in the attic worth a small fortune. There are exceptions of course—silver airplane tails, to name one.

One of the appeals of an exclusive item is the possibility of extra future value implied by limiting the circulation of that product.

The power of exclusivity was driven home to me in October of 1980 when I was in Minocqua, Wisconsin. It was right after I had given a seminar.

At the seminar site, for the enjoyment of the participants, I kept a stable of six snowmobiles. Whenever I would give a seminar during the winter, I would have these machines available for my students during their breaks. Riding snowmobiles was a lot of fun and everybody loved to drive them. Then one day the president of Mattel Electronics, Jeff Rochlis, broke his arm in a bad snowmobile accident. That ended our snowmobile program.

I now had six snowmobiles in my garage with not many people to use them. Out of curiosity, one day I visited the local snowmobile shop—the same place that sold me the six that I owned. I obviously didn't need any more but wanted to see what small improvements were added in the new models.

I walked into the shop and asked the salesman, "Well, Paul, what's new for this year?"

Paul took me over to a snowmobile that was propped up on a small riser and pointed to it. "This baby is our new oil-cooled model that goes over 100 miles per hour and sells for $2,600."

At the time, snowmobiles were selling for under $1,000 and their top speed was around 40 miles per hour so this new model was obviously special. But regardless of how special it was, I already had six and I certainly did not need any more. I turned to Paul and in a matter-of-fact way said, "Who could possibly want a snowmobile that could go 100 miles per hour and cost $2,600? How ridiculous."

Paul chuckled, "Well, there are only going to be six sold in the entire state this year. We've only been allocated two of them and we already have one sold."

I then quickly blurted out, "I'll take this one." Yes, I ended up buying it. I wanted to be one of the few who owned this powerful new machine. I wanted to feel that I was part of a unique group and that I was special. And even though I didn't need any more snow-mobiles, I ended up buying it and I was proud of the fact that I did.

It was this incident that made me realize the power of exclusivity, uniqueness and rarity.

19. Simplicity

You must keep your advertising copy simple. The position-ing of your product must be simple. Your offer must be simple. In short, you want to keep your entire presentation as simple as possible while still getting across your message.

There are times when you want to turn something simple into something complex. We talked about that in the previous chapter under the topic "Product Explanation." But that rule applies to marketing issues and here we are looking at the basic psychological motivator of simplicity.

What does this mean in terms of your advertising copy? I like to tell my students to focus. Focus on what you are trying to accomplish and eliminate things that either complicate your presentation or aren't necessary.

This doesn't mean you write copy that is so simple a third grader can read it. That's not what we mean by simple. The copy should be able to be read by the less educated people as well as the more educated and come across clearly. It is not good style to write either "up" or "down" to anybody.

The use of big words to impress is one example of writing up to somebody. You're trying to impress with your use of words while somebody else who might not be familiar with your fancy words will be lost. Use simple easy-to-understand words. Words are, after all, stories—emotional images—each having an impact sometimes greater than we think. Using simple words has the greatest impact. Using words that everybody can understand has a greater impact than words that most people have difficulty with.

And keep your layouts simple. Tests have confirmed that things like color bars across an ad, fancy type that is difficult to read and lines that draw your eyes away from the copy can hurt comprehension. Fancy typefaces may look good but they often give the lowest comprehension scores.

Simplicity Is a Powerful Tool

If you have a tendency to complicate things, you're not going to succeed in writing good direct-response advertising copy. Be aware of this important point as you decide which type-face to use, how you want to present your product and the offer you want to make.

A good example of how simplicity works in direct response happened to me when Murray Raphel, a dear friend and a great public speaker, approached me. He had been in touch with the people who had developed the Swiss Army watch and wondered if I would be interested in marketing the product in the United States. Yes, I was. A meeting was arranged in which I was going to see the line of watches.

At the meeting I was presented with three styles and three colors in each style for a total of nine different watches. One was a men's style, the second was for women and the third was for children. The colors were black, red and khaki. I examined the watches, learned the history and in general became very knowledgeable about the watches themselves. Then came the big question.

"Mr. Sugarman, you've examined the watches. What do you think?"

I looked over the watches, thought for a few minutes and answered, "I'd like to run just the men's watch in black in *The Wall Street Journal* to test the concept."

The watch company executives looked perplexed. "Why don't you offer all the styles? Look at how many more people you'll reach if you offer nine different styles. You'll reach women and children in addition to men and you'll give them all a color choice."

I told them that in my experience, keeping it simple was the best approach and that offering a customer too many choices was a very dangerous thing to do.

But no matter what I said, they would not agree. "Logic says, Mr. Sugarman, that offering more of a choice will result in more sales."

I then came up with an idea to prove that I was right. I offered to run two separate ads in what is called an "A/B split." That is where *The Wall Street Journal* will print two separate versions of the same ad—version A and version B—to be delivered in the same area at the same time. So one home will get one version of the ad while the next-door neighbor might get version B. This was a very good way to test two different ads to determine the winning approach.

I offered to do the test and ran the two ads with almost

Both ads were practically identical with ad A (top) offering nine different models and ad B (bottom) offering only one.

identical copy and graphics. One of the few differences was that in ad A, I showed the men's watch along with the child's watch for size perspective, whereas in ad B, I showed just the men's watch. I then listed each one of the choices—nine in all—in ad A and just one in ad B.

When I finished the ads, the A version actually looked better than the version with only one choice. When both versions ran, the ad that featured only one men's watch out-pulled the other version that featured nine models by a surprising 3 to 1 ratio. In short, for every watch we sold from the ad that featured the nine styles, we sold three in the other ad that showed just the one black watch.

I knew almost instinctively that to give the consumer a confusing array of choices meant that the consumer would back off and not buy.

When would I show all these nine watches? Later, in my catalog. Once I've located those people interested in Swiss Army watches, I would then show them all nine models in the catalog. By the time the catalog reaches my customer, he or she has been qualified as a watch buyer. I can now offer a larger selection.

Another good example of the power of simplicity occurred during the production of a half-hour TV commercial I was doing for a pill that reduced wrinkles and improved the skin. Called Miracell, the product was truly revolutionary. I had been taking it for a few months and noticed dramatic results. We did two double-blind studies that proved that the product really did work. But there was one major problem.

For maximum effectiveness, you had to take two pills a day for the first three months and then reduce the intake to one pill a day.

This violated my principles of simplicity and I was very concerned that the consumer was going to be confused. You make it easy initially to buy a continuity product and then later you raise the price. For example, the first video in a video series offered on TV may cost only $5. It is a simple offer and it isn't very expensive. You then buy the video and to get the rest of the series, you must pay $19.95 a month to receive a video each month for the next 12 months.

I was going the opposite way. For the first three months, pills would cost double what they would cost during the fourth month and beyond. And here I was recommending taking two pills a day for three months and then one pill a day for the rest of the time. It was really confusing and not very simple.

So I did two things to ensure the success of this show, which we had already spent hundreds of thousands of dollars to prepare. The first was to have the host in the show verify the dosage and tell how the program worked even after I had explained it. We devoted almost three minutes to explaining the complicated offer in order to answer all anticipated questions.

But somehow I knew that the first offer was too complicated. And so I prepared an alternate offer just in case. For the second version I shot additional footage with just a simple offer: "Miracell costs $25 a box and a box lasts one month." That was it. It was very simple and very easy to understand. I knew that I would have to supply my customers with a double dose for the first three months, so three boxes would be at my own expense if this second version of the ad worked and the complicated first version did not.

Sure enough, after testing, the version that worked was the simple one; it outpulled the first one by a very large number. We ended up giving away an enormous amount of product in order to keep the offer simple and make the program simple as well.

Simplicity in direct response is critical and quite necessary. The two examples above are just a few typical experiences from my many years of direct response marketing in various media.

20. Human Relationships

It is always important to relate the product or service you are offering in human terms. How the product will fit, how it will feel, how it will look—all are just some of the ways you can relate. That may seem pretty obvious.

But there are other ways that copy or graphics can bring a human element to an advertisement. And let's look at why this is important.

Buying is an emotional human experience when we exchange our hard-earned money for a product or service. And because we worked hard for that money, the act of buying represents more than just handing over our money. Buying something becomes an emotional event.

Resonating with Your Prospect

Now let's consider for a moment a physical device—specifically a tuning fork. I'm talking about the ones that look like a U-shaped piece of metal. Clang one of the metal tines and you hear a vibration. Take two tuning forks and if they are of the same frequency and you hit just one, the other one will start vibrating even though it did not come into physical contact with the first one.

Taking this experiment one step further, if you take several tuning forks and put them together and hit them all, they will create a harmonic frequency all their own. And if you just happen to know what that combined frequency is and have a tuning fork that matches that frequency, then it too will start to vibrate in resonance with all the other tuning forks.

In creating a direct response advertisement, it is important that you create a condition where your customer is in perfect harmonic resonance with your copy. We talked earlier in this book about getting the prospect to start nodding his or her head in agreement until the close. And the close becomes easier because the prospect is already nodding yes in agreement. It then becomes easier to say yes when that final question is posed: "May I have your order?"

If you look at all the elements of an advertisement as a series of tuning forks that must resonate with your reader, you've got a valuable picture of the dynamics that take place during the selling process.

One tuning fork might be the headline, another might be the picture, another might be the caption, and on to the first sentence and through the copy to the final offer. In a print ad, the vibrations must be conveyed through the elements in the advertisement.

In order to create these positive vibrations, you first must interest the prospect in reading your copy and then you must really "tune in" and relate to your prospect.

You can add a human element by relating a story in your copy. Stories hold people's interest. I discuss this technique in Chapter 22. Or you can use a byline and write copy in the first person using a conversational tone. This makes your copy a more direct communication from one individual to another. Using humor in a light, nonoffensive way will also develop a human relationship with your prospect. The humor can relate a story in a folksy way as in my ad for the Pet Plane in Chapter 30 or it can bring out the "humanness" of the person marketing their product or service as I've done in my ad for the Magic Stat thermostat in Chapter 29.

Another approach is to use a picture of a human hand holding a small product. The hand adds size and perspective to what is being presented and also adds that human element.

You can use attractive models. People like to relate to pretty women or handsome men even though they may not themselves be attractive. In a subtle sense, they want to belong to the group of people in the picture. On the other hand, you don't want to use a picture of yourself if you think some of your readers may respond negatively to it. Especially if you look like a bearded villain from some B-rated movie.

In short, in your advertising you want to use as many positive human elements as you can without risking any negative vibrations from emotional reactions.

And if you do your job right, your advertisement will have its own vibration—so much so that some people will be able to pick up that vibration and almost feel that they know you.

21. Guilt

Have you ever received mailings from charities that include a small gift? The gifts are usually address stickers, colorful stamps or some other inexpensive token. Or how about those mailings with surveys that include a dollar bill or a reply envelope with a return stamp? In both cases you may have experienced a slight touch of guilt. After all, you've received something of value and you feel an obligation to take some action in return, such as sending in a donation or answering the survey. These are good examples of the use of guilt. But how do you use this technique in a print ad when you can't include stickers or a dollar bill?

I've had many people tell me that after they read one of my ads, they not only are compelled to buy my product, but feel guilty if they don't. Instead of giving them stickers or a dollar bill, I give the reader plenty of compelling information and reading entertainment—so much so that they sense an obligation to respond. In a print ad, often the mere repetition of seeing an ad in several magazines works to create a slight sense of guilt.

Repeated mailings also create guilt. Keep sending somebody mailings and after a while, they may feel guilty that they haven't responded. I used this technique when I sold ski lifts for a company called Ski Lift International. Each week I sent out a small mailing with a premium gift enclosed. One mailing would have a button, another an unusual mailing piece and still another an involvement device. After a while, many of the recipients felt guilty and responded. Some even apologized for not responding earlier.

22. Specificity

Being specific in your explanations is very critical and can establish your credibility. Let me first give you an example. If I were to say, "New dentists everywhere use and recommend CapSnap Toothpaste," it sounds like typical advertising lingo—puffery designed to sell a product. It's so general that it will probably cause a viewer to discount the statement you have just made and maybe everything else you say. But if I said, "92% of new dentists use and recommend CapSnap Toothpaste," it sounds much more believable. The consumer is likely to think that we did a scientific survey and that 92% was the result.

When people perceive certain general statements as puffery or typical advertising babble, those statements are at best discounted and accepted with some doubts. On the other hand, statements with specific facts can generate strong believability. I once wrote an ad for a company I created called Battram Galleries—a collectibles company. In the ad I stated the exact cost of running the ad, the exact cost of the product and I clearly demonstrated through specific figures that we weren't making any profit from the offering. It was so successful, it was oversubscribed. I've used this technique on video as well.

In my BluBlocker infomercials, I state the specific reasons why blue light isn't good for your eyes. I explain that blue light focuses in front of the retina (which is the focusing screen of the eye) and not on the retina as do the other colors. So when you block blue light, you block those rays that don't focus on your retina and therefore objects appear clearer, sharper and more defined. I'm specific. It sounds believable. And the statement is a lot better than just saying, "BluBlocker sunglasses let you see clearer, sharper and with more definition."

If you're describing a product that is designed for the circulatory functions of the body, you can talk about "242 miles of blood vessels" instead of "miles of blood vessels." When you talk about the bottom of your feet, instead of saying, "There are a lot of nerve endings at the bottom of your feet," you can say, "There are 72,000 nerve endings at the bottom of your feet." You are stating a fact as opposed to a general or vague statement. You are more believable.

You Sound More like an Expert

There's one other benefit to being specific. By being specific you sound like you're an expert on your product—you've really investigated it and are very knowledgeable. And this too builds trust and confidence.

People, in general, are very skeptical about advertising and often don't believe many of the claims stated in ads. But when you make a specific claim using the exact facts and figures, your message is much more credible and often trusted.

23. Familiarity

The Kowloon section of Hong Kong is an exciting but very foreign part of the city. Its storefronts, hordes of people and many sounds and smells make for a very unique and exciting place to visit. It is different. And when you are in Kowloon, America seems awfully far away.

I was walking down the street absorbing the energy of the area and stopping occasionally to look in a store when suddenly, right in front of me, I saw one of my American suppliers walking down the sidewalk.

What a surprise. What a totally wonderful feeling to see somebody you know in a totally lonely and foreign place like Hong Kong.

Although previously I hadn't been that friendly with the supplier, I suddenly felt close. I asked if he was available for dinner and I made an appointment for that evening to get together and spend some time with him. As a result, he ended up selling me a lot more than I normally would have bought. The contrast of seeing somebody with whom you are familiar in a totally foreign setting creates a strong attraction. And so it is with advertising.

An Ad as an Old Friend

If somebody is reading a magazine and sees your advertising format—something they have seen many times before—and recognizes your logo or company name, there is a feeling of familiarity. They see a friend in an environment of foreign advertisers and to them you're not foreign. You are familiar and as a result, there is an attraction to your offering just as I was attracted to my supplier in Hong Kong.

Advertise enough times or sell a product whose name is familiar to your prospect and you will create the same attraction. That is why brand names are so important; that is why the familiarity of a shopping environment is also important.

When I first appeared on QVC, the home shopping channel, we sold out our entire inventory of BluBlocker sunglasses within minutes. When our sunglasses first appeared on retail shelves in the Walgreens drug chain, they quickly sold out within a few days. In short, our product was well known to the consumer. Each time we introduced our product to a familiar shopping environment, the combination of brand name familiarity and a familiar selling environment caused an immediate sellout.

Even the word 'familiar' or 'familiarity' has the word 'family' in it. People feel most comfortable within their own family. They feel confident and trusting and allow themselves to be more vulnerable. So it is with anything people are familiar with. They trust a brand name, are more confident that they are buying the right product and are more inclined to do so.

One of the biggest mistakes traditional advertisers make is to kill campaigns they have been using a long time because they are tired of them. "Fly the friendly skies of United" and "You deserve a break today, at McDonald's" are but a few examples familiar to consumers. In addition, consumers often sang along during these commercials. Too often in traditional advertising, the client gets tired of the commercial long before the public does.

In direct marketing, a decision to drop a commercial approach is not arbitrary. You keep running your product or service ad until the public tells you when to stop by virtue of lower sales. The orders simply stop coming in or you have replaced your ad with something that pulls more response. Good direct-marketing technique calls for continually revising or "tweaking" your ad until it does better. But you never drop a campaign because you are tired of it. Drop it only when the public stops exchanging their hard-earned dollars for your product or service.

Now the traditional agencies will tell you something like, "Well, we asked a focus group what they thought about our slogan and they said that they were getting tired of it, so we are going to pull it." This is a major fallacy too. There is no real way to test the effectiveness of a commercial except by virtue of sales. Focus groups only tell you what they think you want to hear and not how they would act themselves. If the product isn't selling, then look at the campaign. Maybe it isn't even the campaign but rather competition or some other element in the marketing mix.

Use Familiar Words

There are certain words that are more familiar to most people and to the human consciousness. For example, if you ask somebody to give you a number from 1 to 10 right off the top of their head, chances are the number 7 will be chosen more often than any other number—often dwarfing the next choice. Therefore, using the number 7 in a book title such as "The Seven Ways to Improve Your Relationships" or "The Seven Spiritual Laws of Success" is utilizing the most common and familiar integer of the first ten. You are therefore vibrating with the familiar and harmonizing with your reader.

Ask somebody for a color off the top of their head and the answer will be 'red' the majority of the time. Ask them to name a piece of furniture and the answer will likely be 'chair'. There are familiar words that can create a very subtle harmony with your reader and it's up to you to find them and use them. Where do you find them? Many books have been written on the effective use of words that really draw response. Books by David Ogilvy or John Caples are good ones to read. A list can be found in Appendix D. There are some powerful words such as 'sale' or 'free'. And then there are the not so obvious words—the ones that relate specifically to your product and which you, as a passionate devotee of your product, inherently already know. Finally, there are words that aren't in your own consciousness and aren't in any books but will only be discovered by testing. Sometimes, changing just one word in a thousand-word ad will double response.

As a copywriter, be aware of the powerful force of familiarity to make a person comfortable with your product or service. Realize the importance of a familiar brand name, a logo that appears many times and becomes well known, a layout that people instinctively know is yours, familiar phrases (not clichés) and words that your public can harmonize with—all of these create the bond that familiarity creates between you and your prospect.

24. Hope

Hope can be a great motivator in the buying process. A woman buys a new face cream that offers the hope it will make a difference in her wrinkles. An intense golfer buys a new golf ball that offers the hope it may take a few strokes off a golf game. In short, there is an implied possibility that using a product or service will provide a future benefit. The future benefit is not assured nor is it guaranteed; it is a dream, a fantasy or, at the most, a possibility. The hope replaces the reality of an already-delivered benefit or guarantee that you receive when you buy other products such as a radio or a computer. Let me cite a few personal experiences and describe how hope applies to specific products.

I was introduced in 1996 to a very successful scientist. He had supposedly invented a formula that cured a great many human ills. The formula contained what he called "biological repair machines" that went to the source of a malfunction in your body and repaired it. If an organ was damaged, these miniature "machines" would repair the organ even if it meant regenerating a new one.

You placed a few drops of this product under your tongue twice a day and it was absorbed into your body.

In a discussion with the scientist, it occurred to me that if people took this product they would never die, if indeed it repaired any defective body part. He agreed. "I'm taking it and honestly feel I am getting younger. Look, my gray hair is starting to turn black again."

The scientist continued claiming that there was no reason why his formula couldn't keep us alive until the age of 300. This sounded incredible to me. If this was true, this man had indeed discovered the fountain of youth.

The scientist appeared to be very credible. He had several Ph.D.'s, and I honestly thought he was one of the smartest people I had ever met. He had three manufacturing facilities in different parts of the world. He had a reputation that extended all the way to Europe and Asia, and he told me how he helped an Asian country cure many of its citizens of a specific form of cancer.

His discovery of the biological repair machines came to him from uncovering formulas that were hidden in coded ancient artifacts and through the process of what he called "sacred geometry." He had apparently cracked the code and opened up a wealth of information. He spent two hours showing me photograph after photograph to substantiate the information he had received from the artifacts.

I had a health problem that was not serious but for whatever reason, doctors did not know its cause or cure. The problem was a few small growths beneath the surface of my skin. They were not cancerous, others hardly noticed them and they posed no health threat. But they were there and they were not normal.

Surgery Was the Only Way

The only method doctors had for eliminating these growths was to cut open the skin and surgically remove them—a relatively easy procedure that was done on an outpatient basis.

I was told by this scientist that indeed his formula could eliminate the problem completely. "In just a few months they'll be gone," he said. In short, I received from him an explicitly clear time frame during which my growths were going to melt away and disappear. The promise wasn't in the form of a hoped-for result or a dream or even a possibility. It was a definite warranty that they would disappear.

I was so impressed by him and his discoveries and he seemed so credible that I decided to put his product to a test. A 750 ml bottle (the size of a wine bottle) of his formula sold for $600. It was rather expensive but it lasted a long time as you only used a few drops each day and it was less costly than the surgical procedure.

A Few Months Go By

After a few months, I noticed that the growths were not gone as I had been promised. I was then advised to buy his stronger formula—the one with a higher concentration of biological repair machines. I did, at a cost of $2,000. Still no improved results after two more months.

I was then told that there was a $20,000 bottle that would do the job (boy, they saw me coming) and believe it or not, I was tempted to get a bottle. I didn't.

Note: In all fairness to the scientist, there were clinical studies done on rats with his formula by a credible pharmaceutical company and there were very positive results with the rats. The research is continuing now on humans and he may have indeed created a powerful new medical concept.

What did I learn from this experience? The doctor should have simply told me about how his formula improved his life. I trusted him. He had all the credibility I needed for me to ingest this foreign substance into my body. What if I could live to 300 years of age? What if indeed I could become younger? I would have gladly taken the formula and continued purchasing bottles of it with the hopes that I was right about him.

Scientist Made Fatal Error

But the scientist made a fatal error. Had he not made any claims to me about specific expected results, I would not have been disappointed but would have continued taking the product waiting and hoping that the stuff would kick in and dissolve those growths. I would, on the basis of hope, have continued taking it and buying more. But once a specific promise was made and I saw that the formula didn't work within that time frame, I immediately refused to invest further. The scientist's credibility was questioned even though he may have had a great product.

When using the psychological trigger of hope, you must avoid the trap of making a specific claim that can be measured or guaranteed. You want to allude to what the product is used for without making any promises of an exact outcome.

There are other products people buy repeatedly, on hope. Let's take vitamins for example. Can people tell if taking vitamins makes a difference in their health? Yes, some can. Interview a bunch of people and they'll swear the vitamins are making a difference. Capture those interviews on TV and they are very impressive. Then prospects, impressed with the results shown on TV, start buying the product and continue to buy it regularly with the hopes that it is making a difference in their lives. But the key here is not to make a specific promise but rather to imply results through testimonials.

How does this apply to selling in print? There are some products that are sold using hope as a strong motivational tool. You need to determine the nature of your product and find something that you can imply about a future result without stating a specific guarantee (particularly if you want to stay in business for a long time).

Many product categories lend themselves to the power of hope. The entire health food industry is a good example, including vitamins, food supplements and even brain enhancers. Lowering your golf score, finding a new relationship, preventing wrinkles, impressing your date—all are good opportunities to recognize the psychological trigger of hope at work.

Focus on Credibility

One aspect to focus on when you create an ad using the power of hope is credibility. If you present yourself as a credible person representing a credible company, then what you say will elicit a feeling of confidence on the part of your prospect. Then, whatever you say your product did for you or for your previous customers will be taken as a possibility for your prospect, and the power of hope will compel your prospect to order. And reorder. It might be a book on relationships and how the information changed your life and those of previous readers. It might be on a formula you take to live a long life and how wonderful you feel. Whatever you are selling, with the proper credibility, you will automatically engage the power of hope to sell.

The preceding chapter is very important in your understanding of the underlying reasons why people buy. Some of the 24 psychological triggers to buying may not have been obvious to you before. Nevertheless, an awareness of each of these points will give you a tremendous boost in becoming a great copywriter. The following chapter is also very important in understanding the mental process that takes place in your prospect's mind. It will help supercharge the information you have already learned.

Have you ever gone to a movie and known how it was going to end after watching the first few minutes? Or a movie where every action can be easily anticipated? These movies tend not to be very enjoyable.

However, the opposite is true when you watch a movie that keeps you in suspense until the very end when it reaches a credible surprise ending. Any movie that is not predictable is more enjoyable.

What forces in our mind are in effect that make one movie seem a lot better than another?

I have a theory—one that I strongly believe in—which I feel comes pretty close to the answer.

Axiom 15

The more the mind must work to reach a conclusion successfully, the more positive, enjoyable or stimulating the experience.

I taught this concept at my seminar for many years, and one day one of my participants brought me a copy of a media newsletter which confirmed what I had been teaching. The article claimed that a missing element was responsible for advertising failure—a lack of whole-brain appeal.

The article went on to explain how science is rapidly discovering that different parts of the brain perform different functions and how some brain researchers are suggesting that human beings experience the most pleasure when all parts of the brain are engaged in pleasurable levels of stimulation and activity.

The four parts of the brain discussed were those that control thinking, intuition, sensation and emotion. The theory suggests that advertising which pleasurably engages the senses, emotions and thought process as well as our innate intuition will tend to be successful, while advertising which merely grabs the attention of the senses will tend to be only temporarily attractive. Most advertising tests today reflect the power of day-after recall but fail to predict the response from whole-brain advertising.

Anything that causes the mind to work hard to reach a conclusion creates a positive, enjoyable or stimulating effect on the brain.

Let's look at how whole-brain advertising applies to copywriting. If you make your copy too obvious, the reader is feeling either looked down upon or bored. Provide a little suspense so that the reader has to come to a conclusion on his or her own using intuition, thinking, sensation and emotion and you've got a very good force working for you. Let me cite an example from an ad I wrote on digital watches.

The ad was for an alarm chronograph digital watch. At the time, Seiko was the standard of comparison for this type of watch. They were the first out with the new technology.

The following paragraph from the ad best exemplifies what I am talking about:

> The Seiko chronograph alarm sells for $300. The watch costs jewelers $150. And jewelers love the item, not only because of the excellent reputation of the Seiko brand, but because it's probably America's best-selling new expensive digital watch. And Seiko can't supply enough of them to their dealers.

Now note what I didn't say but what was rather obvious. Read the quote again to see if you pick it up. What I didn't say was that the jewelers were making a small fortune each time they sold a Seiko. I didn't have to say it, yet the readers could come to their own conclusion all by themselves using their intuition, thinking and emotions. Had I made it too obvious by adding the line "and jewelers are making a small fortune," it would not have been as powerful. The mind had to work a little to reach a conclusion through its own thought processes.

This is a very subtle but powerful concept. It's the difference between talking down to a prospect and making the prospect think along with you. And it is one of the most difficult theories to understand.

Working Hard Brings Appreciation

To get a better appreciation for the theory, think back in your life to those times when you had to work hard to achieve something and how much more you appreciated what you achieved.

I remember all the work I had to go through to get my instrument rating after getting my private pilot's license. It took me months of flying and study, not to mention thousands of dollars in expense. And when I finally received my instrument rating, it was one of the thrills of my life.

On the other hand, when I took my commercial rating test, it was simple. Not that much study, very little flying and within a few weeks I had the rating. Sure I was proud that I was finally a commercial pilot, but nowhere near as proud as I was of my instrument rating. Working hard for a successful conclusion brings a great deal of personal satisfaction.

The same holds true for the mind and the thinking process. Anything that causes the mind to work hard to reach a conclusion creates a positive, enjoyable or stimulating effect on the brain. The opposite is true if the mind does not have to work hard and the conclusion is obvious.

You appreciate that sale to a difficult client a lot more than the one to the pushover who bought the very first minute. When a very difficult product is given to me to sell and I am successful, I get great pleasure from it. But give me a really easy product—something that is already in demand—and I don't have the same feeling of satisfaction.

Vague Descriptions Promote Work

When Hemingway described beautiful women in his books, he was never very specific. He used general terms and let his readers picture them in their imagination.

And so it is with copywriting. If you make your copy too obvious, the reader feels either patronized or bored. Make the reader think to come to a conclusion, and you create a very stimulating mental effect.

Another good example is the experience I had with a jogging machine. It was a small flat platform on which you jogged in place, with a separate unit that had a digital readout showing the distance you were jogging. It was an inexpensive solution that allowed you to jog indoors. I showed a dramatic view of the unit and the readout and explained its use without showing the readers a picture of how it actually looked with somebody jogging on it. I felt that showing a jogger was showing too much and that the drama of the unit was all that was needed to sell it.

It sold fairly well. But then I started getting pressure from my Japanese supplier who couldn't understand why I didn't have somebody jogging on the unit, thereby showing clearly how the product was used. They were convinced that sales would increase. I disagreed but decided to do as they recommended and even put the ad in color, whereas before it had just appeared in black and white. The ad bombed.

Telling Too Much Will Hurt a Sale

Telling too much in copy or even in photography can actually harm a sale. Have you ever met salespeople who said too much when selling? I'm sure we can all remember one who didn't know when to stop talking.

How do you write copy that doesn't say too much? You do it in the editing process. You go over your copy after you've written it and you edit with the thought in the back of your mind, "Am I saying more than I have to? Am I challenging my readers' minds? Am I being too obvious?"

I'm convinced there is a chemical process that takes place in the mind that secretes wonderful-feeling hormones each time we have to stretch our minds a little. And the results can make a dramatic difference in how effective you are at getting your prospects to exchange their hard-earned money for your product or service.

Chapter 21 | Selling a Cure, Not Prevention

One of the least understood reasons why many products fail is due to one aspect of human nature. Understand this aspect and not only do you hold the key to creating a successful direct response ad, but you will also understand clearly why some products just plain don't sell.

The key to successfully marketing certain products lies in the nature of that product and the way that product is viewed in the marketplace. The guiding principle can be summed up very clearly: Always sell the cure and avoid selling prevention.

Now what does this mean? Let me explain. If you were my prospect and I tried to sell you a magic pill that contained an extract of carrots and various tinctures of leafy vegetables because it would help prevent cancer, chances are it would be a difficult sale. On the other hand, if you suddenly discovered you had cancer and I said to you that I had a magic pill that would cure the disease, you would be not only willing to try it, but willing to pay considerably more. In the first instance, you might be willing to pay $20 a bottle to prevent the disease but in the other you might be willing to pay $1,000 if it would cure the disease.

Human Nature at Play

The above is an extreme example. But let's take something less extreme. You're a traveling salesperson and stay at hotels a lot. Somebody tries to sell you a spray that you put on your feet before you go to sleep to prevent athlete's foot which might come from walking on a floor that hasn't been cleaned thoroughly. You ignore the sales message because you rarely get athlete's foot, and besides, it's a bother to use. The next week you get athlete's foot and you're at the corner pharmacy trying to find the strongest thing they've got to cure it.

The two situations illustrate two general principles. The first: It is human nature to think you're never going to get the disease or affliction that the preventative can prevent, so it becomes a very tough sell. The second: If you do get the disease or affliction, you're willing to pay a whole lot more for the cure than you were for the preventative and it's easier to sell.

I have been talking in medical or health terms. But this theory also applies to several other products and concepts. I'll go into those in a moment, but let's examine the first step in breaking through the cure/preventative theory and see if you can make the appeal of the preventative as strong as the appeal of the cure.

It can be done, but only if you can position the product to make the preventative the cure. Let me cite an example:

When the Midex burglar alarms were first sold by JS&A in the late '70s, it was definitely a product that was more of a preventative. However, I also knew that there were people who were recently robbed or whose neighbors were recently robbed, and to these people, the Midex alarm was more of a cure. Think about it. At first they thought, "Naw, our neighborhood is safe. I don't need one." And then after their neighborhood was robbed and they needed a cure, "Boy, I'd better get one of those Midex alarms or else I may be next." And of course, there was the prospect who had just been robbed: "Where did I see that ad for that burglar alarm?"

HELLO.,,. BURGLAR ALARM COMPANY ? I NEED ONE... *QUICK!!*

The consumer waited until he felt threatened before he bought.

I also knew that if I advertised in a professional manner and explained the quality and value of my product and its quick and easy installation, as opposed to using the scare tactics expressed through quoting crime statistics, I would attract a different kind of customer. I would attract the person not quite threatened but concerned—a person to whom the product did not currently represent prevention or a cure. In short, it was for somebody who hadn't been robbed and whose neighbor hadn't been robbed, but who realized that there was a problem out there. This last group would save my ad, and when they needed it, they would take it out of their files—often after several months—and call. This actually did happen a lot.

Twenty years ago, The Club automotive steering wheel locking device would have been a tough sale. Back then, car theft was not as big a problem as it is now. But with the increase in drug traffic today and with thousands of cars being stolen every hour, The Club has become more of a cure against your fear of having your car stolen.

The big rage in health food and prevention as I write this today is the melatonin craze. This is a hormone secreted naturally by the pineal gland—a pea-sized object at the center of the brain. It is supposed to help prevent aging. With millions of baby boomers turning 50, it has suddenly become a very big product— more of a cure than a preventative.

Many Products Make Powerful Cures

When I sold my wrinkle pill, Miracell, it too was a cure. If you have wrinkles, you are a great prospect for wrinkle creams and treatments. They represent cures, not preventatives. And think about it. Don't the preventatives like creams to moisturize your skin and sunscreens to avoid sun damage cost a lot less than the cures? But some of the effective wrinkle eliminators cost plenty for a small jar. Miracell sold at $25 for a month's supply.

Insurance is another preventative. "Keep your family from going through hard times after you die." What could be tougher than thinking you're going to die someday? But the older you get, the more you think about it. And remember the story about my friend, the insurance salesman, who always tried to sell me insurance and finally succeeded when my next-door neighbor died suddenly at an early age? I couldn't wait to sign the papers.

You must first make a decision when evaluating a product. Is this product a preventative or a cure? Can the product be positioned as a cure rather than a preventative? Is the market trend changing the perception of your product from being a preventative to being a cure? Or do you simply have a preventative that does not have a broad enough market?

If you've got a cure and the market is large enough, you've got a powerful product. If you've got a preventative, think in terms of how you can change it into a cure. Let me show you how this can be done.

Make a Preventative a Cure

Another pill I have been selling for the past few years, called simply "The Pill," is a fuel conditioning treatment for automobiles. It is a pill you put in your gas tank, and it is both a preventative and a cure.

First, as a preventative, it helps you avoid engine problems by cleaning out your engine before anything serious happens to your car from impurities that could lodge in your fuel injectors. It reduces pollution to help you pass the many mandatory emission tests conducted throughout the United States, and it prevents you from having to visit the repair shop. Again, these are the preventatives.

But when I go on TV at QVC to present The Pill, I don't talk that much about what it prevents but rather what it cures. It cures engine knock, it eliminates ping, it saves up to 10% on gas. If you flunk your emissions test, use The Pill and you'll pass the next time. In short, I emphasize the curative aspects of the product and underplay the preventative features. And The Pill is truly a miracle product. (I swear, it really works.) This brings me to my next point.

Notice how I have to swear that The Pill mentioned above really works. Selling truly breakthrough products is the toughest marketing job in the world because people find it difficult to believe that these products really work. And belief is one of the strongest motivational factors in human nature. If your prospect believes in something, he or she will move mountains to obtain it, but if he or she doesn't believe in something, you won't move that prospect an inch.

In this chapter you've learned that you sell the cure, not the preventative, that preventatives don't sell very easily and that some products can be changed from preventatives to cures. You've also learned that you can charge a lot more for a cure than you can for a preventative. And finally, I've demonstrated that you can successfully market a product that is both a preventative and a cure by emphasizing its curative aspects while underplaying its preventative aspects. So let's summarize what you've learned in a simple statement that we can refer to in the future:

Axiom 16

Selling a cure is a lot easier than selling a preventative unless the preventative is perceived as a cure or the curative aspects of the preventative are emphasized.

The information presented in this chapter will be very helpful for you in evaluating products in the future. Simply understanding that the cure/preventative factor exists will help you to select and then position your next product for selling.

But now it is story time. And if a sudden rush of interest now perks you up and you are already waiting eagerly for the story, you're not alone. Everybody loves a good story. And the effective use of telling a story in your advertising is explained in the next chapter.

Chapter 22 | Telling a Story

People love stories, and one of the really good ways to relate to your audience is to tell a story. Just as a picture is worth a thousand words, a story can be invaluable and often provides an emotional relationship that keeps the reader riveted and reading. Stories create human interest and in our childhood, stories read to us by our parents influenced the way we fantasized or even saw the world. In short, we've been primed for stories ever since we were very young.

Telling a story is a powerful tool to create a bond between you and your prospects.

Think of the public speaker who starts a speech with a story or uses stories throughout the presentation. It makes for a more interesting presentation and helps hold the interest of the audience. In fact, very often after I've been listening to a boring speaker and start to doze, I wake up when I know a story is about to be told.

Stories Have Lessons to Teach

Stories usually have lessons to teach or experiences to share or even endings that can excite and surprise. And so it is with advertising. If you can tell a story in your advertisement that is relevant to either selling your product, creating the environment or getting the prospect well into your copy and into the slippery slide, you are using this wonderful and powerful tool as a very effective way to sell your product or service.

And finally, some stories add that human element which allows you to relate more closely with your prospects.

Kathy Levine, one of QVC's top TV salespersons, wrote in her book *It's Better to Laugh*, "I realized early on that selling is a matter of capturing people's attention and holding it with a good story." The most interesting salespeople I knew always had a story to tell. It was their way of relating to their customers and entertaining them as well. One in particular has a repertoire of a thousand jokes—each relevant to the selling environment and what he has to sell. And, as you would imagine, he is very effective. Remember, selling in print is similar in principle to selling in person. And if telling a story is a very good sales technique face to face, then chances are you can translate this concept into writing effective copy.

My most successful print campaigns all had stories as the basis for my presentation—the BluBlocker sunglasses, the Bone Fone, Magic Baloney (the Magic Stat thermostat) and several others are examples. Let's take a closer look at the use of this technique in a few ads.

The following paragraphs from my BluBlocker ad will give you a flavor of how a story can be very helpful in creating that human interest which will cause your prospects to read your entire message. The full ad is in Chapter 33.

> **Headline:** Vision Breakthrough
>
> **Subheadline:** When I put on the pair of glasses what I saw I could not believe. Nor will you.
>
> **Byline:** By Joseph Sugarman
>
> **Copy:** I am about to tell you a true story. If you believe me, you will be well rewarded. If you don't believe me, I will make it worth your while to change your mind. Let me explain.
>
> Len is a friend of mine who knows good products. One day he called excited about a pair of sunglasses he owned. "It's so incredible," he said, "when you first look through a pair, you won't believe it."
>
> "What will I see?" I asked. "What could be so incredible?"
>
> Len continued, "When you put on these glasses, your vision improves. Objects appear sharper, more defined. Everything takes on an enhanced 3-D effect. And it's not my imagination. I just want you to see for yourself."

The story continues as I personally see the sunglasses and learn more about them from Len. The ad uses a conversational tone which covers all the important points on the sunglasses, the danger from the sun and the danger caused by blue light. A story is used very effectively to build curiosity and cause the reader to read all the copy and eventually read the final sales pitch.

The ad worked extremely well and from this ad we sold 100,000 pairs of sunglasses at $59.95 each for a total sales volume of $6 million. This was before I presented the product in an infomercial first at $39.95 and then later at $49.95 and sold close to 8 million pairs over a six-year period from 1987 through 1993.

Then there was an ad I wrote in which I offered a $6 million home. The "tell a story" concept in this ad ran almost the entire length of the advertisement:

> **Headline:** Mail Order Mansion
>
> **Subheadline:** It's only 6 million dollars and comes complete with swimming pool, tennis court and a breathtaking view.
>
> **Byline:** By Joseph Sugarman
>
> **Copy:** Have I got a deal. And even if you don't buy this home, you'll love the story.
>
> It all started with an invitation. I was invited by one of the top real estate developers in the country to attend a party at his home in Malibu, California. I didn't know why. All the developer would say is, "Just come."
>
> The jet was waiting for me at O'Hare Airport in Chicago and his chauffeur-driven limousine met me at Los Angeles for the drive to Malibu. It was class all the way.
>
> When I drove up to the home, there was a party going on. Rolls Royces were lined up everywhere and the noise and music from the house made it clear that something special was going on.

The story continues almost the entire length of the ad with the purpose of not only selling the house but offering a videotape of the house which people could order. The entire ad involved me telling this story well into the very last column of the ad where I summarized the offer. The story was the compelling vehicle driving you through the entire ad. You'll find the full ad in Chapter 31.

These ads tell a story. And each story is so compelling that you've got to find out what the payoff is, so you are encouraged to keep reading.

Often the best stories are told in the first person and sound like a personal message from the writer to the prospect. Other stories are told in the third person, but because they are in story form, they still sound quite personal and very compelling.

Frank Schultz wrote his highly successful grapefruit ad after finishing my very first seminar. In fact, his ad almost sounds like the beginning of a fairy tale. The ad copy he wrote was used in one form or another for over 18 years from the time Frank attended the seminar in 1977. It stood the test of time. Here's what he said:

> **Headline:** A Fluke of Nature
>
> **Subheadline:** A new grapefruit discovery may change your concept of fruit.
>
> **Copy:** I'm a farmer. And the story I tell you is the absolute truth, as incredible as it may seem.
>
> It all started in a grove owned by Dr. Webb, our family doctor. One of the men who was picking fruit in the doctor's orchard came up to the Webb house holding six of the strangest grapefruit anyone had ever seen. A single branch of an ordinary grapefruit tree had produced these six unusual fruit.

The story goes on for five paragraphs explaining the discovery and what it meant. And of course, later in the copy the grapefruit was explained further. By the time you finished the fifth paragraph you were hooked. You had to read the rest of the ad as the product took on an almost mystical character. I cover the ad completely in Chapter 25.

Once again, if you can weave a story around your product, it makes for both interesting reading and a way to develop your slippery slide and that perfect buying environment. Storytelling can be best expressed in the following axiom:

Axiom 17   *Telling a story can effectively sell your product, create the environment or get the reader well into your copy as you create an emotional bonding with your prospect.*

Chapter 23 | Rating Your Writing Level

You've gained a tremendous amount of knowledge reading this book. And in Section Three you will use this knowledge to evaluate my mail order ads and those of others who attended my seminar.

But how are you going to rate yourself in the future? Is there some measure you can apply to your writing to determine if you are communicating at the level you need to in order to reach your audience?

Well, fortunately there is a way, thanks to Robert Gunning who created the Fog Index for newspaper writers to help them avoid "foggy writing" and determine for themselves the grade level of the copy they were writing. In short, were they writing with enough clarity so that a fifth grader could understand their copy or must a reader be in high school or even college to understand it? The lower the grade level, the wider the audience.

Reaching a Mass Market

For example, if I wanted to reach a mass market, I would keep my ad copy simple, my sentences short and I wouldn't use big words. On the other hand, if I wanted to reach a very upscale audience, I might use bigger words and longer sentences.

Best-selling books are written for the 8th to 10th grade level. *Time, Business Week* and *The Wall Street Journal* are 11th grade level. The Gettysburg Address and *Reader's Digest* have a 10th grade level in common. And for the most part, the average American audience reads between the 11th and 12th grade levels.

The following are the rules for determining the Fog Index, or grade level of the copy you write:

1. Take a sample of your copy—start with 100 to 125 words from the very beginning of the ad.
2. Count the words in each sentence. Dates and numbers equal one word and independent clauses count as separate sentences (e.g.: "We studied, and we learned" would be two sentences).

3. Divide the total number of words by the number of sentences to get the average sentence length.

4. Count the number of long words (those of 3 or more syllables), but:

>   **a.** Do not count short-word combinations like 'pawnbroker' or 'yellowtail'.
>
>   **b.** Do not include proper names.
>
>   **c.** Do not include verbs that have become 3 or more syllables by adding 'ed' or 'es'.

5. Divide the number of long words by the total number of words in the selection to get the percentage of long words.

6. Add the average sentence length to the percentage of long words.

7. Multiply this total by 0.4 to get the grade level.

Now let's use as an example the Vision Breakthrough ad we saw in the previous chapter. The ad is presented in full in Chapter 33. I will take the first 102 words of copy, and show you how to determine the grade level.

> I am about to tell you a true story. If you believe me, you will be well rewarded. If you don't believe me, I will make it worth your while to change your mind. Let me explain.
>
> Len is a friend of mine who knows good products. One day he called excited about a pair of sunglasses he owned. "It's so **incredible**," he said, "when you first look through a pair, you won't believe it."
>
> "What will I see?" I asked. "What could be so **incredible**?"
>
> Len **continued**, "When you put on these glasses, your vision improves. Objects appear sharper, more defined.

I have put the three long words in bold type. There are 102 total words in this selection and 11 sentences. This means that the average number of words per sentence is 9.3.

The next step is to divide the number of long words (3) by the total words (102) to get the percentage of long words: 2.9%.

Now add the average sentence length of 9.3 words to the percentage of long words, which is 2.9, and you have the number 12.2. Then multiply the number 12.2 by 0.4 and you end up with the number 4.9. In short, this ad started out being understandable to a very large segment of the market by virtue of the fact that it was quite comprehensible to anybody reading at about the 5th grade level and above.

Incidentally, the next block of copy in that same ad had about the same reading level. The third block of copy jumped to 7.2, but by that time the reader was well into the copy. I would suggest that you take different 100-word blocks from different parts of your ad to see how consistent your style is.

Try this with one of your ads or with one of the many ads in Section Three. It is an easy way to determine the level of comprehension of your writing and it will also make you aware of the effect that multi-syllabic words and long sentences have on the comprehensibility of your ad and the level of reader that will resonate with your copy.

The ad that we just tested was one of JS&A's most successful. And it seemed that with many of my ads, the greater the clarity, the broader the appeal and the greater the response. After you've tried it with some of the ads in this book or other ads, you'll be amazed at how easily you will be able to guess the Fog Index from reading just the first few paragraphs of any ad.

Clarity is one of the most important factors in writing copy and the Fog Index gives you an insight into how important short sentences and simple words can be. But don't be obsessed with achieving low Fog Index scores at the expense of common sense. You need to vary the length of sentences and use 3-syllable words when you need them and realize that every audience is different.

You've Learned a Great Deal

You have learned what it takes to be a great copywriter in Section One. You have learned in Section Two what works and why it works.

In the first two sections of this book I have taught you most of the copywriting techniques I taught my seminar participants. You have learned techniques that took me many years to develop. You have learned concepts that I didn't discover and personally use until well into my career. And most importantly, you have learned from my failures—an education that has cost me dearly but that you do not have to experience on your own. Finally, you did not have to pay $3,000 to get this knowledge as my seminar participants did.

In Section Three we take all that you have learned and crys-tallize it into practical knowledge by examining many of the ads that were used as examples in our seminar. This is an important section, for here you see how all the pieces you have learned fit together. We also examine a few ads where the pieces didn't quite fit together and we show you how they could have been done more effectively.

In addition to examining a few ads from beginning to end, I also reproduce a few of the JS&A ads that show my principles in action.

If you've had a problem understanding any of the principles, this is where you'll get greater understanding and clarity. It was during this part of my seminar when participants would often comment, "Now I feel I can do a great ad myself." And they often did.

Section Three

You've learned the principles and theory of copywriting and you've had a chance to see how it all works through my many personal experiences. Now it's time to show you how these principles actually work in some of the complete ad examples that follow. This is the fine-tuning you'll need to perfect your newly learned skills.

During the course of my seminar I showed slides of various ads to illustrate the theories I was presenting. In my first seminars, the ads were mine and those of my competitors—the very companies who were copying my format. But as the course continued and more and more of my students succeeded with the knowledge I gave them, many of the ads I showed at subsequent seminars were created by my former students themselves.

Finally, I used illustrations to show the best and the worst of mail order advertising and even non-mail-order advertising. By the end of the course, not only were my students able to tell me what was wrong with each of the ads that I showed but they were producing great advertising copy and even helping their fellow seminar participants in crafting and improving their advertisements.

Hundreds of ads were presented during the seminar—each on slides. Several of the classic examples were duplicated and passed around. For the book I have selected only a few of the best ads to illustrate the principles I taught—all examples that will solidify everything you've learned so far and add even more to your insights and copywriting skills.

"But hey," you might wonder. "What about those famous JS&A mail order ads that were the hallmark of mail order advertising in the '70s and '80s? Don't they point out some really important principles and aren't they good examples of the best in copywriting?"

Shucks. Well, if you insist. OK, I'll include some of those as well.

Starting in Chapter 29 are some of the JS&A ads that really drive home various points. Not only are they examples of successful copywriting but they are entertaining as well. The fact that I wrote them might come through in my enthusiasm and commentary, so please bear with me. Deep down, I'm really a modest kinda guy.

If your future is in TV marketing, these examples will help you understand marketing in that medium as well. For as you have already learned, my copywriting and marketing principles can be applied to any form of advertising communication.

But now it's time to solidify everything you've learned in Sections One and Two with some classic ad examples to prove many of my points.

Chapter 24 | The Lazy Man's Way to Riches

The Lazy Man's Way to Riches

'Most People Are Too Busy Earning a Living to Make Any Money'

I used to work hard. The 18-hour days. The 7-day weeks.

But I didn't start making big money until I did less—a *lot* less.

For example, this ad took about 2 hours to write. With a little luck, it should earn me 50, maybe a hundred thousand dollars.

What's more, I'm going to ask you to send me 10 dollars for something that'll cost me no more than 50 cents. And I'll try to make it so irresistible that you'd be a darned fool not to do it.

After all, why should you care if I make $9.50 profit if I can show you how to make a lot more?

What if I'm so sure that *you will* make money my Lazy Man's Way that I'll make you the world's most unusual guarantee?

And here it is: I won't even cash your check or money order for 31 days *after* I've sent you my material.

That'll give you plenty of time to get it, look it over, try it out.

If you don't agree that it's worth *at least a hundred times* what you invested, send it back. Your uncashed check or money order will be put in the return mail.

The only reason I won't send it to you and bill you or send it C.O.D. is because both these methods involve more time and money.

And I'm already going to give you the biggest bargain of your life.

Because I'm going to tell you what it took me 11 years to perfect: How to make money the Lazy Man's Way.

O.K.—now I have to brag a little. I don't mind it. And it's necessary—to prove that sending me 10 dollars... which I'll keep "in escrow" until you're satisfied... is the smartest thing you ever did.

I live in a home that's worth $100,000. I know it is, because I turned down an offer for that much. My mortgage is less than half that, and the only reason I haven't paid it off is because my Tax Accountant says I'd be an idiot.

My "office," about a mile and a half from my home, is right on the beach. My view is so breathtaking that most people comment that they don't see how I get any work done. But I do enough. About 6 hours a day, 8 or 9 months a year.

The rest of the time we spend at our mountain "cabin." I paid $30,000 for it—cash.

I have 2 boats and a Cadillac. All paid for.

We have stocks, bonds, investments, cash in the bank. But the most important thing I have is priceless: time with my family.

And I'll show you just how I did it—the Lazy Man's Way—a secret I've shared with just a few friends 'til now.

It doesn't require "education." I'm a high school graduate.

It doesn't require "capital." When I started out, I was so deep in debt that a lawyer friend advised bankruptcy as the only way out. He was wrong. We paid off our debts and outside of the mortgage, don't owe a cent to any man.

It doesn't require "luck." I've had more than my share, but I'm not promising you that you'll make as much money as I have. And you may do better; I personally know one man who used these principles, worked hard, and made 11 million dollars in 8 years. But money isn't everything.

It doesn't require "talent." Just enough brains to know what to look for. And I'll tell you that.

It doesn't require "youth." One woman I worked with is over 70. She's travelled the world over, making all the money she needs, doing only what I taught her.

It doesn't require "experience." A widow in Chicago has been averaging $25,000 a year for the past 5 years, using my methods.

What *does* it require? Belief. Enough to take a chance. Enough to absorb what I'll send you. Enough to put the principles into action. If you do just that—nothing more, nothing less—the results will be hard to believe. Remember—I guarantee it.

You don't have to give up your job. But you may soon be making so much money that you'll be able to. Once again—I guarantee it.

The wisest man I ever knew told me something I never forgot: "Most people are too busy earning a living to make any money."

Don't take as long as I did to find out he was right.

I'll prove it to you, if you'll send me a card or letter telling me where to send your material. I'm not asking you to "believe" me. Just try it. If I'm wrong, all you've lost is a couple of minutes and an 8-cent stamp. But what if I'm right?

Sworn Statement:

"I have examined this advertisement. On the basis of personal acquaintance with Mr. Joe Karbo for 18 years and my professional relationship as his accountant, I certify that every statement is true."

[Accountant's name available upon request.]

Bank Reference:
American State Bank
675 South Main Street, Orange, California 92668

Joe Karbo
17105 South Pacific, Dept. 512-H
Sunset Beach, California 90742

Joe, you may be full of beans, but what have I got to lose? Send me the Lazy Man's Way to Riches. *But don't deposit my check or money order for 31 days after it's in the mail.*

If I return your material—for any reason—within that time, return my uncashed check or money order to me. On that basis, here's my ten dollars.

☐ Please send Air Mail. I'm enclosing an extra dollar.

Name _____

Address _____

City _____ State _____ Zip _____

© 1973 Joe Karbo

This classic mail order ad sold 3 million books.

This is a classic example of a mail order ad. There are some people who spend their entire career creating hundreds of ads, and then there is Joe Karbo.

Joe Karbo wrote only a few ads. He wrote the one I've featured here right off the top of his head. There was practically no editing involved. As he later claimed at my seminar, "I just sat down and wrote the ad in a matter of a few minutes and then looked back at it, made a few changes, and that was it."

The ad Joe created ran in hundreds of magazines for many years. In later years, it was rewritten to reflect more current mail order approaches, but it was basically the same ad. And it has become a classic.

First, a little background on Joe. Joe Karbo was discharged from the Army in 1945, and at age 20 with a wife and child, no money and only a high school education, he started his business career. Karbo was modestly successful in the scrap paper business and then he moved on to acting, followed by advertising, radio and finally television.

Karbo had his own TV show in Hollywood and, along with his wife Betty, was on the air from midnight to 8 AM. Since sponsors were hard to come by, Karbo started a direct mail business and sold a variety of products on his show. Joe soon mastered direct-response advertising and flourished.

In 1973 Joe formalized his personal philosophies in a book called *The Lazy Man's Way to Riches* in which he shared his beliefs and principles both on success and on direct-response advertising. The ad shown above is the one he wrote to market his book.

Let's examine the ad, as it will confirm many of the things

you have already learned. We'll start at the headline and systematically work our way through the entire ad.

> **Headline:** The Lazy Man's Way to Riches
> **Subheadline:** 'Most People Are Too Busy Earning a Living to Make Any Money'

The headline is provocative. At the time, this was a novel approach and a novel headline. Prior to this, ads such as these were only found in the group of magazines classified as "income opportunity." Magazines such as *Income Opportunity, Success* and *Entrepreneur* had dozens of offers such as the one Karbo was making, but the category of advertising hadn't yet made it into the mainstream. Joe's was one of the first to break through. The headline grabbed you and got you to read the subheadline. And the subheadline got you into the copy.

Let's start with the copy and see if he is creating that slippery slide. First, notice how he gets you into the copy by the use of short sentences. Notice how short the first sentence is and how short all his sentences are. Also notice how he is identifying with his prospect—the guy or gal who is serious about succeeding and wants a good life but finds himself or herself working hard and not getting anywhere. The copy starts out as follows:

> I used to work hard. The 18-hour days. The 7-day weeks.
> But I didn't start making big money until I did less—a *lot* less.

The ad continues and you're compelled to read further.

> For example, this ad took about 2 hours to write. With a little luck, it should earn me 50, maybe a hundred thousand dollars.

Remember, this was written in 1973 and the equivalent of $100,000 today might be close to a half-million dollars. Once again, Karbo is building curiosity. What is he offering? Why will this ad earn him so much money? You've got to read further. Notice also that there are no big words, no complicated long sentences. He's leading his reader into the copy slowly and easily, building curiosity as he goes. He tells a story as he progresses.

> What's more, I'm going to ask you to send me 10 dollars for something that'll cost me no more than 50 cents. And I'll try to make it so irresistible that you'd be a darned fool not to do it.

Here Karbo is establishing trust with his readers. His honesty is almost disarming. He tells you up front that he has something he wants to sell you for 10 dollars that only costs him 50 cents. He's also building curiosity. He's using basic and simple statements, and the copy has you slowly slipping down his slippery slide right to the next paragraph. Then note how he justifies the purchase.

> After all, why should you care if I make $9.50 profit if I can show you how to make a *lot* more?
>
> What if I'm so sure that you *will* make money my Lazy Man's Way that I'll make you the world's most unusual guarantee?
>
> And here it is: I won't even cash your check or money order for 31 days *after* I've sent you my material.
>
> That'll give you plenty of time to get it, look it over, try it out.

Note the flow of the copy. Again he builds on the reader's curiosity, justifying the $10 purchase even if he hasn't yet told you about the offer. Now you are really curious. He wasn't going to cash the check for 31 days, which at the time was a novel approach. It was what I call a "satisfaction conviction" because your reaction might have been, "Boy, a lot of people are going to rip him off. They're going to get his book, read it and then return it and get their uncashed check back in the mail." You already know how important a good satisfaction conviction can be from Chapter 19, and Karbo uses it here, early in his copy. He also shows a degree of enthusiasm and confidence in his concept that raises your curiosity even more. He continues.

> If you don't agree that it's worth *at least a hundred times* what you invested, send it back. Your *uncashed* check or money order will be put in the return mail.
>
> The only reason I won't send it to you and bill you or send it C.O.D. is because both these methods involve more time and money.
>
> And I'm already going to give you the biggest bargain of your life.
>
> Because I'm going to tell you what it took me 11 years to perfect: How to make money the Lazy Man's Way.

Again, Karbo is justifying the purchase without even telling you what it is. And he is justifying why accepting payment by check is the only way he'll sell it to you, giving you an economic basis for his decision. The curiosity builds. But instead of telling you about his offer, he now changes directions completely to establish credibility for his offer by presenting himself as an example of how successfully this program has worked.

> O.K.—now I have to brag a little. I don't mind it. And it's necessary—to prove that sending me ten dollars...which I'll keep "in escrow" until you're satisfied...is the smartest thing you ever did.
>
> I live in a home that's worth $100,000. I know it is because I turned down an offer for that much. My mortgage is less than half that, and the only reason I haven't paid it off is because my Tax Accountant says I'd be an idiot.
>
> My "office," about a mile and a half from my home, is right on the beach. My view is so breathtaking that most people comment that they don't see how I get any work done. But I do enough. About 6 hours a day, 8 or 9 months a year.
>
> The rest of the time we spend at our mountain "cabin." I paid $30,000 for it—cash.
>
> I have 2 boats and a Cadillac. All paid for.
>
> We have stocks, bonds, investments, cash in the bank. But the most important thing I have is priceless: time with my family.
>
> And I'll show you just how I did it—the Lazy Man's Way—a secret I've shared with just a few friends 'til now.

Here in these last paragraphs he is obviously whetting your appetite and telling you what the results of his system produced for him. But there is another very subtle thing he has done as well. He is trying to personally identify with his audience. He doesn't talk about driving around in a Rolls-Royce but rather a Cadillac. He talks about having a mortgage which most of his readers, if they own their own home, probably have. He keeps his wealth to a modest level, for if it was too far out of the reach of his readers, they would not be able to relate to Karbo.

He is also selling the sizzle, not the steak. He is relating a number of things, most of which sound pretty inviting to you and represent the results of buying his system—the many material things in life that most of his readers dream of having. He is identifying with his prospects. And then at the end of the list, he talks about the most priceless thing his system has created, "time with my family." All of this resonates with the reader, who by now can't stop reading and might be saying, "What does this guy have to offer that can make it possible for me to live the life of Joe

Karbo?" So you read on. You read the secret that he's shared with only a few friends.

In the next paragraph you find one of the truly important highlights of his ad copy. He is very subtly trying to expand the appeal of his offer to the broadest possible segment of the market. Think about it. If he said that one person made millions, you might not identify with what he is saying if you honestly didn't believe that you could earn millions. But you might relate to the little old lady who is now able to travel wherever she wants or the widow who is earning $25,000 extra a year. Or the guy who doesn't have much of an education.

As you read the following copy, see how he appeals to the mass market—probably the single reason that this ad had such widespread appeal and was not confined to just the income opportunity area. Also see where he again builds on his integrity when he talks about almost declaring bankruptcy—thus relating to many in his audience who may also be facing financial difficulty.

> It doesn't require "education." I'm a high school graduate.
>
> It doesn't require "capital." When I started out, I was so deep in debt that a lawyer friend advised bankruptcy as the only way out. He was wrong. We paid off our debts and, outside of the mortgage, don't owe a cent to any man.
>
> It doesn't require "luck." I've had more than my share, but I'm not promising you that you'll make as much money as I have. And you may do better: I personally know one man who used these principles, worked hard, and made 11 million dollars in 8 years. But money isn't everything.
>
> It doesn't require "talent." Just enough brains to know what to look for. And I'll tell you that.
>
> It doesn't require "youth." One woman I worked with is over 70. She's travelled the world over, making all the money she needs, doing only what I taught her.
>
> It doesn't require "experience." A widow in Chicago has been averaging $25,000 a year for the past 5 years, using my methods.

These last sentences are very important. In short, he appealed to a very broad segment of the opportunity market and even went beyond it to people who might not be looking for an opportunity but would find this message compelling. And Karbo comes across as being incredibly honest. Remember, he told you the cost of what he was going to send you and he seems to be very honest throughout his ad, even to the point of being disarming. Remember, honesty is a powerful psychological selling tool.

Now comes the closing pitch, with complete and total enthusiasm for his concept and his book. Once again, Karbo realizes that many of his readers have jobs and at this point in the copy are wondering if they will have to give them up to learn what he has to offer. He uses a little sage wisdom given to him by a wise man he met. And then he wraps up the entire ad with a question that builds the final level of curiosity to a point that compels you to respond in order to find out what this man has to offer.

> What *does* it require? Belief. Enough to take a chance. Enough to absorb what I'll send you. Enough to put the principles into *action.* If you do just that—nothing more, nothing less—the results *will* be hard to believe. Remember—I guarantee it.
>
> You don't have to give up your job. But you may soon be making so much money that you'll be able to. Once again—I guarantee it.
>
> The wisest man I ever knew told me something I never forgot: "Most people are too busy earning a living to make any money."
>
> Don't take as long as I did to find out he was right.
>
> I'll prove it to you, if you'll send in the coupon now. I'm not asking you to "believe" me. Just try it. If I'm wrong, all you've lost is a couple of minutes and an 8-cent stamp. But what if I'm right?

It is interesting to see the cost of a first class stamp back in 1973. Today as I write this book a stamp costs 32 cents, so the cost of his book relative to the cost of a postage stamp was equivalent to $40 in today's dollars.

Then you examine the coupon. But right above the coupon you first read a sworn statement from his accountant:

> "I have examined this advertisement. On the basis of personal acquaintance with Mr. Joe Karbo for 18 years and my professional relationship as his accountant, I certify that every statement is true." (Accountant's name available upon request.)

He also includes his bank reference. Once again, this really is very convincing as prior to Karbo, nobody had ever put anything like this in an ad. He was strongly establishing his credibility by using the bank's name as an indirect testimonial on his honesty— something his prospects needed in order to feel confident to reach for their checkbooks and send him their hard-earned money.

The coupon is a summary of the offer.

Joe, you may be full of beans, but what have I got to lose? Send me the Lazy Man's Way to Riches. *But don't deposit my check or money order for 31 days after it's in the mail.*
If I return your material—for *any* reason—within that time, return my *uncashed* check or money order to me. On that basis, here's my ten dollars.

He even has a small box you can check if you want his "material" sent by airmail for only one dollar more.

Note that he is sending "material" and not just a book. "Material" makes the program appear much more valuable—more like a course as opposed to a book. It has much more sizzle than just saying "book."

If you sent in your money, you received a wonderful book that actually looked like it cost about 50 cents to print. But it contained both a motivational message and the direct marketing techniques necessary to make money the "Lazy Man's Way."

Karbo ran these ads for several years. I had been establishing the fact in my national advertising that there was no such thing as too many words. By 1973 we were really cranking out our advertising, but mostly in *The Wall Street Journal*. One year later when we advertised in many national magazines, we noticed that Karbo's copy was expanding to include testimonials and more examples to cover the broad market he was trying to reach. The ads became more wordy with each passing year.

But it was Joe's very first ad—the first major mass market advertising campaign to come from the income opportunity area in many years—that was the purest example of what I was teaching in my seminar.

Joe Karbo attended my seminar in 1978. At my seminar he shared his background and told the story of how he wrote this one ad.

Joe died in 1980 from a massive heart attack. He was being interviewed at a local TV station near his home in California when the interviewer decided to unfairly attack Joe, thus changing entirely the premise of the interview. Joe's first reaction was a heart attack from which he never revived. Joe was survived by his wife Betty and eight children.

His work and efforts have been continued in an excellent recently revised version of his book including a workbook. Any student of mail order needing some really good motivation should purchase it. Please see the listing in Appendix D for this course as well as several other good direct-marketing books.

The Karbo ad was a classic. It was his biggest and best shot in the mail order business and its significance was felt by the many millions who bought his book and later indeed profited by it. But if this seemed like a real fluke—a once-in-a-lifetime experience that would be impossible to duplicate—you're wrong. It is happening even as you read this, with other entrepreneurs using direct marketing as a method to market their products.

The next true story tells of somebody who never wrote print mail order copy before he sat down and wrote one of the classic long-running mail order ads of the decade, and he did it right after attending my seminar. Read on.

It was Frank's first ad and it became a classic.

Frank Lewis Schultz is a farmer who grows grapefruit in the Rio Grande Valley of Texas. For years he had used a simple letter or direct mailing to build his customer base into a nice-sized business which sold grapefruit by mail. But something always seemed to elude him. He couldn't get print mail order advertising to work for him.

He realized that space advertising (the idea of reaching millions of people for the same price it takes to reach thousands by mail) sounded like a great concept. And along with reaching millions, he could add credibility to his company and more profit to his bottom line.

It all sounded great until Schultz hired one of the nation's most respected direct response agencies. The first ad bombed. So did the second. In fact, his gross sales didn't cover the raw cost of the ad space. Schultz was discouraged.

When I announced my first seminar in 1977, Schultz was one of the first to sign up. During the seminar, he was very quiet, but he seemed to be absorbing everything I had to say. I didn't know at the time that he had a degree in marketing from the University of California at Berkeley.

After the seminar, with the information fresh in his mind, he went to the local Holiday Inn in Minocqua, Wisconsin, and started drafting his first print ad.

He based it on both the successful letter that he had run for years and the information I had taught. And the result was sent to me in Northbrook, Illinois, upon my return home after the seminar.

The ad was great. It wasn't the very technical style of the JS&A ads, but it had a homespun feel that grabbed you at the start and drew you through the copy all the way to the very end. As Frank later said about the seminar and what he had learned about writing copy, "It was actually pretty easy because suddenly everything was clear. I knew what I had to say and how to say it. I learned that you don't have to be a professional copywriter to write effective copy."

When I received Schultz's ad, I called him on the phone and told him, "Your ad is great. I only have a few changes to suggest but they are minor. Your big problem is the headline." I suggested "Fluke of Nature" instead of "A Stroke of Luck from Mother Nature"—the one he had written. I suggested the subheadline: "A new grapefruit discovery may change your concept of fruit." I also suggested he take out a line, "The zesty flavor of Royal Ruby Red grapefruit juice will help start your day with a smile," as it seemed almost a cliché—something an ad agency might have written. And there were several other small changes, but again, they were minor.

There were two pictures captioned with copy explaining the offer, and of course, all the elements were designed to get you to read the first sentence. Let's examine the copy as we did with the Karbo ad and see how Schultz captured the essence of what I taught, and in a very simple yet persuasive way. The copy starts out with a first paragraph that was printed in bold type to act almost as a subheadline, thus drawing you further into the copy:

> I'm a farmer. And the story I tell you is the absolute truth, as incredible as it may seem.

This is a classic opening for an ad. Remember we talked about how each word has an emotion and a story attached to it? What does the word 'farmer' bring to mind? How about honesty, hard work and integrity? Simply by stating that he is a farmer, he has established a degree of credibility right from the start of the ad. And then look at the curiosity he creates right away in the second sentence. How could you not continue?

> It all started in a grove owned by Dr. Webb, our family doctor. One of the men who was picking fruit in the doctor's orchard came up to the Webb house holding six of the strangest grapefruit anyone had ever seen. A single branch of an ordinary grapefruit tree had produced these six unusual fruit.
>
> These were big grapefruit, unusually big. And they had a faint red

blush on their skin. When Dr. Webb sliced open the grapefruit, the fruit was a brilliant ruby red in color.

Dr. Webb decided to taste this strange new grapefruit. The fruit was perfect, juicy and luscious. It wasn't sour like other grapefruit either—it was naturally sweet without sugar.

For some reason, we'll never know why, nature had chosen to produce an entirely new kind of grapefruit here in our Magic Rio Grande Valley. It was incredible—men had labored for years to produce the ideal grapefruit, and had failed. But suddenly on a single branch of one tree in one grove, Mother Nature had done it all by herself!

The copy reads almost like a fairy tale with the use of the Magic Rio Grande Valley name and the story of this unexpected discovery. Schultz created this environment—all woven through a compelling and interesting story that holds your attention and keeps you reading. You can't stop now. You've got to see where this all takes you. Schultz now goes into more detail on the fruit itself. And he uses one technique that you would never believe could be applied to fruit. He makes his product a rarity—a limited edition to be shared by very few people. Read the following and see what I mean.

YOU CAN IMAGINE THE EXCITEMENT

From the fruit on that one branch, grove after grove now produces our own Texas Ruby Red Grapefruit. When I say, "not one man in a thousand has ever tasted this grapefruit"—you can easily understand why.

To begin with, Ruby Reds are rare. You can look for them in stores but I doubt if you'll find one. You may find pink grapefruit, but seldom if ever do you see the genuine Ruby Reds.

So you start with the rarity of Ruby Reds, and to get to ROYAL Ruby Reds you have to get rarer yet. Only 4 to 5 percent of the entire crop will qualify as a "Royal Ruby Red."

Schultz graphically brought out the true rarity of what he was selling. You can certainly do that with a collectible, but the simple way Schultz made his fruit rare was ingenious. After he told you that "not one man in a thousand has ever tasted this grapefruit," you might have thought he was going to pitch you on the fruit. Instead he started to explain what makes it even more rare. And it got so rare that it seemed quite plausible that few people indeed have tasted this fruit.

In the next passage, Schultz continues to build the story but now he makes his message a very personal one. It almost sounds like he goes right into the grove with his men to pick the fruit. He is personally involved in every step of the growing and picking process, and he uses this approach to make his message personal. Secondly, he even uses a technical explanation—something that really builds confidence in the expertise he brings to his farming. A technical explanation in selling electronics would make sense, but see how he does it here with a very nonscientific product— grapefruit. And he also gets you totally involved with the fruit itself. Your taste buds are activated and you can almost savor the grapefruit as you read the copy. He is actually using your sense of taste as an involvement device. Instead of turning the knobs of a TV set or clicking on the keys of a calculator to involve you, he's getting you to salivate. The copy continues:

> Each Royal Ruby Red weighs a pound—or more! Each has a rich red color, flowing juices, luscious naturally sweet flavor, and the ability to stay this way for many weeks.
>
> Why, we won't even consider harvesting a grove until I've checked out the fruit for tree-ripened maturity myself. I check for "natural sugar," low acid balance and high juice content. I check to see that the fruit is plump and meaty, and I even check to see that the skin is thin. Not only does each factor have to check out, but all the factors have to be in a proper relationship to each other before I'll harvest a grove.
>
> And when we pick the fruit, we're just as fussy. Every one of us takes a 'picking ring' when we harvest. If the fruit is small enough to pass through this ring—we don't pick it! It simply isn't big enough to qualify as a Royal Ruby Red!
>
> Even after picking there are other careful inspections each fruit must pass before I'll accept it. I size the fruit. And I grade it for beauty. Sometimes the fruit will be wind scarred. I won't accept it. Or sometimes it will have a bulge on the stem and that we call "sheep nose." I won't accept it. You can see I really mean it when I say I accept only perfect Royal Ruby Reds.

By now you can just picture Frank Schultz out in the grove with his picking ring rejecting wind-scarred grapefruit or fruit that has sheep nose. By now you are actually convinced that this fruit is very carefully selected—not only chosen for its juice content but also for its beauty. Beauty? Yep, beauty.

Probably the one thing that he uses with great skill is the

personal nature of his presentation. His company sounds small—as if it is made up of just Schultz and a few other pickers. And they all go out with their picking rings, spend the day gathering only the prettiest and juiciest grapefruit, and then return with their harvest for shipping to just a few of their customers the next day. It is a beautiful example of the personal one-to-one selling technique that you want to capture in print, and Schultz has managed to do this in a very simple and masterful way.

Think also about the nature of grapefruit. This is unquestionably a simple product and this chapter is a good example of my "simple vs. complicated" rule. When something is simple, like a grapefruit, you make it complex. If it's complex, you make it simple. What could be more simple than a grapefruit? But look at how Schultz has brought out all the features and the complexities of his selection process and even his own expertise by telling you more than you've ever wanted to know about grapefruit.

Schultz is now ready for the pitch. The grapefruit could not get any better. It is rare, it is delicious, it is beautiful and it has value. It's now up to Schultz to make his customers reach into their pockets and exchange their hard-earned dollars for his grapefruit, and he makes it as simple as possible.

Frank does this by offering a sample shipment—a low-priced no-risk opportunity just to try his product. He makes it so simple that you begin to wonder if he's going to be ripped off. And what does that signify? That's right—a satisfaction conviction—something that is so compelling, you wonder if people are going to take advantage of him.

> When I realized that the Royal Ruby Reds were the ultimate fruit, I decided to form a club and sell only to my club members. In this manner, I can control my production to insure that nobody will be disappointed.
>
> But before I ask you to join my club, I want you to sample my Royal Ruby Reds for yourself, at no cost to you whatsoever. Let me send you a box prepaid of 16 to 20 Royal Ruby Reds. Place four of them in your refrigerator until they are thoroughly cool. Then cut them in half and have your family sample this unusual fruit.
>
> You decide whether or not Royal Ruby Reds are everything I say. You determine whether or not eating a Royal Ruby Red is the fantastic taste experience I promise.

You decide. I'm confident that you and your family will want more of this superb fruit and on a regular basis, too. If the four Royal Ruby Reds make you say "yes," then keep the remaining fruit. Otherwise return the unused fruit (at my expense) and you won't owe me a single penny.

But you are never going to know just how wonderful genuine Royal Ruby Reds are unless you place your order right quick.

This way you are sure to receive your package containing 16 to 20 Royal Ruby Reds for you and your family to sample. But since the supply is strictly limited it's important to place your order now.

Note the use of the words 'right quick'. That's the way farmers talk, isn't it. And it is this homey-sounding copy that captivated his audience. In fact, Schultz asked me if he should leave it in. "It isn't really good English" was his concern. "By all means, leave it in," I suggested. "It sounds great to me."

His offer then went on to give the terms of the purchase. The first box was going to cost $5 less than the standard shipment— a further incentive to at least try his grapefruit. In fact, you actually didn't pay anything up front, as he also included a bill for $9.95. You only paid if you wanted to keep the shipment and you then were enrolled in his monthly club. His copy continued:

Now suppose you do like Royal Ruby Reds—suppose you love them—can you be sure of getting more?

You surely can. By saying "yes" to my first shipment you have the privilege of automatically joining my Winter Fruit Club. Please be assured you pay nothing in advance. But each month during the winter, I'll ship you a pack of 16 to 20 orchard-fresh, hand-selected, hand-picked Royal Ruby Reds.

Every Royal Ruby Red you receive will pass my tough tests. Each will weigh a pound or more. Safe delivery is guaranteed. This fruit is picked, packed and shipped each month, December through April.

You pay only after you have received each shipment. And you can skip or cancel any shipment, simply by telling me your wishes.

He summarized his offer. He restated most of the points he told you in the previous copy at the very end of the ad. And then he goes into the close:

Remember, it obligates you to nothing except making a taste test of the best grapefruit that has ever been grown. And this taste test is on me!

Of course, as you can well imagine, when I say supplies are limited—I'm not kidding! There's just so many club members I can accept before I must close my membership this year.

In this statement, he is giving you a sense of urgency that is both believable and true. Production is limited and getting your order in quickly is very important to ensure that you'll be part of the membership program. He also makes it sound risk free and easy to test.

So to taste this 'miracle' grapefruit and have the opportunity to savor it each month during the growing season, be sure to place your order at no obligation, today.

Frank was pleasantly surprised when he ran his test ad in *The Wall Street Journal:* "Our cost per order was the lowest of any outside list we've ever used, and I realized that a single advertisement held the key to the rapid growth of our company."

But Frank Schultz didn't stop there. He continued to advertise in *The Wall Street Journal, The New York Times, Parade* and *TV Guide* to name only a few. "When you're a farmer you always worry about the crop. It's growing too slow—you worry. It's growing too fast—you really worry," said Frank later in a letter to me.

"I find it to be about the same when a farmer gets into space advertising. The orders are coming in so good from our space ads, I'm beginning to worry. A high-class worry, I'll admit."

In December 1980, an article on Schultz appeared in *Texas Monthly* magazine. The story talked about his wonderful copy and how the copy made his business seem small and personal. Yet it also explained that the business was quite large by then. He harvested 26,000 tons of grapefruit in 1979 with only 4% passing Schultz's rigorous standards for Royal Ruby Red grapefruit. The rest were sold to the grocery chains. And he now had 80,000 customers in the 48 continental states. He owned 14,000 acres of orchards spread out from Brownsville to McAllen, Texas, and had hundreds of employees. He truly was a success story—all created from the power of his pen.

And yet, his customers visualized Frank with his picking ring out in the orchard picking those perfect Royal Ruby Red grapefruit free of sheep nose and wind scarring.

From time to time, Frank would send me some of the letters he received complimenting him on his copy. One came from Stanley Marcus, then the chairman of Neiman Marcus. Some were from other copywriters who recognized his ad as brilliant. And for many years Schultz ran the ads until they finally wore out.

I myself was in Schultz's grapefruit club for many years. And from my orders alone, he probably made back all the money he had spent on my seminar. If you'd like Royal Ruby Red grapefruit sent directly to your door, call Frank toll free—(800) 477-4773 between 8 AM and 6 PM Central time. But do it "right quick."

Lingerie for Men

How a Group of Very Special Men Made It All Possible

WE WERE ASTOUNDED! When we opened the doors of our new business, we thought most of our customers would be women. After all, beautiful designer lingerie is the kind of luxury a lady can't resist.

How wrong we were.

That first Valentine's Day, the men came in droves! Hundreds of men, who had secretly been dying to visit our boutique. At last, they had the perfect excuse—Valentine's Day gifts for their favorite ladies.

They loved the merchandise.

Can you imagine how shocked we were? All those men—milling about our Victorian boutique. Admiring the silk stockings and lacy garter belts from France. Totally smitten by the luxurious silk and satin kimonos from London. Crowding around the bra and bikini sets from Italy. They couldn't wait to surprise their wives or girlfriends with something truly special.

Weren't they embarrassed?

The truth is, they were. But not enough to keep them away! They had seen our exciting, full-color catalogue. A breathtaking picture book of beautiful women, wearing enticing creations. Besides, a few men became our first satisfied customers. And in a short time, they had managed to spread the good word. Victoria's Secret wasn't like shopping for lingerie in a department store. No mutterly saleslady to make a man feel uneasy. No raised eyebrows or pursed lips asking about sizes. No racks of flannel and terrycloth to wade through. And no clanky, plastic boxes overflowing with boring white foundation garments.

The men in our life.

Since that first Valentine's Day, we've learned a lot about our male customers. Mainly, they can't be stereotyped. Some are conservative, some far from it. Some are rather old, while others are much younger. Whether doctors, accountants, salesmen or bankers ... they all have one thing in common. They are true connoisseurs of beauty. They know how sensuous and

lovely a lacy camisole or elegant gown looks on a woman. And what's more, they know how wonderful a woman feels to receive something beautiful and intimate from a special man. And it takes a very special man to shop from Victoria's Secret.

Our luxurious photo album ....

If you're like our male patrons—sensitive and fashion-conscious in your own right—you've been dying to find a place like Victoria's Secret. However, if you live outside of Northern California, you won't find it. But for $2.00 you can have the next best thing. Our luscious, four-color catalogue of alluring designer lingerie.

What if you don't like our style?

We guarantee you'll be the first man who didn't. But ... if after you receive our catalogue, you find our fashions too sensuous or too luxurious for the lady in your life, you haven't lost a thing. Our lush, full-color catalogue is an elegant collector's item—a conversation piece your friends will adore! (Already, our customers are requesting previous editions of the Victoria's Secret catalogue.)

To receive your own personal copy, send $2.00 to Victoria's Secret, dept. W500, P.O. Box 31442, San Francisco, CA 94111. We'll send you our colorful catalogue of fashion romance via first class mail.

The ad drew a lot of attention but missed a few major points at the end.

Victoria's Secret is now a major chain with 800 stores, $569 million in sales and a major catalog division. But back in 1979, it consisted of just three small stores and a catalog run by a gentleman by the name of Raymond. And that is when Barbara Dunlap attended my seminar.

The ad she wrote helps illustrate many of the points you've learned in this book and also points to a few she overlooked. Let's start with the headline and subheadline. If you were a man or a woman reading through a newspaper, you might stop dead in your tracks if you saw the following:

Headline: Lingerie for Men

Subheadline: How a Group of Very Special Men Made It All Possible

Note that the headline was just three words— short, concise and certainly enough to get you to read the subheadline. Then notice that the subheadline did not give away the premise of the ad; you still don't know what it is. In fact, it might sound like some men got together and made the wearing of lingerie possible. You just don't know, so you keep reading.

Now read the first paragraph, which is in large type and actually draws you into the copy. Also note the storytelling feel of the first few paragraphs.

> WE WERE ASTOUNDED! When we opened the doors of our new business, we thought most of our customers would be women. After all, beautiful designer lingerie is the kind of luxury a lady can't resist.
>
> **How wrong we were.**
>
> That first Valentine's Day, the men came in droves! Hundreds of men, who had secretly been dying to visit our boutique. At last, they had the perfect excuse—Valentine's Day gifts for their favorite ladies.

They loved the merchandise.

Can you imagine how shocked we were? All those men—milling about our Victorian boutique. Admiring the silk stockings and lacy garter belts from France. Totally smitten by the luxurious silk and satin kimonos from London. Crowding around the bra and bikini sets from Italy. They couldn't wait to surprise their wives or girlfriends with something truly special.

Once again as the story is told you can visualize the scene. You can almost see the merchandise and appreciate how the variety of merchandise is woven neatly into the story. But now a question might pop into your mind as you are reading this. And this very question is brought into the copy at precisely this moment.

Weren't they embarrassed?

The truth is, they were. But not enough to keep them away! They had seen our exciting, full-color catalogue. A breathtaking picture book of beautiful women, wearing enticing creations. Besides, a few men became our first satisfied customers. And in a short time, they had managed to spread the good word. Victoria's Secret wasn't like shopping for lingerie in a department store. No matronly saleslady to make a man feel uneasy. No raised eyebrows or pursed lips asking about sizes. No racks of flannel and terrycloth to wade through. And no clunky, plastic boxes overflowing with boring white foundation garments.

There were a number of good issues just covered. First, Dunlap comes across as being truthful when she admits that the men were embarrassed. In short, she raises an objection in the paragraph heading ("Weren't they embarrassed?") and then answers it honestly. But then she brings in the fact that they were motivated by a full-color catalog that she refers to as a "breathtaking picture book." Here she very subtly brings in the catalog as the motivational factor that prompted all these men to come to the store.

Another objection you might raise if you decided to go to the store is the store environment itself and the human element in the store—the salesclerks. If you were a man, would you be embarrassed? Here in this same paragraph (which really should have been a new paragraph) she raises the objection and resolves it by pointing out that the store has none of the embarrassments found in a department store. In short, this is a store that would not embarrass a man at all.

In this ad, Dunlap first got your attention and raised all the objections that you might have if you were a man and wanted to buy lingerie for your wife or girlfriend in a women's lingerie store. In the next paragraph, Dunlap broadens the market from just a few men to all men, similar to the way Karbo broadened his income opportunity ad to include anybody interested in bettering his or her life. Here's what she said.

The men in our life.

Since that first Valentine's Day, we've learned a lot about our male customers. Mainly, they can't be stereotyped. Some are conservative, some far from it. Some are rather old, while others are much younger. Whether doctors, accountants, salesmen or bankers . . . they all have one thing in common. They are true connoisseurs of beauty. They know how sensuous and lovely a lacy camisole or elegant gown looks on a woman. And what's more, they know how wonderful a woman feels to receive something beautiful and intimate from a special man. And it takes a *very* special man to shop from Victoria's Secret.

Not only does Dunlap include a broad range of men but she then compliments the men on their taste and understanding of women in general.

In the next paragraph we finally get the real pitch of the ad. Since the only Victoria's Secret stores were located in northern California at the time, the real purpose of this ad, which ran nationally, was to attract catalog customers from the other 49 states. So after the paragraph heading "Our luxurious photo album . . ." comes the pitch. Note the colorful and sensuous language which only helps to create the environment for this ad.

If you're like our male patrons—sensuous and fashion-conscious in your own right—you've been dying to find a place like Victoria's Secret. However, if you live outside of northern California you won't find it. But for $2.00 you can have the next best thing. Our luscious, full-color catalogue of alluring designer lingerie.

What if you don't like our style?

We guarantee you'll be the first man who didn't. But . . . if after you receive our catalogue, you find our fashions too sensuous or too luxurious for the lady in your life, you haven't lost a thing. Our lush, full-color catalogue is an elegant collector's item—a conversation piece your friends will adore! (Already, our customers are requesting previous editions of the Victoria's Secret catalogue.)

To receive your own personal copy, send $2.00 to Victoria's Secret, dept. W500 [address went here]. We'll send you our colorful catalogue of fashion romance via first class mail.

There was one main problem with this ad and unfortunately it came at the most critical part—at the end. The objection some prospects might raise is, "What if I'm not pleased with the $2 catalog or any of the merchandise?" Nothing was indicated about their return policy. And a nice hook could have been to allow customers to use their $2 investment in buying the catalog toward the purchase of their first order. Or even allowing them $10 toward their first order.

From what I understand, the first ad was moderately successful in bringing in catalog requests, which in turn brought in sales. This was a two-step process—to scan the market for possible customers and then make them customers through the catalog. This is a very good application of a print ad and a good example of many of the principles.

The principles that you should particularly pay attention to are the excellent timing of the objections and how they were resolved and the beautiful use of words that told a story and created the perfect environment for the offer. The real offer was the catalog, but the story that was told gave men permission to get the catalog and buy from it—a lot less embarrassing than going into the store.

"Lingerie for Men" was brief, interesting and flowed quite nicely. And although its ending could have been more compelling and more effective, it brought you through the copy like a slippery slide all the way to the very end. I would have also added a byline to the ad to make it even more personal.

The catalog Victoria's Secret published back in 1979 was a lot more sensuous than the catalog they put out today. If I had to classify it, I would say it was an upscale version of a Frederick's of Hollywood lingerie catalog. And indeed, they were quite popular with the men.

Two advertising people from Victoria's Secret attended my seminar before the franchise was sold to The Limited. The two women used their copywriting skills to write the colorful catalogs. They both claim that the seminar was one of the turning points in their careers and a major factor in the early success of Victoria's Secret.

The lesson to be learned from this example is that you can write a great ad but then miss some great opportunities at the end. And the end of the ad is when the buying decision has to be made—it's a critical point in any advertisement.

In the next chapter, I give you an example of a company trying to resolve a problem without first raising it. It will clarify the important method of always raising an objection and then resolving it.

"The more you learn about our DC-10, the more you know how great it really is."

Pete Conrad
Former Astronaut
Division Vice President, McDonnell Douglas

"I've watched airplanes and spacecraft take shape for much of my adult life. I'm certain that nothing made to fly has ever been designed or built to more exacting standards than our DC-10.

"Eighteen million engineering man-hours were invested in this plane's development. That includes 14,000 hours of wind tunnel testing, as well as full-scale fatigue testing for the equivalent of 40 years of airline service.

"I'm convinced that the DC-10 is the most thoroughly-tested jetliner ever built. Along with U.S. Government certification, the DC-10 has passed structures tests just as demanding, in their own way, as those required of U.S. Air Force fighter planes.

"The DC-10 fleet demonstrates its dependability flying more than a million miles a day and serving 170 cities in 90 countries around the globe."

To learn more about the DC-10, write "DC-10 Report," McDonnell Douglas, Box 14526, St. Louis, MO 63178.

MCDONNELL DOUGLAS

This ad had a major flaw. The entire first part was missing.

This is a good example of an advertising message that could have been quite powerful if it weren't for one fatal flaw. Let me explain.

I was flying back from Rockford, Illinois, in my own private plane. I was about 50 miles from the Pal-Waukee airport where I was scheduled for an instrument landing even though the weather was perfect for flying. The air traffic controllers were unusually quiet as I approached Pal-Waukee. It was a bright clear day—one of those rare days when you could see for miles.

As I got closer to Pal-Waukee, I could see off in the distance a big fire near Chicago's O'Hare airport. I landed my plane, parked and walked into the airport office where I learned from a television broadcast that American Airlines flight 191 had just crashed on takeoff from O'Hare and that all its passengers had died. That was May 25, 1979, and it was one of those memories that remains indelibly etched in my mind.

The plane that crashed was a DC-10—one of McDonnell Douglas's largest and most popular aircraft. Immediately after the crash, it was determined that there was a hydraulic problem that, under certain circumstances, could cause loss of control and consequently a crash. McDonnell Douglas quickly corrected the problem, but for a while all DC-10s were grounded.

If that weren't enough, the DC-10 was involved in two more crashes within a relatively short period of time. The last two were unrelated to any fault of the airplane, but the stigma of the American Airlines crash was still on the mind of the public. McDonnell Douglas realized that it had to do something to offset the negative publicity.

They picked Pete Conrad to act as spokesman in an advertisement to address the public's concern. But instead of raising the objections of the plane crashes and then resolving the problem with the excellent copy that was written, the objection was totally ignored. The resulting ad was hollow. The following is the copy as it was written:

> **Headline:** "The more you learn about our DC-10, the more you know how great it really is."
>
> **Byline:** Pete Conrad, former astronaut, Division Vice President, McDonnell Douglas
>
> **Copy:** I've watched airplanes and spacecraft take shape for much of my adult life. I'm certain that nothing made to fly has ever been designed or built to more exacting standards than our DC-10.
>
> Eighteen million engineering man-hours were invested in this plane's development. That includes 14,000 hours of wind tunnel testing, as well as full-scale 'fatigue testing' for the equivalent of 40 years of airline service.
>
> I'm convinced that the DC-10 is the most thoroughly-tested jet-liner ever built. Along with U.S. Government certification, the DC-10 has passed structure tests just as demanding, in their own way, as those required of U.S. Air Force fighter planes.
>
> The DC-10 fleet demonstrates its dependability flying more than a million miles a day and serving 170 cities in 90 countries around the globe.

The ad then ended with a place to write McDonnell Douglas to get more information.

The copy was good copy—very persuasive in terms of building confidence in the plane. And all this was presented by a former astronaut to add credibility. But it lacked an important opening that would have made the copy many times more effective.

What if the ad had started out differently? If I were given the assignment of writing the ad it would go as follows:

> **Headline:** DC-10's Big Secret
>
> **Subheadline:** You've heard a lot of bad publicity about the DC-10. But here's something you may not have known.
>
> **Byline:** By Pete Conrad
>
> **Copy:** It was horrible. When American Airlines flight 191 crashed at O'Hare in Chicago last May 25th, hundreds of people lost their lives in what was considered one of the worst plane crashes in American history. The plane—a DC-10.
>
> But as the facts emerged, it was learned that a series of coincidences resulted in a hydraulic malfunction which in all likelihood

may never happen again. But it did happen. And in the subsequent weeks, a series of fail-safe systems were installed that make the DC-10's hydraulic system among the safest of any jetliner.

In addition, two other recent crashes of DC-10s were determined to be totally not the fault of the airplane but of the pilots. But because of the negative publicity generated by the American Airlines crash and these other two crashes, we have been even more diligent. All airlines are required to give each DC-10 a complete inspection every 50 hours instead of the required 100 hours of flying. The plane's hydraulic system is checked before each flight instead of waiting until a required inspection. And the plane's structural system is checked not only by each mechanic but by the pilots themselves. You couldn't fly a safer plane.

Then I would pick up the copy from the existing ad so it would continue,

I've watched airplanes and spacecraft take shape for much of my adult life. I'm certain that nothing made to fly has ever been designed or built to more exacting standards than our DC-10. [Then I would put the rest of his copy here.]

Do you see the difference? What I have done is to raise the real problem (or as I call it, the "objection") and then resolve it. Conrad's copy, which could easily go at the end of my ad, would then contribute to resolving the problem.

After reading my version of the ad, you would leave with a positive, good feeling about both the company and the message. You would think, "That was a sincere effort to dispel those false impressions on the safety of the DC-10." The message is an emotional presentation which shows concern, integrity and leadership.

Now compare that with the way the ad was originally written, which might have left you with the sarcastic impression, "Sure it's a safe plane. . . ." Or maybe, "They are just trying to cover themselves from all the heat they've been taking."

Keep in mind that the copy they had was very good. They just left off the entire front end of the ad and were avoiding the real issue—the events that actually happened that prompted their ad. They just spent most of their copy resolving the objection without acknowledging and addressing it directly.

The lesson to be learned here is to realize the importance of raising an objection, regardless of how embarrassing or detrimental it may seem, and then doing your best to resolve it. You'll find that the public really appreciates your candor, honesty and frankness and will respond to your message in a positive way, whether it be to buy your product, to develop a good feeling about your company or, as in the case of the DC-10, to restore confidence in an airplane.

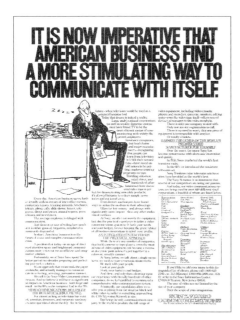

The theme of this ad was "boring." They accomplished their goal.

Even if you never wrote a piece of copy in your life, one look at this ad from Sony Video Communications and you would feel pretty much like the cartoon character shown in it. You'd feel like falling asleep.

The advertising agency that created this ad probably thought they had a very clever idea. Their concept—show the contrast between typical types of boring communications and a new, more stimulating video presentation (new back in the mid '70s when this ad appeared).

In keeping with the theme, the headline in the ad was inadvertently boring in that it was hard to read with its bold capitalized type. The ad layout was boring. And finally, the copy was monotonous and did not follow many of my principles. So whoever created this ad was certainly being consistent with the theme in their presentation. It was boring.

But being consistent while going in the wrong direction is not a great strategy either. Very few people would want to read a boring ad. There are thousands of ad messages out there on a daily basis, and to stand out you need a message that grabs people's attention and causes them to read your entire ad. And to get them to read your entire ad, you must use many of the techniques I've presented throughout this book, even if the ad you are creating is not a mail order ad.

In the Sony ad they are first trying to sell the concept of using video and then of using Sony video, once they have convinced their reader to try this new medium. My approach would have been to create a story of somebody who switched to video and saw a dramatic benefit—more sales, greater productivity or more awareness.

Here are the first few paragraphs to give you the sense of

how the copy flowed. The ad had no subheadline, no cartoon caption and started out with a very long and boring first sentence.

> Every day, American business spews forth a virtually endless stream of inter-office memos, conference reports, training manuals, brochures, telexes, phone calls, slide shows, letters, telegrams, direct mail pieces, annual reports, press releases and newsletters.
>
> The average employee is deluged with communication.
>
> And there is no way of telling how much of it is either ignored, forgotten, misplaced or summarily disposed of.
>
> In short, American business is in the throes of a vast and complex communication crisis.
>
> A problem that today—in an age of shortened attention spans and heightened communications costs—cries out for an efficient and imaginative solution.

The first sentence is too long and the copy is boring. But then again, isn't "boring" the theme of the ad? (I'm being facetious.)

The ad then tells how video is being used and what Sony has to offer the new and emerging industry. If you thought the first few paragraphs were boring, so was the rest of the copy. And since I get bored typing it into my computer for this book, I'm not going to include any more for you to read. Just trust me, it was boring.

Chances are, unless you were totally interested in video communications and were actively searching for everything you could find on the subject, you wouldn't even consider reading the entire ad.

And here's my final point. The ad was created by a professional ad agency using professional copywriters, layout artists and art directors. After reading this book, you could act as a consultant to that ad agency and improve its advertising by 1,000% and you may not even be a professional anything. The ability to write good advertising copy is not limited exclusively to professionals. Often even the most inexperienced person can write an incredibly effective ad. And certainly after reading this book, you can criticize even the most professionally prepared ads.

I brought out the worst aspects of this product and turned them around.

This JS&A mail order ad for the Magic Stat thermostat basically tells a story but with a unique twist. The story starts out with us hating the product, and then as the story unfolds, the product takes a quantum leap in our approval to become the best product on the planet. How I get there is an interesting process.

First I realized that the number one drawback in purchasing a thermostat was the installation. It's not one of those things that consumers relate to. It could be dangerous handling all those wires and there's a lot of extra expense in having an installer put one in. So one of the first good features we finally like in our story is the ease of installation. In short, we recognize that consumers don't like to be bothered with installation and we hit this feature right at the start of the ad.

The copy itself raises many objections—the case design, the look of it and even the name. We realized that these would be some of the same objections consumers would raise when they looked at the product. And we resolved them one by one as we floated through the copy.

A good portion of the copy explained in a light sort of way the features of the product. And then near the end we built up the company selling us the product to add credibility and make the consumer feel more secure. Our competition, after all, was Honeywell—a company with an established name and reputation.

The Magic Stat ad ran in print for almost three years starting in 1983 and made the product into a very successful brand name. The company eventually was sold to Honeywell.

The following is the complete text of the ad:

Headline: Magic Baloney

Subheadline: You'll love the way we hated the Magic Stat thermostat until an amazing thing happened.

Caption: It had no digital readout, an ugly case and a stupid name. It almost made us sick.

Copy: You're probably expecting our typical sales pitch, but get ready for a shock. For instead of trying to tell you what a great product the Magic Stat thermostat is, we're going to tear it apart. Unmercifully.

When we first saw the Magic Stat, we took one look at the name and went, "Yuck." We took one look at the plastic case and said, "How cheap looking." And when we looked for the digital readout, it had none. So before the salesman even showed us how it worked, we were totally turned off.

REAL LOSER

So there it was—at first blush a real loser. But wait, we did find one good feature—a feature that led us to a discovery. The Magic Stat installs in a few minutes and no serviceman is required. Thermostat wires in your wall follow standard color codes. So when you install Magic Stat, you attach the red wire to the red location and the white to the white. That's play school stuff. And it's safe. Conventional thermostats installed over the past 20 years are generally only 24 volts, so you can either turn off the power or work with the "live" wires without fear.

OK, LET'S TEST IT

The Magic Stat installation was so easy that the least we could do was test it. And that's when we made an incredible discovery. We discovered that the Magic Stat was probably the most consumer-oriented, technologically-advanced and most sophisticated thermostat ever developed on the face of this earth and in our galaxy for all times ever. What made us switch from hating the thing to loving it? Read the following:

The Magic Stat has six setback settings per day and a seven day program. That means that you could set it for 70 degrees when you get up in the morning, drop the temperature to 54 degrees when you go to work, raise it to 68 degrees when you return for dinner, raise it up to 70 degrees after dinner as you watch TV and then drop it down to 62 degrees when you go to sleep. Count them—five settings with one to spare.

In one day the Magic Stat is programmed for the whole week and for the weeks to come. If you want a different schedule for weekends, you can individually program the thermostat for those days, too. "Big deal," you might think. "What's so great about that?" Read on.

You set most electronic setback thermostats to the time you want the furnace to go on in the morning, so when you wake up, your room is once again warm. But what if one morning it's bitter cold outside and the next morning it's much warmer? This means that setting your furnace to go on at the same time may, on one morning, leave you cold and on the next morning cause you to waste energy by warming up your house too soon.

By golly, the Magic Stat has everybody beat on this one too. Throughout the night it senses and computes the drop in temperature and the time it will take to get your room to your exact wake-up temperature. So if you want to wake up at 7 AM to 70 degrees—that's the temperature you'll wake up to every time. Because it's a patented concept, no other thermostat has this feature. But wait. There is also a patent on the setting feature.

SIMPLE TO SET

To set the thermostat, you press just one button. A small LED light scans the temperature scale until you reach your desired temperature and then you release the button. You change the temperature naturally, throughout the day, up to six times. The unit responds and remembers that exact living pattern. The present temperature is displayed by a glowing red LED on the scale.

The system also computes the ideal length the furnace should stay on to keep the temperature within a range of plus or minus one and one-half degrees. A battery backup lets you keep your stored program in its memory so power outages as long as eight hours won't let your unit forget. And if something happens and your power is out for a few days, the unit will automatically maintain 68 degrees when the power is restored.

Quite frankly, we were so impressed with the unit, its ease of installation and setting plus its many energy-saving features, we seriously considered advertising it until we realized that our customers would probably not want to trust their future comfort to a product called Magic Stat. What if something went wrong with the unit? How substantial was this Magic Stat outfit? Remember, a thermostat is something you live with as long as you live in your home, and they're supposed to last ages. After all, your comfort depends on it.

Well, we did our homework. We found the company to be a sound, well-financed organization. They have been in business for several years, and they back their products with a three-year limited warranty. In addition, the company has a policy of buying back your unit in one year if you haven't saved its full cost in energy savings. We were satisfied with the company, the people, the product, its incredible features, the company's commitment to the product and above all, the energy savings.

We are so impressed now with the Magic Stat that we're going to make buying one irresistible. Buy one from us for only $79.

Install it yourself in a few minutes or hire a handyman to install it.

Or order the new deluxe unit for $99 with the exact same features as the regular model, but with a beautiful new case.

Then enjoy the savings this next winter. Not only will you save up to 30% on your heating bills, but you're eligible for the 15% energy tax credit. Then if you're not absolutely in love with this product one year later, return it to JS&A. You'll get all your money back and you can reinstall your old thermostat.

REALIZE SAVINGS

But we're counting on a few things. First, you will realize an energy savings and a comfort that will far surpass what you are currently experiencing. Secondly, you probably will sleep better breathing cooler air yet wake up to just the right temperature.

Beauty is only skin deep and a name doesn't really mean that much. But we sure wish those guys at Magic Stat would have named their unit something more impressive. Maybe something like Twinkle Temp.

To order, credit card holders call toll free and ask for product by number below or send check plus $4 delivery for each unit ordered.

Magic Stat (0040C) $79
Deluxe Magic Stat (0041C) 99

The ad drew your attention and brought you into the copy with the way I knocked the product. Your question might have been, "What's the gimmick? Why is he knocking the product?"

You started to read the ad. And then you discovered the one feature that we liked, which happened to be installation—the most difficult obstacle we had to overcome in selling this product.

From then on selling the Magic Stat was all downhill. Once we had the product installed, we could then discover its great features, raise and resolve the remaining objections (the name and the appearance) and then sell all the product's benefits. And indeed we did for more than three years.

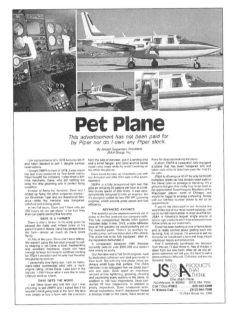

Pet Plane

This advertisement has not been paid for by Piper nor do I own any Piper stock.

By Joseph Sugarman, President
JS&A Group, Inc.

They said I'd never get my asking price, but it only took one customer.

At JS&A we had three corporate aircraft. Like having a lot of cars, you can only fly one airplane at a time. So I decided to get rid of the plane I used the least—my Aerostar.

I paid close to $240,000 for it and everybody told me that it was now worth only $190,000 at best. I couldn't believe this fine aircraft had dropped so much in value, so I decided to take out a single ad in the *AOPA Pilot*—one of the private pilot magazines—and find out if I could get my asking price.

The basic format of the ad was a story about my lack of use of the airplane and my concern for our mechanic/pilot Dave. And I use the story to weave in all the good features of the plane. Then, at the end, to add a little humor, I offered to give away a small steer to anybody who buys the plane. I finished the ad with a classic ending. In this ad the humor worked. My Aerostar sold quickly for $240,000—I got back exactly what I paid for it minus the cost of the ad, around $5,000. It was well worth the effort. Humor can work if it is done in a friendly sort of way. In essence I was poking fun at myself, but the serious message of the ad didn't get overlooked. And, remember, I only needed to sell one to break even.

Headline: Pet Plane

Subheadline: This advertisement has not been paid for by Piper nor do I own any Piper stock.

Byline: By Joseph Sugarman, President, JS&A Group, Inc.

Copy: I am a proud owner of a 1978 Aerostar 601P and have decided to sell it despite serious reservations.

I bought 296PA in April of 1978. It was one of the last ones produced by Ted Smith before Piper bought the company. I also hired a full-time mechanic, Dave, who did nothing but keep the ship gleaming and in perfect flying condition.

Instead of flying the Aerostar, Dave and I ended up flying the other corporate planes—our Grumman Tiger and our Beechcraft Bonanza—while the Aerostar was hangared, polished and looking pretty.

In two full years, Dave and I have only put 350 hours on our pet plane—a lot less time than can justify owning this fine ship.

DAVE IS A FARMER

Dave is also a farmer. In his early years he plowed the fields and milked cows at his parents' farm in Illinois. Dave has always loved the farm—almost as much as Dave loves flying.

In July of this year, Dave and I were talking. We weren't using the Aerostar enough to justify keeping it, yet Dave, a loyal, hard-working and excellent mechanic, would not have enough to keep him busy to continue working for JS&A if we sold it and he only had the other two planes to work on.

I personally love flying too. I am an instrument-rated commercial pilot with a multi-engine rating. Unlike Dave, I was born in the big city. I didn't know what it was like to raise crops or work on a farm.

DAVE GETS THE WORD

I sat Dave down and told him that I was planning to sell 296PA and I asked him if he wouldn't mind going back to the farm. My idea was simply to buy a farm with the proceeds from the sale of the Aerostar, put in a landing strip and a small hangar, and Dave and his family could raise crops while he wasn't working on the other two planes.

Dave loved the idea, so I decided to part with our Aerostar and offer it for sale in this advertisement.

296PA is a fully pressurized light twin that gets an amazing 28 gallons per hour at a realistic cruise speed of 200 knots. It was aerodynamically designed to take jet engines, but its designer settled for two 290 HP Lycoming engines which provide great speed and fuel efficiency.

ADVANCED AVIONICS

The avionics on the airplane remind me of many of the fine products our company sells. The fully computerized Bendix 2000 system includes radar, R-Nav, DME, a radar altimeter plus all the goodies we could possibly put on the beautiful panel. There's an auxiliary hydraulic pump, surface de-ice plus a flight phone. The plane had to be fully equipped—after all, my reputation demanded it.

A comparably equipped 1980 Aerostar currently sells for over $350,000 and doesn't look nearly as pretty.

Our Aerostar was a Ted Smith original—built by dedicated craftsmen who took great pride in their work. But with any new plane, there are always small bugs that surface. The JS&A Aerostar is so debugged that we doubt you'll see one soon. Dave spent an enormous amount of time tightening, greasing, cleaning and examining every system in the plane. In addition to 100 hour inspections, Dave conducted 50 hour inspections. In addition to yearly inspections, Dave conducted semi-annual inspections. And if I mentioned I heard a strange creak on the plane, Dave would be there for days decreaking the plane.

In short, 296PA is a beautiful, fully-equipped airplane that has been hangared and well taken care of for its short two-year life. And it's for sale.

JS&A is offering our 601P for only $240,000 complete (sales tax has already been paid on the plane) plus no postage or handling. It's a genuine bargain that really has to be seen to be appreciated. Dave hangars the plane at the Waukegan airport, north of Chicago, and would be happy to arrange a showing. Simply call our toll-free number below to set up an appointment.

If you're not interested in our Aerostar but would like one of our most recent catalogs, call us on our toll-free number or drop us a line too. JS&A is America's largest single source of space-age products and I'd be anxious to have fellow pilots as our customers.

Dave has been looking at a lot of farms lately and is really excited about getting back into farming. And, of course, I'm anxious to sell my Aerostar so I could own a farm and keep a loyal employee happy and productive.

And if somebody purchases my Aerostar from this ad, I'll also throw in, free of charge, a steer from our new farm. After all, as any airplane salesman will tell you, it's hard to sell a plane without a little bull. Call early and see my Aerostar, today.

As I mentioned, the plane sold very quickly. And for the asking price. It was only later, after a call from the FBI, that I discovered the plane was used for running drugs from South America and had been confiscated.

Mail Order Mansion

It's only 6 million dollars and comes complete with swimming pool, tennis court and a breathtaking view.

By Joseph Sugarman

We accepted Visa, MasterCard and American Express. And even Japanese Yen.

After my success with the airplane, I had a chance to really push the mail order envelope. Could I sell a $6 million home? The exposure might find one buyer—just as it did with my airplane—and all I needed was one buyer.

So in 1987 I created the ad as a complete story almost all the way to the end. The marketing strategy was to offer the house or a video. If the house didn't sell, maybe I would sell enough videos to cover the space costs. But I didn't sell enough videos and the ad was a loss, as the house did not sell either.

Headline: Mail Order Mansion

Caption: It looked like a setup to me.

Subheadline: It's only 6 million dollars and comes complete with swimming pool, tennis court and a breathtaking view.

Byline: By Joseph Sugarman

Copy: Have I got a deal. And even if you don't buy this home, you'll love the story.

It all started with an invitation. I was invited by one of the top real estate developers in the country to attend a party at his home in Malibu, California. I didn't know why. All the developer would say is, "Just come."

The jet was waiting for me at O'Hare Airport in Chicago and his chauffeur-driven limousine met me at Los Angeles for the drive to Malibu. It was class all the way.

When I drove up to the home, there was a party going on. Rolls Royces were lined up everywhere and the noise and music from the house made it clear that something special was going on.

VERY FAMOUS GUESTS

After I entered and was introduced to the host and his wife, they took me around and introduced me to some of their guests. "This is Joe Sugarman, that famous mail order copy writer who writes all those interesting mail order ads."

I met a famous movie star, a nationally famous sports broadcaster, a soap opera TV star, a few famous baseball players and two famous California politicians. I recognized everybody and a few even knew who I was. In fact, some of them were my customers. But why was I there? I still didn't know.

I had a chance to look around the house. Now I've seen beautiful homes in my life but this one had to be the most impressive I've ever seen. First, it was on top of a 90 foot bluff overlooking a sandy beach and the Pacific Ocean. Secondly, it was night and I could see the entire shoreline of Los Angeles. It was as if I were on a cruise ship at sea and I could look over the Pacific and back at the city.

Then I recognized the cliff. Was this the site of the most publicized wedding in show business where seven helicopters hovered above taking pictures? I found out later that it was.

The home took complete advantage of the view. Practically every room faced the ocean. And the sliding glass doors completely opened so you had an unobstructed view of the ocean—no partitions, no supporting beams.

The sound that filled the house with music first appeared to be live. But later I found that the home had the best acoustics ever designed into a personal residence with a sound system that rivaled a recording studio. And what a personal residence.

There was a sunken tennis court, a swimming pool, whirlpool bath and solid state electronic lighting system that was controlled from any place in the house. The ceilings were 25 feet high and the interior decor was so tastefully done that I could easily understand why it won all sorts of awards. But why was I here? Why were all my expenses paid for? Then I found out.

The developer and his wife set me up in one of the five bedrooms and after the guests had left invited me into the living room. "Joe, the reason we've invited you here is that we want you to write an advertisement to sell our house. You're one of the nation's top copywriters, and since this house is an award-winning world-class residence, we wanted a world-class copywriter to do it justice."

Now I'll admit, I was flattered. "But I'm a mail order copywriter. How could I possibly sell a house this expensive?"

VERY SPECIAL

"Easy," replied the developer. "By its value. This property is very special. It's on a peninsula that sticks out of the curved part that faces Los Angeles. When you look from the cliff you see Los Angeles as if it were rising out of the ocean. And because we are on a point, we do not get the harsh winds off the ocean but rather gentle breezes all year long. The property itself is so valuable that our next door neighbor paid close to 9 million dollars for his one bedroom house."

I was starting to feel uneasy. "I'm sorry, but there's no way I can sell your home. I refuse to write anything except under my own company name. And I'm not in the real estate business." But the developer persisted.

"Joe, you really can be. This house is an investment. There's a lot of foreign money out there. And all it takes is that special person looking for a celebrity-status world-class home on one of the best sites in America and presto, it's sold."

FINAL REFUSAL

I refused and it was my final refusal. "I'm sorry, I cannot sell anything without a 30 day return privilege. My customers all have the opportunity to return anything we sell them for a prompt and courteous refund. And then there's the credit card issue. We make it easy for them to purchase with either Master Card, Visa or American Express."

Well, the rest is history. I am indeed offering the house for sale. Please call me at (312) 564-7000 and arrange for a personal showing. Then I urge you to buy it. We accept Visa, Master Card, American Express, American dollars, Japanese Yen or any negotiable hard currency.

After you buy the home, live in it for 30 days. Enjoy the spectacular view, walk on the beautiful beaches, experience the spacious living. If, after 30 days, you aren't completely satisfied, return the home to the original owner for a prompt and courteous refund.

The developer and his wife are thrilled that I am selling their home. They realize that the mail order business is a lot different than the real estate business and are willing to compromise. But don't you compromise. If you truly are one of those rare people in search of a spectacular home on the best location in America, call me personally at no obligation, today.

PS: If you don't have time for the showing, please order a video tape of the home. (Please refer to product number 7077YE.) Send $20 plus $3 postage and handling to the address below or credit card buyers call our toll-free number below.

Malibu Mansion $6,000,000

As I mentioned, the house did not sell. And, as a matter of fact, we didn't sell enough videos to break even either. But that was part of the risk I was willing to take. We did get a lot of publicity from the ad including an invitation to appear on the David Letterman show, which I declined.

I also got a call from the Disney estate asking me if I would sell Walt Disney's old home in the same fashion I offered the Mail Order Mansion. I didn't accept the opportunity as one crazy real estate ad was enough for me.

Chapter 32 | Hungarian Conspiracy

After completely insulting my prospects, I still did well.

Some of my ads were never even published. Others were not that successful and some appeared only in our catalog. From this last group I have selected one that I felt struck out in a very unique direction and had an interesting story. Hungarian Conspiracy appeared only in our catalog and was moderately successful. It was, however, one of my favorites.

I actually traveled to Hungary, did all the photography in Budapest and even met with Professor Erno Rubik, the inventor of Rubik's Cube—a three-dimensional puzzle in the shape of a cube that was a fad in the early 1980s.

What was unique in this ad was the message. Consumers were urged not to buy the product through a tongue-in-cheek explanation of why purchasing one could cause another major recession. It is only in the last paragraph of the ad that I actually offer the product for sale.

Keep in mind that when this was written in 1983, we still had the Berlin Wall and the Soviet Union with all the associated paranoia.

The environment created in the ad for the product is both a story and a tease. "What's the gimmick here if they aren't selling the product?" is one of the questions you might ask yourself as you slowly slip through the copy. And you don't get the answer until the very last paragraph. What do you think of the ad copy?

Headline: Hungarian Conspiracy

Subheadline: Hungary plans massive assault on America with new computer weapon. Exclusive report from Budapest.

Caption 1: Warn your neighbors not to buy this dangerous Hungarian secret weapon.

Caption 2: Thomas Kovacs caught holding the XL-25 in this special photo smuggled out of Budapest. "You think the last recession was bad?"

Copy: Note: Reproduction or any reprints, in whole or in part, of the following material is strictly forbidden without the express written permission of JS&A. All rights reserved.

BUDAPEST (JS&A)—Reporters have smuggled intelligence reports out of Hungary on a conspiracy that may have far-reaching consequences for all Americans.

In the coming year, Hungarians will be shipping to the United States, via Hong Kong, a game with the code name "XL-25."

The game at first may look innocuous—a typical electronic game that could come from Mattel, or any of the other big electronic game manufacturers. But beware. Whatever you do, don't buy it.

MASSIVE CONSPIRACY

The game is part of a massive conspiracy to weaken the United States by destroying our productive work force and eventually putting the entire free world into a major depression. Here's what we've discovered.

In 1980 when Erno Rubik, the Budapest University professor, unleashed the now famous Rubik's Cube, the United States economy was growing at a nice clip. Shortly after the cube was introduced, America entered into a major recession. Our gross national product dropped, factories started laying off people by the thousands and the economy took a big nosedive.

The exact reasons for the recession are varied, but our theory is quite simple. JS&A contends that millions of Americans were so busy twisting that small cube that they were not paying attention to their jobs. Productivity dropped, profits plunged and consumer spending fell to new lows.

It was obvious to Russian intelligence sources that the cause of the American recession was the Rubik's Cube. The Russians reasoned that if the Hungarians could invent games and then flood the American market with them, they could cause a massive depression—one that would permanently weaken America thus making us easy targets for a communist takeover. If you think this theory is farfetched, please read on.

THANK YOU

Hungarians everywhere, proud of the huge success of the Rubik's Cube, were now inspired. Hungarians are quite a creative bunch to start with. They were responsible for such things as glass fiber optics, the micro floppy disk and the science of holography. Hungary always had creative people, but their potential was never really unleashed until Rubik.

The Hungarian government wanted to not only encourage this pent-up creativity, but help Hungary develop their game industry for specific communist purposes.

A new private company was set up last year for the sole purpose of developing computer games for the American market. Funded by banks and run by successful Budapest business types, the company developed the XL-25 through the efforts of three game designers shown to the left.

The bearded communist shown in the picture is Laszlo Mero, 33, a winner of the 1968 International Mathematical Student Olympiad held in Moscow. He's bright, intelligent and one of the top puzzle and game designers in Hungary.

AUTO PARTS DEALER

The man in the middle is Thomas Kovacs, a Hungarian auto parts dealer. At least that's what our investigators turned up. We suspect auto parts is only a front.

The man to the left is Ferenc Szatmari, a physicist and a real genius. He graduated from the University of Budapest with a doctorate degree in elementary particle physics.

The incredible game they invented and the one we must stop from being sold in this country is quite fascinating. The XL-25 is an electronic game with five rows of five squares or 25 squares in all. Each square is actually a button with a built-in light-emitting diode.

When you start, lights light up under five of the buttons. The object of the puzzle is to get all the lights under the buttons to light up. But there's a catch, and here's where the frustration comes in.

Each time you press a button, the four buttons immediately surrounding the button you push change state. If they're lit, they go off. If they're off, they'll go on. If you're a little confused, it doesn't matter anyway. Just remember that the object of the game is to get all the buttons to light up with the least number of keystrokes.

The unit counts the number of button entries and you can ask the XL-25 what your score is and still return to your game.

Once you try the XL-25, you'll be immediately sucked into the Hungarian conspiracy. But don't worry. You're in good company. Texas Instruments was so impressed with its design that they developed the integrated circuit. A group in Hong Kong became so obsessed with it that they built the game with the quality you'd expect from a Mattel or Atari game.

Quite frankly, we were so hooked that we bought thousands and even dispatched a reporter to Budapest where we made our shocking intelligence discovery.

YOU CAN HELP

So there's the story. A communist game, whose circuit was designed by a good ol' American company, carefully assembled by one of our best friends in the Far East—all part of a massive conspiracy to prepare Americans for a major communist takeover.

Prevent other Americans from falling into this scam. Order a unit from JS&A. When you receive it, whatever you do, don't play with it. Instead, immediately take it to all your neighbors and urge them not to buy one. Tell them about the real cause of our last recession, the communist plot and the Hungarian conspiracy. And then make sure you give them the ultimate warning. "Anybody who buys this thing is a real idiot."

XL-25 (3045C 4.00) $29

This was a really good example of pushing the envelope. The ad copy was strong enough to get my prospects to read all the copy and hopefully the curiosity was strong enough to cause them to purchase the product. Even if I did call anybody who bought one an idiot.

Vision Break-through

When I put on the pair of glasses what I saw I could not believe. Nor will you.

They look like sunglasses.

By Joseph Sugarman

JS&A

One JS&A Plaza, Northbrook, IL 60065
CALL TOLL FREE 800 228-5000

This single ad started an entire business that eventually created a brand name.

The Vision Breakthrough advertisement was among the most successful in my company's history, so it merits a close look.

In this ad I did not want to present the product as another pair of sunglasses, so I presented it as a vision breakthrough that protects you from the harmful rays of the sun. It was one of the first ads that provided a real educational message about the dangers of UV rays on the eyes. Before this ad ran, there was really nothing in the popular press about UV ray damage.

The approach I used was to tell the story of how I discovered the glasses and all the facts I learned about them as well as the sun's light. I did it in a simple yet powerful way.

I also used a tremendous dose of curiosity. You can't experience the pair unless you personally try them on. Thus, you must buy them to satisfy your curiosity.

The BluBlocker advertising campaign was a major success that started with this print ad in 1986 and continued on television for several years. Today BluBlocker is a recognized brand name that is sold in retail stores throughout the country.

Headline: Vision Breakthrough

Subheadline: When I put on the pair of glasses what I saw I could not believe. Nor will you.

Caption: They look like sunglasses.

Byline: By Joseph Sugarman

Copy: I am about to tell you a true story. If you believe me, you will be well rewarded. If you don't believe me, I will make it worth your while to change your mind. Let me explain.

Len is a friend of mine who knows good products. One day he called excited about a pair of sunglasses he owned. "It's so incredible," he said, "when you first look through a pair, you won't believe it."

"What will I see?" I asked. "What could be so incredible?"

Len continued, "When you put on these glasses, your vision improves. Objects appear sharper, more defined. Everything takes on an enhanced 3-D effect. And it's not my imagination. I just want you to see for yourself."

COULDN'T BELIEVE EYES

When I received the sunglasses and put them on I couldn't believe my eyes. I kept taking them off and putting them on to see if what I was seeing was indeed actually sharper or if my imagination was playing tricks on me. But my vision improved. It was obvious. I kept putting on my $100 pair of sunglasses and comparing them. They didn't compare. I was very impressed. Everything appeared sharper, more defined and indeed had a greater three dimensional look to it. But what did this product do that made my vision so much better? I found out.

The sunglasses (called BluBlockers) filter out the ultraviolet and blue spectrum light waves from the sun. Blue rays have one of the shortest wavelengths in the visible spectrum (red is the longest). As a result, the color blue will focus slightly in front of the retina which is the "focusing screen" in our eye. By blocking the blue from the sunlight through a special filtration process and only letting those rays through that indeed focus clearly on the retina, objects appear to be sharper and clearer.

The second reason is even more impressive. It is harmful to have ultraviolet rays fall on our eyes. Recognized as bad for skin, UV light is worse for eyes and is believed to play a role in many of today's eye diseases.

SUNGLASS DANGER

But what really surprised me was the danger in conventional sunglasses. Our pupils close in bright light to limit the light entering the eye and open wider at night like the lens of an automatic camera. So when we put on sunglasses, although we reduce the amount of light that enters our eyes, our pupils open wider and we allow more of the harmful blue and ultraviolet light into our eyes.

DON'T BE CONFUSED

I'm often asked by people who read this, "Do those BluBlockers really work?" They really do and please give me the opportunity to prove it. I guarantee each pair of BluBlockers to perform exactly as I described.

BluBlocker sunglasses use Malenium™ lenses with a hard anti-scratch coating. No shortcuts were taken.

The black, lightweight frame is one of the most comfortable I have ever worn and will comfortably contour to any size face. It compares with many of the $200 pairs you can buy from France or Italy.

There is a clip-on pair that weighs less than one ounce and fits over prescription lenses. All models include a padded carrying case and a one-year limited warranty.

I urge you to order a pair and experience your improved vision. Then take your old sunglasses and compare them to the BluBlocker sunglasses. See how much clearer and sharper objects appear with the BluBlocker pair. And see if your night vision doesn't improve as a direct result. If you don't see a dramatic difference in your vision—one so noticeable that you can tell immediately—then send them back anytime within 30 days and I will send you a prompt and courteous refund.

DRAMATIC DIFFERENCE

But from what I've personally witnessed, once you wear a pair, there will be no way you'll want to return it.

Our eyes are very important to us. Protect them and at the same time improve your vision with the most incredible breakthrough in sunglasses since they were first introduced. Order a pair or two at no obligation, today.

Credit card holders call toll free and order by product number below or send a check plus $3 for postage and handling.

BluBlocker Sunglasses (1020CD) . . . $59.95

Clip-On Model (1028CD) 59.95

The main feature of this ad is the storytelling approach which wove an educational message—the first of its kind. It brought the awareness of the dangers of sunlight to the attention of the public who were unaware of these dangers.

In addition, it launched the BluBlocker brand name and created a new business which continues to this day. It is a perfect example of the power of the pen—the same power you will have upon completion of this book and with enough practice.

JOY TO THE WORLD

Gold Space Chains

Dress her in style for that next trip through outer space with America's first space-age gold chains.

This controversial ad was a complete departure from our normal offerings.

This was the ad that created a lot of controversy when it appeared in our catalog in 1978. A number of women complained vehemently. It is a good example of the insensitivity to women's issues that I had at the time. But, hey. I'm human and I learned.

I also received a lot of mail congratulating me on the incredible piece of copy that I had written. So for its controversial response and for the sake of presenting some interesting and entertaining copy, I have included it here.

Another interesting factor was the timing of this ad. When we placed it in our catalog, prices for gold were pretty low. Right after the ad appeared, the price of gold skyrocketed, the response grew like crazy and we sold out. So it proved to be quite a successful ad too—but probably due to the serendipity of our timing.

Notice the use of the editorial 'we' in the ad copy. It would have been more personal had I used the word 'I' instead. Also see if there is one place in the ad that might offend a woman currently employed in a primarily male job category.

Headline: Gold Space Chains

Subheadline: Dress her in style for that next trip through outer space with America's first space-age gold chains.

Copy: Our good friend, Bob Ross, is one of America's top wholesale jewelry representatives.

A few months ago, Bob approached us with a suggestion, "Why not offer gold chains to your customers?" We rejected the idea, for our catalog must only contain products that relate to space-age technology. And besides, it was too late; we had just passed our deadline.

But Bob persisted, "Most of your readers are men. Why not give them something they could buy for their wives or loved ones?

After all, you offer them all sorts of neat things to buy for themselves, but other than a good watch, there's nothing for the lady."

SUGGESTION REJECTED

We could not accept Bob's argument. Although we have a 90% male readership, and although we felt that our customers might indeed want to buy jewelry from our catalog, we felt that our strict adherence to the principles of space-age product selection precluded our making any variation in our philosophy.

Then Bob tried to appeal to our sense of profit. "Your customers are wealthy and smart. Offer them gold chains at very low prices. You'll sell a ton because they have the money to spend, and they have the brains to recognize good value."

Again we had to disappoint Bob. True, our customers earn an average of $50,000 a year, higher than practically any other buying group in the country. And true, our customers include some of the nation's leading businessmen, politicians, newscasters, doctors, and even movie stars. But we could not justify the violation of our principles and take advantage of an opportunity just because our customers are above average. "Sorry Bob," we said. "JS&A has an important reputation to maintain."

HE DOESN'T GIVE UP

Bob is quite a successful salesman. He never gives up until he has exhausted all arguments. A good salesman is persistent, and Bob certainly persisted. He just wouldn't give up.

"Why don't you call the gold chains 'Space Chains'—space-age jewelry for the lady you want to take on that trip through outer space? After all, giving it a space-age theme really makes it tie nicely into your catalog, and besides, gold is a valuable metal found on many of the planets in outer space."

"That would be deceiving," we told Bob. To think that we could use a flimsy theme like that to tie such an unrelated product to space-age technology was almost an insult. It was at this point that we thought seriously of asking Bob to leave. "Bob, you're a nice guy and we've known you for years, but you'll have to leave now."

ENTER BOB'S COUSIN

But Bob pleaded, "Let me show you one thing before I leave. My cousin Joy is very pretty, and I'm sure she would be happy to model the jewelry for you in your advertisement." Bob then took a photograph from his wallet and showed it to us.

At this point, Bob had worn out his welcome. We were surprised to discover that he would stoop so low as to use one of his relatives as a means of getting his products displayed in our catalog. But then we gave the whole matter some very serious thought.

"Actually Bob, space-age jewelry isn't a bad idea for our catalog.

After all, the only items we have for women are watches. Gold Space Chains might go very well. Of course we would keep our prices low to provide some real bargains, and I'm sure our customers would appreciate the convenience of being able to buy such a valuable gift. Bob, can she be at our photographer Tuesday so we can make our extended deadline?"

"Sure," said Bob. "But what about the selection?"

"Who cares about the selection? Why don't you just pick the most popular styles in various price ranges, and we'll have those photographed too."

Bob left quickly. He selected the chains and his cousin is shown above.

We did keep our prices considerably less than any jewelry store or catalog discount showroom. In fact, if you have a chance, you might compare. Or compare them after you receive the chains. 14 carat gold makes a nice gift for any lady and with our space-age theme, what a combination!

Bob's a funny guy. He probably thinks he's quite a salesman. Actually, if it weren't for our open-mindedness, our keen ability to recognize outstanding new space-age-oriented products, and our compelling desire to satisfy the needs of our customers, Bob wouldn't have a chance.

[*Prices were then listed for different styles on the order form.*]

In the above ad, I mentioned that our customers earn, on average, $50,000 a year. In 1978 when this ad was written, a $50,000 salary was very high.

Did you find the offending passages? What could I have said that would have made it less offensive without changing the basic premise of the ad? And what was the premise of the ad? Let me answer this last question.

The premise of the ad was to introduce a product that had nothing to do with our product line and could not be justified as an offering in our catalog—unless we created a very strong reason for including it. The strong reason was Bob's beautiful cousin, Joy, who agreed to model the jewelry for us. After all, we were human and Joy was a beautiful girl.

As I mentioned, the ad did quite well but it was primarily because of the dramatic increase in the price of gold right after our catalog was published.

Chapter 35

Consumers Hero

Once you started reading this ad, you couldn't put it down.

This ad was one of the best examples of the slippery slide theory. If you just read the headline, subheadline and the bold "Impossible-to-trace Guarantee," you would be compelled to read the first sentence.

Once you started to read, you wouldn't be able to stop until you reached the end of the copy. It was a highly effective piece of advertising copy that I wrote in 1976.

This was one of my favorite ads in that it was not the typical JS&A ad. In the JS&A ads I was the expert in space-age products. In the Consumers Hero ad I was a consumer advocate speaking the language of the consumer. It showed that I could write copy for two totally diverse businesses. Each ad had its own set of expressions and method of delivery. It was also a good example of relating in a human way without being humorous. It remains one of my personal favorites.

Headline: HOT

Subheadline: A new consumer concept lets you buy stolen merchandise if you're willing to take a risk.

Copy: We developed an exciting new consumer marketing concept. It's called "stealing." That's right, stealing!

Now if that sounds bad, look at the facts. Consumers are being robbed. Inflation is stealing our purchasing power. Our dollars are shrinking in value. The poor average consumer is plundered, robbed and stepped on.

So the poor consumer tries to strike back. First, he forms consumer groups. He lobbies in Washington. He fights price increases. He looks for value.

So we developed our new concept around value. Our idea was to steal from the rich companies and give to the poor consumer, save our environment and maybe, if we're lucky, make a buck.

A MODERN DAY ROBIN HOOD

To explain our concept, let's take a typical clock radio retailing for $39.95 at a major retailer whose name we better not mention or we'll be sued. It costs the manufacturer $9.72 to make. The manufacturer sells the unit to the retailer for $16.

THE UNCLE HENRY PROBLEM

Let's say that retailer sells the clock radio to your Uncle Henry. Uncle Henry brings it home, turns it on and it doesn't work. So Uncle Henry trudges back to the store to exchange his "lousy rotten" clock radio for a new one that works ("lousy" and "rotten" are Uncle Henry's words).

Now, the defective one goes right back to the manufacturer along with all the other clock radios that didn't work. And if this major retail chain sells 40,000 clock radios with a 5% defective rate, that's 2,000 "lousy rotten" clock radios.

CONSUMERS PROTECTED ALREADY

Consumers are protected against ever seeing these products again because even if the manufacturer repairs them, he can't recycle them as new units. He's got to put a label on the product clearly stating that it is repaired, not new and if Uncle Henry had his way the label would also say that the product was "lousy" and "rotten."

It's hard enough selling a new clock radio, let alone one that is used. So the manufacturer looks for somebody willing to buy his bad product for a super fantastic price. Like $10. But who wants a clock radio that doesn't work at any price!

ENTER CONSUMERS HERO

We approach the manufacturer and offer to steal that $39.95 radio for $3 per unit. Now think of it. The manufacturer has already spent $9.72 to make it, would have to spend another $5 in labor to fix and repackage it, and still would have to mark the unit as having been previously used. So he would be better off selling it to us for $3, taking a small loss and getting rid of his defective merchandise.

Consumers Hero is now sitting with 2,000 "lousy rotten" clock radios in its warehouse.

Here comes the good part. We take that clock radio, test it, check it and repair it. Then we life test it, clean it up, replace anything that makes the unit look used, put a new label on it and presto— a $39.95 clock radio and it only costs us $3 plus maybe $7 to repair it.

Impossible-to-trace Guarantee

We guarantee that our stolen products will look like brand new merchandise without any trace of previous brand identification or ownership.

We take more care in bringing that clock radio to life than the original manufacturer took to make it. We put it through more tests, more fine tuning than any repair service could afford. We get more out of that $10 heap of parts and labor than even the most quality-conscious manufacturer. And we did our bit for ecology by not wasting good raw materials.

NOW THE BEST PART

We offer that product to the consumer for $20—the same product that costs us $3 to steal and $7 to make work. And we make $10 clear profit. But the poor consumer is glad we made our profit because:

1) We provide a better product than the original version.

2) The better product costs one half the retail price.

3) We are nice people.

BUT THERE'S MORE

Because we are so proud of the merchandise we refurbish, we offer a longer warranty. Instead of 90 days (the original warranty), we offer a five-year warranty.

So that's our concept. We recycle "lousy rotten" garbage into super new products with five-year warranties. We steal from the rich manufacturers and give to the poor consumer. We work hard and make a glorious profit.

To make our concept work, we've organized a private membership of quality and price-conscious consumers and we send bulletins to this membership about the products available in our program.

Items range from microwave ovens to TV sets to clock radios, digital watches, and stereo sets. There are home appliances from toasters to electric can openers. Discounts generally range between 40 and 70 percent off the retail price. Each product has a considerably longer warranty than the original one and a two week money-back trial period. If you are not absolutely satisfied, for any reason, return your purchase within two weeks after receipt for a prompt refund.

Many items are in great abundance but when we only have a few of something, we select, at random, a very small number of members for the mailing. A good example was our $39.95 TV set (we had 62 of them) or a $1 AM radio (we had 1,257). In short, we try to make it fair for everybody without disappointing a member and returning a check.

EASY TO JOIN

To join our small membership group, simply write your name, address and phone number on a slip of paper and enclose a check or money order for five dollars. Mail it to Consumers Hero, Three JS&A Plaza, Northbrook, Illinois 60062.

You'll receive a two-year membership, regular bulletins on the products we offer and some surprises we would rather not mention in this advertisement. But what if you never buy from us and your two-year membership expires. Fine. Send us just your membership card and we'll fully refund your five dollars plus send you interest on your money.

If the consumer ever had a chance to strike back, it's now. But act quickly. With all this hot merchandise there's sure to be something for you. Join our group and start saving today.

Since the time I wrote the Consumers Hero ad I have written many different ads for many different companies. The point I wish to make is simply this: A good copywriter can write to fit any market. His or her ads can sound very upscale for one client and then very downscale for the next. Simply by understanding and applying the principles, one can rise to any copywriting challenge—through understanding the jargon of the customer and using the appropriate words that will resonate with that customer.

There were 25 misspelled words in this ad and some pretty bad grammar.

Imagine writing an ad with dozens of misspelled words and bad grammar and running it in *The Wall Street Journal.* That's exactly what I did in what was one of my most unusual advertising approaches.

I was presented with a closeout product. The Nautilus Lower Back machine had stopped selling at retail. As a result, the manufacturer, loaded with inventory, decided to liquidate the entire load to one of the barter companies in New York.

There was only one proviso in the closeout sale. The manufacturer did not want the product offered at a discount because it would embarrass his retailers who sold customers this product at its full retail price. "If it had to be advertised, it had to be at the full retail price," was the directive from the barter company who called me on the phone.

The product was going to cost only around $100. And I could easily sell it for $250 and make a nice profit. But I was being forced to offer it for $485. If it died at retail, chances were slim to none that I could sell any at $485.

So I created a novel strategy. I would offer the product at $500, even more than the full retail price. I would then allow readers of the ad to circle any misspelled words and I would give them $10 off the retail price for each misspelled word they found. I could then misspell 25 words and sell the machine for $250 without creating a problem with my vendor. Nobody would know the actual price I was selling it for, as it depended on the spelling skills of my readers.

So in June of 1985, I ran the following ad. I had fun writing it—purposely misspelling words as well as using bad grammar. Read the ad and see how you would have done in the Nautilus Spelling Sale.

Headline: Nautilus Spelling Sale

Subheadline: Every mispelled word you find in this advertisement is worth $10 towards the purchase of this popular exercise product.

Bold Copy:

Americans have two weaknesses. The first is spelling and the second is in our lower backs. JS&A intends to do something about both problems.

Byline: By Joseph Sugarman, President

Copy: This advertisment has several mispelled words. Some of them are intentionally mispelled and others are because my spelling is pretty lousy. (My grammar's bad too.)

For every mispelled word you find in this advertisment, I'll reduce the price of the product shown here by $10. If you find 10 words mispelled, you get $100 off the price. If you find 25 words mispelled, you get $250 off the price. And if you find 50 words mispelled, you get the product for absolutely nothing. Why such generosity?

TOO COSTLY

Hundreds of retailers throughout the country have been selling the Nautilus Lower Back machine for its full retail price of $485. Nautilus designed it for the consumer market. Their $3,000 hospital version, used for rehabilitation purposes was too costly for the average consumer.

So Nautilus designed one for the home and sold thousands. Then JS&A got hold of a few thousand and felt that an entirely new market would develope if the unit could sell for $250 or less. But the manufacturer would obviously be concerned as the machine would upset those who had sold the unit for its full price.

So by running this special sale and listing the full retail price and with nobody really knowing what price we're really offering the unit for anyway (I told you my grammar wasn't good), we can make everybody happy—especially those of you with good spelling skills and with lower backs you want to strengthen. The rules are really quite simple.

THE RULES

Look through this ad trying to find several mispelled words, Circle each mispelled word you find and put the total number of mispelled words in the circle above. Please don't correct my grammar. Then multiply the number of mispelled words by $10 and then deduct that amount from the $500 price show in this advertisement. We promise to deliver a unit to you for the price you earn. But be careful. If you circle a word that is not mispelled, we reserve the right to return your order and have you arrested. All orders must be mailed in and paid for by check or money order. (We can't afford the credit card charges, and COD's are more bother than they are worth and at this price we don't need the extra espense.)

If you just want to enter this sale without purchasing anything, simply send the ad in with the number in the circle. If you guess the correct number of mispelled words, you will get a $10 credit towards all the products listed in our catalog which we will also send you (not all the products, just our catalog).

There are a few disclamers. We only have a few thousand of these machines so we reserve the right to run out of them. We also reserve the right to return any order that claims more mispelled words than we've actually made. We will ship each unit freight collect with charges usually running around $50 east of the Mississippi or a little more in California. And finally, a little clue. There are three mispelled words in this paragraph.

DESIGNED FOR THE LOWER BACK

The Nautilus Lower Back machine is designed to strengthen your lower back. If you're an executive who sits at a desk for long hours, your back muscles soon grow weak and cannot support your spine and your skeletal frame as it was designed to do.

What I like about the back machine is how easy it works to strengthen the back. As little as five minutes a day and three days a week is all the exercise you need to start the program. And since the exercise time is so short and not very strenuous, you can exercise anytime of the day or night.

There are ten tension positions. You start at the smallest setting and gradually build up as you increase your strength. In a relatively short time, you'll be able to feel the difference. I can't guarantee that your lower back problems will be gone forever, but the Nautilus Lower Back machine can really make a difference. And even with its low price, the Nautilus comes with a 30-day exercise trial period. If the unit doesn't make a big difference in your exercise program, return the unit to JS&A for a full refund of your purchase price. But act quickly. Once we sell all these units, that's all we can get. One last thing. Please don't call our operators to find out the number of mispelled words.

The Nautilus Lower Back machine is made out of tubular steel that will take a tremendous amount of abuse. All the contact surfaces are cushioned and covered with black Naugahyde. It takes only a few minutes to assemble it with a screwdriver and wrench and it measures 34 1/2" x 51" x 54" and weighs 150 pounds. The unit comes with a 90-day manufacturer's limited warranty and complete instructions.

Take advantage of this unique opportunity to own one of the

finest pieces of exercise equiptment at the lowest possible cost for just being able to count our mispelled words.

To order, ask for product by number shown below or send a check to the address below.

Nautilus Back Machine (7068) $500
Better Speller Cost (7069) . . . . ?

I had two surprises with the results from this ad. The first was the number of people who missed many of the words. We made more profit than I had anticipated. There were exactly 25 misspelled words, but on average most people found around 20 of them.

The second surprise was the number of people who called me to tell me that they had spent hours reading and rereading the ad to find the number of misspelled words even though they had no intention of buying the unit.

I then used this technique to sell the Franklin Spelling Computer. For the spelling computer, it certainly made sense as it tied nicely into the product. But it was this first Nautilus ad that really launched the concept.

One of the strong points of this ad was the involvement that it created on the part of the reader. I received mail months later asking me for the correct number of misspelled words. People were spending hours reading my ad. How many ads can claim that distinction?

The people who found all the words really had a bargain too. And we eventually sold all of our inventory in what was a very successful ad. Bad spelling, bad grammar, who cared? We broke a few rules and came up with a very unique marketing concept that could still work today.

A Note | The Power of Your Pen

In Section Three you took all your new copywriting knowledge and saw how it could be applied in actual mail order advertisements. You also saw how these principles could work in ads that weren't mail order ads and you saw what copy elements were missing in others.

You can now write a great mail order ad using my approach to writing copy. You can create the goose that lays the golden egg. And you know that with this new knowledge you have the potential skill to start businesses and earn millions of dollars—all through the power of your pen.

But it takes practice. And the more you practice, the greater your skill and the closer you will come to the wonderful and exhilarating feeling of writing an ad that the public responds to in massive numbers. Good luck and best wishes in your quest for success.

You may have a special technique or learning experience that I can add to this book when it is reprinted sometime in the future. Why not share it with me? Any insights, experiences or novel theories would be welcome too. I look at this book as a work in progress and your input will be most appreciated. You can mail your comments to me, Joseph Sugarman, at DelStar Books, 3350 Palms Center Drive, Las Vegas, NV 89103.

Finally, if you'd like to be on my mailing list, drop me a short note with your name, address, city and zip code and I'll make sure you receive all of our future announcements.

Epilogue | Some Final Thoughts

The material which you have read was based on an exclusive seminar I conducted from 1977 through 1988. During this time I taught many students who went on to build great companies and fortunes for themselves. I'm proud of them all.

And you should be proud of yourself too for having read this book. You have had to read and learn a great deal. I hope you will use this material to contribute to your community and to your country in a positive and productive way through the informative, entertaining and effective use of advertising.

There are many businesses to build in the future. There's the Internet and all the opportunities associated with it. There's the combination of direct marketing and the new technologies that are only now being developed even as you read this. Congratulations for making the effort to succeed.

I am not the smartest of men. Had I been smarter I would not have made many of the mistakes I did. I would have read more of the direct marketing books and learned more that would have prevented those mistakes from ever happening. I would have tested more. I would have thought more carefully before risking my money and my time.

I never graduated from college, my grades were not great and I practically flunked English. I've never taken an advertising course (although that may have been the best educational break I ever had) and I'm not formally educated in many of the subjects necessary to ply my craft.

I am also not that much more talented than others. There are many great writers, marketers and entrepreneurs. If you work longer hours, if you risk more of your time and capital, eventually you learn. I worked and risked a lot. And I learned a lot.

Then what do I have? I would say three things could sum me up. The first is the skill I have to take a very complex issue and present it in a very simple, understandable way—in short, my communications skill. Because of it, I therefore became a good teacher and was able to pass along to my students the underlying reasons for why things work. I was able to share the many experiences I've had and point out the real lessons that I learned. Very often a teacher does not make a good practitioner and a practitioner does not make a good teacher. I like to think I can do both.

The second thing I have is persistence. I don't easily give up. And if I do, it is not without a very good reason. To me, it wasn't whether I won or lost that was important. It was whether I played the game. And I played hard.

And finally, as a writer, I am an originator. To best understand what I mean by an originator, let me explain the difference between compilers and originators.

Compilers: These are the writers who compile their information from the works of others. Jack Canfield and Mark Victor Hansen, co-authors of *Chicken Soup for the Soul,* are good examples. They compiled a book of short stories, anecdotes, cartoons and commentaries that has sold millions and has enriched the lives of those who have read it. Reporters and editors are other examples of compilers. Their articles and commentaries in magazines, in newspapers and on television reflect the current thoughts of the day.

Originators: These are the people from whom the compilers take their information. Originators may or may not write about their own experiences but they provide the material that the compilers compile. These are the people in the trenches who have constantly reinvented themselves. They have not been afraid to fail and have fought the good war and have battle scars to prove it. Their many personal experiences are the stories people find fascinating, for once you have achieved the status of an originator you become newsworthy. The press soon creates your public image and you are constantly copied or imitated. My favorite examples range from software mogul Bill Gates to the music group the Beatles, all the way to Nobel Prize economist Milton Friedman and back to singer and movie personality Madonna.

My role in life always has been and always will be that of an originator. Although I have subtly put myself in some pretty good company above, I have nowhere near their renown. That's not the point of my commentary. I'm simply saying that this book has been written by an originator. In fact, I live to originate. It is my sole purpose in life—the energy that has fueled my very being. If I cannot originate, innovate, or break new ground, I am not living to my full potential. I am not whole.

And through the years, when the compilers have written about me and a story has appeared in *Forbes* or on the front page of *The Wall Street Journal* or in an entire chapter of a book, usually the article or story is mostly correct, mostly reaches the right conclusion but all too often misses the true essence of what I have originated. And this is one of the reasons I have been so motivated to write this book.

There comes a time in your life to step out of the trenches and share the knowledge that you have acquired in your years of battle—to examine the scars and reflect on the lessons and the often odd directions you've taken. For me, that time is right now and this book is a product of that introspection.

Claude Hopkins, one of the early pioneers in advertising, explained why he wrote his book *My Life in Advertising*: "Any man who by a lifetime of excessive application learns more about anything than others owes a statement to successors."

If I had to pick another motivation for writing this book, it would be my strong desire to give of myself to others. I learned more at my seminars by giving and sharing than I did at any time before or after. And aside from acquiring many insights from the seminar participants themselves, I was forced to organize and articulate my concepts to present them properly—which made me a better copywriter and marketer, as I soon started following my own advice.

Many of the seminar participants were highly motivated. You had to be motivated to spend up to $3,000 to attend. And to get to know over 200 of them personally—their successes, their failures and the lessons they learned—simply added to my base of knowledge and experience. You learn from the mistakes and failures of others, and as I was sharing my mistakes and failures, so were they sharing theirs.

Edwin Land, the inventor of the Polaroid camera and also an originator, once said, "A mistake is a future benefit, the full value of which is yet to be realized." And in that spirit many of my mistakes became learning tools which I shared with my students and which inspired them.

I have helped many entrepreneurs build outstanding businesses and go on to contribute greatly to their industry and their community. That is my greatest thrill. For if I can continue that achievement with this book, I will have left a legacy that can live long after I am gone.

Being able to write a great mail order ad is a tremendous skill that will help you achieve a level of success that will amaze you when it happens. But there is much more to achieving success than simply creating the goose that lays golden eggs.

You first have to have a product. And then once you have a product and a great ad, you need to run it in the media and then you need to evaluate the response and respond to your customer orders.

All of these steps are encompassed in my next book, *Marketing Secrets of a Mail Order Maverick,* in which I present the seminar teachings that focused on marketing. How to pick a great product and then evaluate it for potential sale, how to pick the right media at the right price, how to handle the response—all are covered with the same style and unique approach you've read in this book. It's a marketing book unlike any other. Get one at your favorite bookstore or write DelStar Books at 3350 Palms Center Drive, Las Vegas, NV 89103. In addition, you might like the cassette course available with *Advertising Secrets of the Written Word* along with a workbook to help hone your skills. Just call (800) 323-6400 or fax (702) 597-2002 for particulars.

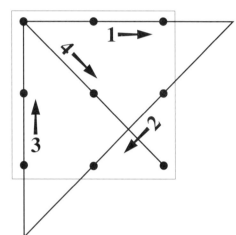

As you can see from the diagram, by not assuming any constraints the answer to the puzzle on page 56 becomes quite simple. All too often we assume constraints that aren't really there. By breaking out of the box you can come up with incredibly effective answers—whether you're writing copy or simply solving everyday problems.

Assumed Constraint Examples

The following are examples of assumed constraints from history. When somebody tells you it can't be done, recall these historical examples before you become discouraged.

1. "Drill for oil? You mean drill into the ground to try and find oil? You're crazy." This was said by drillers whom wildcatter **Edwin L. Drake** tried to enlist in his project to drill for oil in **1859.**

2. "Airplanes are interesting toys but of no military value." **Ferdinand Foch, professor of military strategy, Ecole Superieure de Guerre,** later commander of Allied Armies in World War I.

3. "Stocks have reached what looks like a permanently high plateau." **Irving Fisher, professor of economics, Yale University, 1929.**

4. "I think there is a world market for maybe five computers." **Thomas Watson, Sr., president of IBM, 1943.**

5. "So we went to Atari and said, 'Hey, we've got this amazing thing, even built with some of your parts, and what do you think about funding us? Or we'll give it to you. We just want to do it. Pay our salary, we'll come work for you.' And they said, 'No.' So then we went to Hewlett-Packard, and they said, 'Hey, we don't need you. You haven't got through college yet.'" This was related by **Steven Jobs, Apple Computer co-founder,** on his attempts in the mid '70s to get Atari and Hewlett-Packard interested in his and Steve Wozniak's personal computer.

6. "A cookie store is a bad idea. Besides, the market research reports say America likes crispy cookies, not soft and chewy cookies like you make." This was a response in the mid '70s to **Debbi Fields'** idea of starting **Mrs. Fields Cookies.**

7. "640K ought to be enough for anybody." **Bill Gates, Microsoft founder, 1981.**

You couldn't wait, could you? You had to turn to the back of the book before you read the next line of copy in Chapter 10. Well, you just fell for the seeds of curiosity theory big time:

Your message must always be so compelling that you motivate the reader to do things normally not done.

I realize that you might think this is a dirty trick and the story never took place. You're wrong on both counts. This is exactly what happened and this is no dirty trick. But to get people to reach into their pockets and exchange their hard-earned dollars for your product is not a natural act. It's one of the most difficult things a copywriter must do to sell a product. It requires tremendous motivation—motivation that needs to be generated by a compelling message, a message so compelling that people will become totally involved with your copy, slide down the slippery slide and call or write to place an order or feel guilty that they haven't.

I guess it wouldn't be fair, now that I've proven my point, to leave you hanging. After all, you were so involved with my text that you skipped all the rest of the chapters in this book (something you normally wouldn't do) to find out exactly what Ginger said to me at that dramatic moment in my office.

"Joe, I want only you to help me. I want you as my mentor—my guide through this direct marketing jungle. I don't know what I can do to motivate you to help me, but I do know what most men appreciate. I've had men proposition me all my life but I've never openly propositioned a man. What I'm saying, Joe, is that—"

"Wait," I said, fumbling for words as I held up one hand as if to say stop. "You've got the wrong guy. Don't embarrass yourself any further. I can no longer accept what I think you're trying to say. I can't do the work for you. I'm really too busy to take outside projects. But attend my seminar. I'll let you attend for free on the condition that you pay me back after you make your first million."

Ginger left the office, maybe a bit embarrassed. And I never heard from her again. I suspect that she thought she could entice me into writing copy by flaunting her body. And would she have really followed through? I guess I will never know.

When I returned home that evening and my wife asked me how the day went, I replied, "Oh, I was almost seduced by a gorgeous blonde who was willing to give me her body for my copywriting ability."

Appendix C | Summary of Axioms and Major Points

The following lists summarize the Axioms and major points of copywriting that have been presented throughout this book.

Axioms

Axiom 1: Copywriting is a mental process the successful execution of which reflects the sum total of all your experiences, your specific knowledge and your ability to mentally process that information and transfer it onto a sheet of paper for the purpose of selling a product or service. (page 24)

Axiom 2: All the elements in an advertisement are primarily designed to do one thing and one thing only: get you to read the first sentence of the copy. (page 29)

Axiom 3: The sole purpose of the first sentence in an advertisement is to get you to read the second sentence. (page 32)

Axiom 4: Your ad layout and the first few paragraphs of your ad must create the buying environment most conducive to the sale of your product or service. (page 38)

Axiom 5: Get the reader to say yes and harmonize with your accurate and truthful statements while reading your copy. (page 44)

Axiom 6: Your readers should be so compelled to read your copy that they cannot stop reading until they read all of it as if sliding down a slippery slide. (page 49)

Axiom 7: When trying to solve problems, don't assume constraints that aren't really there. (page 58)

Axiom 8: Keep the copy interesting and the reader interested through the power of curiosity. (page 63)

Axiom 9: Never sell a product or service. Always sell a concept. (page 71)

Axiom 10: The incubation process is the power of your subconscious mind to use all your knowledge and experiences to solve a specific problem, and its efficiency is dictated by time, creative orientation, environment and ego. (page 80)

Axiom 11: Copy should be long enough to cause the reader to take the action you request. (page 85)

Axiom 12: Every communication should be a personal one, from the writer to the recipient, regardless of the medium used. (page 92)

Axiom 13: The ideas presented in your copy should flow in a logical fashion, anticipating your prospect's questions and answering them as if the questions were asked face-to-face. (page 97)

Axiom 14: In the editing process, you refine your copy to express exactly what you want to express with the fewest words. (page 102)

Axiom 15: The more the mind must work to reach a conclusion successfully, the more positive, enjoyable or stimulating the experience. (page 175)

Axiom 16: Selling a cure is a lot easier than selling a preventative, unless the preventative is perceived as a cure or the curative aspects of the preventative are emphasized. (page 182)

Axiom 17: Telling a story can effectively sell your product, create the environment or get the reader well into your copy as you create an emotional bonding with your prospect. (page 188)

Emotion Principles

Emotion Principle 1: Every word has an emotion associated with it and tells a story. (page 66)

Emotion Principle 2: Every good ad is an emotional outpouring of words, feelings and impressions. (page 66)

Emotion Principle 3: You sell on emotion, but you justify a purchase with logic. (page 66)

Graphic Elements

The following are the 10 graphic elements to consider when designing a mail order ad. (Chapter 4)

1. Headline	6. Paragraph Headings
2. Subheadline	7. Logo
3. Photo or Drawing	8. Price
4. Caption	9. Response Device
5. Copy	10. Overall Layout

The Powerful Copy Elements

The following are the 23 copy elements that should be considered when writing an ad. (Chapter 18)

1. Typeface
2. First Sentence
3. Second Sentence
4. Paragraph Headings
5. Product Explanation
6. New Features
7. Technical Explanation
8. Anticipate Objections
9. Resolve Objections
10. Gender
11. Clarity
12. Clichés
13. Rhythm
14. Service
15. Physical Facts
16. Trial Period
17. Price Comparison
18. Testimonials
19. Price
20. Offer Summary
21. Avoid Saying Too Much
22. Ease of Ordering
23. Ask for the Order

The Psychological Triggers

The following are the 24 psychological triggers to remember or review when you are writing your ad copy. (Chapter 19)

1. Feeling of Involvement or Ownership
2. Honesty
3. Integrity
4. Credibility
5. Value and Proof of Value
6. Justify the Purchase
7. Greed
8. Establish Authority
9. Satisfaction Conviction
10. Nature of Product
11. Current Fads
12. Timing
13. Desire to Belong
14. Desire to Collect
15. Curiosity
16. Sense of Urgency
17. Instant Gratification
18. Exclusivity, Rarity or Uniqueness
19. Simplicity
20. Human Relationships
21. Guilt
22. Specificity
23. Familiarity
24. Hope

Appendix D | Recommended Reading

Reading a number of books on a variety of subjects prepares you to become a good direct marketer and helps you avoid many of the mistakes others have made. That's one of the benefits you have realized from reading *Advertising Secrets of the Written Word*. Many other people in the direct marketing industry have also written books that might be helpful to you. By reading other perspectives on advertising and copywriting, you can further your education and avoid costly errors that many before you have made. I wish I had read many of them earlier in my career.

How to Sell Anything to Anybody, Joe Girard. The world's greatest salesman shares his secrets on how he made a fortune selling cars in Detroit. The book details how he eventually was listed in the *Guinness Book of World Records* for having sold the most cars in one year. An interesting read and some valuable insights from a friend and powerful salesman. ISBN 0-446-38532-8. Warner Books. 192 pages.

Sales Magic, Steve Bryant. Bryant is one of QVC's top show hosts and a master at selling. Here he talks about his proven techniques for selling that will give you new insights on what works and why. Here's your chance to increase your sales dramatically through many of the techniques this popular and effective salesman shares with you. I've personally seen him use many of these techniques on QVC in the sale of BluBlocker sunglasses. ISBN 0-936262-24-9. Amherst Media. 152 pages.

My First 65 Years in Advertising, Maxwell Sackheim. One of the former deans of direct mail advertising shows you how to attract attention, create interest, carry conviction, and get action. Sackheim shows you how to write a good ad and a selling headline and then gives you many firsthand experiences. One of the true pioneers in the business, he is often quoted by others. ISBN 0-8306-5816-5. Tab Books. 200 pages.

Ice to the Eskimos, Jon Spoelstra. This is one of my favorite marketing books of all times. And not because Jon was one of my former seminar participants. When Jon gave me the draft of his book to read, I took it with me thinking, "Oh well, just another marketing book," but I was totally wrong. It is one of the most interesting, witty and well-written marketing books I've ever read and there's a wealth of great ideas in its pages. Jon's premise is how to market products nobody wants because if you can do that, you can market anything. After several successful years with the Portland Trail Blazers basketball team as their general manager, Jon left to become the president of the New Jersey Nets basketball team—one of the worst franchises in the league. He had his work cut out for him. As the NBA's top marketer, Jon shares his battle-tested secrets he used with the Nets—secrets that can help you jump-start your sales, excite your customers and improve your bottom line. An absolute must to read. You won't regret it. ISBN 0-88730-851-1. HarperCollins. 280 pages.

Commonsense Direct Marketing, Drayton Bird. Hailed as "the authoritative textbook" on direct marketing, this book is packed with global case histories of how companies using Bird's ideas have managed to grow and prosper. His writing is witty and practical but never boring. A great book to read and reread and one that I wish I had read a lot earlier in my career. ISBN 0-7494-0996-7. Kogan Page, London. 375 pages.

Elephants in Your Mailbox, Roger Horchow. A classic book on the experiences of one of the nation's top catalog entrepreneurs and the 25 mistakes he made in building his company. Filled with insights on what really goes on in an upscale catalog house, this very honest and disarming book is a must-read for any catalog entrepreneur. ISBN 0-8129-0891-0. Times Books. 250 pages.

To Catch a Mouse, Lewis Kornfeld. Take somebody who was responsible for spending in excess of $600 million in advertising over his career at Radio Shack and add his 65 rules of marketing, and you've got the mix that makes this book a great read. Kornfeld is intimate, witty and tells you how to do it better, cheaper, quicker, with less hocus and more focus, with or without an ad agency. ISBN 0-13-922930-2. Prentice-Hall. 360 pages.

Selling the Invisible, Harry Beckwith. This is a field guide to modern marketing with many of the principles applying to direct marketing. A really down-to-earth, practical guide on how markets work and how prospects think. Beckwith presents hundreds of quick, practical and easy-to-read strategies with most no more than a page long. An eye-opener to new ideas in the critical area of marketing. ISBN 0-446-52094-2. Warner Books. 252 pages.

Breakthrough Advertising, Eugene M. Schwartz. One of the really creative marketing and copywriting geniuses of his time. A compendium of his philosophies. He shows how to develop an entirely new market for a new or old product in a number of clearly defined steps. Schwartz takes you through those steps and shows you how to write effective copy in the process. ISBN 0-932648-54-1. Boardroom Books. 240 pages.

MaxiMarketing, Stan Rapp and Tom Collins. Rapp and Collins take you in a new and exciting direction in promotion, advertising and marketing strategy. Reading almost like a novel, this wonderful book challenges you to seek your own applications of its principles and ideas—to get your juices flowing and to open your eyes to what advertising and, in particular, direct marketing will be like in the future. Many of their predictions have already come true. ISBN 0-07-051191-8. McGraw-Hill. 280 pages.

Direct Marketing, Edward L. Nash. One of the most complete books on direct marketing available. This step-by-step tells you everything you need to succeed in every aspect of direct marketing—from writing a basic marketing plan to writing direct mail copy. Nash guides you through planning an offer to planning a layout and even designing the product. You'll discover the analytical methods for forecasting and you'll get a good dose of list selection. Even infomercials are discussed. A great reference book you'll refer to often. ISBN 0-07-046032-9. McGraw-Hill. 480 pages.

The Golden Mailbox, Ted Nicholas. Here's some great advice on how to write ads, evaluate copywriting and layout and systematically test your ads and analyze the results. Nicholas is a direct marketing practitioner who has been on the firing line for the past 25 years. His advice comes from having been through the trenches and knowing what works and what doesn't. The author of 14 books and a catalyst in the starting of several companies, Nicholas is the entrepreneur's Entrepreneur. Learn from an experienced practitioner. ISBN 0-79310-486-6. Enterprise Dearborn. 215 pages.

Direct Mail Copy That Sells! Herschell Gordon Lewis. One of the most prolific copywriters in the industry has put together a book with his step-by-step formulas on how to write effective direct mail copy. If you want a different perspective on ad copy written in Lewis's light, humorous and often witty style, pick up a copy. It contains a lot of plain truth and good common sense. ISBN 0-13-214750-5. Prentice-Hall. 260 pages.

Tested Advertising Methods, John Caples. One of the true bibles of the direct marketing industry, this commonsense book on direct marketing talks about everything from writing effective copy and the power of words to testing and the effectiveness of the right concept. Caples was also famous for many of his successful ad campaigns, among which was the classic "They laughed when I sat down at the piano." If you had to read just one book on direct marketing, this is the one to read cover to cover. ISBN 0-13-244609-X. Prentice-Hall. 300 pages.

My Life in Advertising/Scientific Advertising, Claude C. Hopkins. He was the founding father of modern advertising and these two reprinted classics together in one paperback book are a must-read for any advertising practitioner. Hopkins covers all of the scientific approaches he utilized in the '20s when he wrote these books—approaches that are still used today in direct marketing. This book will be an essential and vital guidepost for present and future generations of advertising professionals. ISBN 0-8442-3101-0. NTC Business Books. 320 pages.

The Lazy Man's Way to Riches, Richard Gilly Nixon. One of the classic books originally written by Joe Karbo, the mail order legend whose ad we featured in Chapter 24 of this book. This completely revised edition covers the spiritual and motivational aspects involved in making a success of yourself and starting a successful business. Using a commonsense approach, this book combines motivational exercises to build self-esteem with worksheets to define your goals. Then it gives you a moneymaking guide to success in mail order. Very well done and a help to any beginner in the direct marketing business, or any business for that matter. ISBN 0-14-024936-2. Penguin Books. 385 pages.

Influence: The Psychology of Persuasion, Robert B. Cialdini, Ph.D. A great book for understanding the tools of influence at work in today's marketplace. Cialdini takes us through a journey exploring some of the very subtle ways to influence a customer, a loved one or even the mass market with many of the techniques he's tested and personally used. A consultant to many Fortune 500 companies, Cialdini offers insights that will amplify your marketing knowledge. ISBN 0-688-12816-5. Quill. 325 pages.

Confessions of an Advertising Man, David Ogilvy. I read this classic when I first started my career in advertising in the '60s and it has been an influence ever since. Ogilvy strongly believed in the disciplines direct marketers utilized to ply their craft. Much of his knowledge and wisdom was acquired from being a student of direct marketing. As a brilliant adman he created great advertising for such clients as Rolls-Royce, Sears, Campbell's Soup and IBM. He was also responsible for creating campaigns for the governments of Britain, France and the United States. ISBN 0-8442-3711-6. NTC/Contemporary. 170 pages.

Positioning: The Battle for Your Mind, Al Ries and Jack Trout. The concept sparked a revolution in advertising and it is also very important in direct marketing. You've got to find that unique selling proposition—that big idea that will position your product or service to outclass and outsmart the competition. Ries and Trout show you how with many lessons that relate to direct marketing. ISBN 0-446-34794-9. Warner Books. 220 pages.

Magic Words That Bring You Riches, Ted Nicholas. This is a book that covers the gamut on how to use effective words in a multitude of situations. It covers the words that will get you the best table at a restaurant. The best words to use when making a business sale. Several examples are used in direct marketing situations, and there are many other everyday insights on the power of words. ISBN 1-887741-00-3. Nicholas Direct. 325 pages.

Million Dollar Marketing Secrets, David L. Deutsch. This is a very well written book with plenty of good ideas written by a marketing consultant and excellent direct response copywriter. Any successful direct marketing copywriter has a lot of valuable information to share and Deutsch shares a lot in his self-published book. He reveals 20 powerful techniques that he guarantees will turbocharge your marketing abilities. At the end of each chapter he also lists resources where you can get more information to further your knowledge. This 200-page book can be purchased directly from Deutsch at (804) 379-6855.

Marketing Secrets of a Mail Order Maverick, Joseph Sugarman. A good complement to this book in that it takes you into the next phase of becoming a direct marketer. Filled with insightful stories, examples and strategy, you'll learn how to find a product, protect it, create a mail order ad and then test the ad in a magazine or newspaper. You'll learn some of the tricks in buying media and running a mail order operation. Rich with examples and stories, it reads more like a marketing novel than the textbook it really is. ISBN 1-891686-06-2. DelStar Books. 390 pages.

Television Secrets for Marketing Success, Joseph Sugarman. A comprehensive review told in story form of what it is like selling your product or service through a home shopping channel, an infomercial or spot TV advertising. Many helpful insights not found anywhere else. Learn how to determine if your product is suited for TV, what margins you'll need, the importance of various elements in a commercial and helpful tips for breaking into this, the most rewarding of the direct marketing disciplines. ISBN 1-891686-09-7. DelStar Books. 310 pages.

Success Forces, Joseph Sugarman. A book I wrote in 1980 about those forces that drive you closer to success and those that draw you towards failure. Knowing the forces and controlling them is the goal of any successful person and this book describes how to do it. The first part of the book is autobiographical and the last half contains the basis of the Success Forces concept. No longer available from bookstores but may be found at some libraries. Soon to be updated and reprinted. ISBN 0-8092-7061-7. Contemporary Books. 215 pages.

Other Book Resources

Out of Print: Some of the books listed here might be out of print and no longer available. If you can't obtain a copy and all else fails, try reaching Carl Galletti and his Hard To Get Books and Tapes club. He can be reached at (609) 896-0245 or fax him for his latest catalog at (609) 896-2653. You might even check him out on the Web at: www.magic7/htg.

Hoke Communications: This is another resource for a number of good direct marketing books. Contact them at (800) 229-6700.

Newsletter

The Gary Halbert Letter, Gary Halbert. This monthly newsletter on copywriting and marketing is a must-read for anybody actively engaged in marketing and copywriting. Halbert is one of the nation's top copywriters and entrepreneurs and his newsletter is one of the most helpful around. Each issue contains a new concept or copywriting technique that can be easily implemented. Halbert's copy is both entertaining and fun and I personally look forward to my copy each month. Study and collect them as I do. To subscribe, call (305) 294-8425.

The following ads are some of the most unique and innovative examples of my copywriting style from the mid '70s to the mid '80s. I have included them here not necessarily because they were the most effective or important in my marketing career (those ads are in my next book, *Marketing Secrets of a Mail Order Maverick*) but because they present examples of the typical advertising that made our ads and catalogs so unique.

Exact months listed below show when the ads were first run in a magazine or newspaper. When only the year is listed, those ads appeared in my catalog. I hope you enjoy reading them as much as I enjoyed writing them.

1. Mickey Math (January 1975) This tongue-in-cheek ad pitched business executives for a child's calculator and bombed. The copy read great but the product never sold. The conclusion: calculators are serious business tools and there weren't enough chief executive officers with a sense of humor to go for the offer.

2. Laser Beam Mousetrap (April 1977) Great copy but we didn't sell a single one. And we didn't do well with the pendants either. But the copy was fun. If I had sold just one mousetrap I would have felt better. It was a total failure.

3. Pocket Yellow Pages (June 1978) This was an example of presenting a very complex new product in a very simple way. This Canon calculator sold very well for JS&A. My competitors offered similar products utilizing the same circuitry and explained all of the product's technology in great detail but didn't do too well. The headline capsulized in just a few words the product's concept and the copy reinforced the message.

4. Unfair Copy (August 1978) How do you unfairly sell a knockoff of a famous brand-name watch? You admit that it is a knockoff and that it is also unfair. And that's what I did in this successful ad in a very logical and forceful way.

5. George's Revenge (October 1978) This was one of those ads that just flowed right out of my brain and onto a sheet of paper. It required just minor editing—maybe a word or two—and it was ready to run. It didn't do too well despite the holiday buying season and the fact that we had an exclusive for the product. The product got lots of publicity but died.

6. Soviet Challenge (November 1978) I got the endorsement of Anatoli Karpov, the Russian chess champion, according to my manufacturer in Hong Kong who had negotiated the deal with Karpov's manager. Instead of just saying Karpov endorsed my product, I challenged him to play against my chess computer. This ad almost prompted an international incident as Karpov refused to have any part in the promotion. The ad did very well. It is honest in its tone and quite persuasive.

7. Karpov Accepts (March 1979) We had pretty good sales with the previous "Soviet Challenge" ad and wanted to continue the momentum. It was natural, therefore, to play on the fact that Karpov finally agreed to endorse our computer even though he wasn't going to play against it. I used some of the effective copy from the previous ad and created some good Karpov quotes for my ad. I got him to approve the quotes and ran this ad as a follow-up. Again it did well, selling thousands of these games.

8. Endorsement Battle (September 1979) This tongue-in-cheek takeoff of the endorsement scene compares JS&A's president (me, of course) as the endorser of my Olympus recorder with a very famous golfer named Arnold Palmer who endorses the Lanier recorder and whose name I don't mention in the ad. The comparison logically explains why you get a better value with the Olympus, based on the money Lanier spends for the expensive golfer's endorsement as well as the cost of their direct salespeople (vs. our direct mail selling). It's a good example of a clever way to add humor to make a very valid point and justify why the consumer is getting as good a value with our product even though our price is a lot lower.

9. Computer Violence (1981) This ad was run during my fight with the FTC when I was hoping to liquidate as much outdated equipment as I could to keep afloat. I used the premise of violence to grab attention and then I proposed an outrageous solution if I didn't sell my computer. The copy reflects not only my frustration at having lost so much value in my computer from depreciation, but also my potential customers' frustration at having seen the value of their computers drop too.

10. Cadillac Garbage Truck (1981) How do I sell a new type of headlight that would cause a reader to want to remove from his or her car a perfectly operating headlight and replace it with the one I was offering? First, you grab their attention with the unusual cartoon at the top of the page (drawn by Dick Hafer) and then you get them to start reading the copy. That's logical. But as the prospects read in an effort to find out where I'm headed with my sales pitch, they are learning very important information that will help them understand a lot of the technical stuff they may need in order to make a buying decision that favors the purchase of the headlights I'm offering. It's fun reading and it educates and effectively persuades as you will soon find out. We did quite well with this product.

11. Pickle Power (1982) You see this ad and you're hooked. You wonder, what do I mean by "pickle power"? And as you read the ad you realize that I'm selling not the pickle but the power— a set of unusual rechargeable batteries and a battery charging system. Again, the copy hooks you and leads you to the logical ending. The product sold well in our catalog.

12. Mafia Auto Gadget (1982) Here we explain why, for the Mafia at least, the remote automobile starting device makes a lot of sense. Then of course we extend its practical uses for the rest of us non-Mafia types by explaining the advantages of a product that remotely starts your car. It's great copy and resulted in a large number of these expensive gadgets being sold.

13. Customer Explodes (1982) The headline is an attention-getting device to get the reader into the copy. But once into the copy, there is every reason to think that he or she will read all of it. And many did. This was a very successful ad.

14. Space Shuttle (1982) How do you sell a poster of a scene from outer space? Of course, if you're like me the answer is rather obvious. You charter the space shuttle and then sell seats on it. That's the premise of this ad which takes the reader on a fantasy adventure whose primary purpose is to sell posters. Sure, this was a stretch. But our customers loved the idea and

281

responded in big numbers. And even McDonald's bought 300 posters for one of their promotions.

15. Juki Ooki (1984) What do you do when somebody hands you a great high-tech product but the product does not have a very high-tech name? Simple, you play up the fact that for the sophisticated product you are selling, the name is rather stupid. And that's exactly what we did. But we may have gone a little overboard as you will soon discover. The product did well, but we may have offended a few of our customers in the process.

16. Nuclear Mail Box (1984) How do you express the strength of a galvanized steel plate mailbox? You give it the ultimate test and position the product as capable of withstanding the impact of a nuclear explosion or your money back. Of course, who would be around after a nuclear explosion to call customer service and request a replacement? But again, that's not the point. This ad approach is a way of calling attention to the major advantage of this mailbox—its strength. You read the ad and as you are enjoying the off-the-wall approach, you are being sold on the product's advantages. You are entertained by the disarming copy and hopefully you buy. And many did.

The above are some examples of the approaches I've used to solve a number of marketing problems. These are basically fun-to-read ads, many of which were quite effective. And, of course, some were not very effective. But in the process of publishing these ads over an extended period of time, I developed a customer following that looked forward to every issue of my catalog and every ad we ran in magazines and newspapers. And when they read the ads they bought my products, often in record numbers.

Presenting
Mickey
Math ^{T.M.}

$19⁹⁵

The newest executive calculator will do more than just give answers.

©WALT DISNEY PRODUCTIONS

Impress your friends, figure little deals, close sales and feel smarter with the world's most powerful calculator.

Alco, one of America's largest manufacturers of paper clips and rubber bands, has developed a space-age computer miracle.

HERE'S WHAT IT CAN DO

You're a salesman. You're at lunch with a prospective customer. While discussing prices, your customer pulls out his $400 Hewlett Packard HP-80. You pull out your $19.95 Mickey Math. Two minutes later you walk out with the sale.

You're the financial vice president of a major U.S. corporation. You're at the board of directors meeting. The chairman of the board poses an important financial question and points to you for the answer. You open your briefcase and pull out your Mickey Math. The next day you're promoted to president.

Success stories like the above are real possibilities when you own a Mickey Math calculator. In fact our guarantee of satisfaction clearly states, "If the Mickey Math calculator does not make you rich, famous, more interesting and smarter, return it any time within two weeks for a prompt and courteous refund." And no other calculator company could dare make that guarantee.

FOR LITTLE DEALS ONLY

Mickey Math has six large, yet powerful digits. That's why we recommend it for little deals only. Its full-floating decimal, four-function constant and algebraic logic (you perform the functions as you think) make working complex problems a breeze.

You can do chain calculations, derive negative balances and figure all kinds of answers automatically, all by pressing little round buttons. It's truly the ultimate calculator.

Mickey Math is only 1" x 7½" x 7½" and fits conveniently in your briefcase, suitcase or the trunk of your car. It weighs only 14 ounces and its built-in, space-age handle makes it fun to lug around.

THEY'LL NEVER FORGET YOU

Give Mickey Math to somebody you want to impress: your boss, banker, State Farm insurance salesman or favorite General Motors executive. They'll not only be getting the latest in space-age technology, but they'll never forget you.

It is true that the Mickey Math calculator was designed for children. The instruction booklet with its colorful pictures and clear examples is designed to stimulate math interest and create little geniuses.

But as America's largest single source of electronic calculators and other space-age products, we feel Mickey Math's place is with the executive—as a business tool and as a major element in his day-to-day, decision-making process.

If you're looking for the perfect gift or a great business tool, we urge you to act quickly and order your Mickey Math electronic calculator at no obligation today!

EXECUTIVE ORDER FORM

○ Yes, please rush me____ Mickey Math electronic calculator(s) @ $22.45 each ($19.95 plus $2.50 postage and handling) complete with one year warranty and explicit Mickey Mouse instructions. I understand that if I do not become rich, famous, more interesting or smarter, I may return Mickey Math within two weeks for a prompt and courteous refund.

○ Please add the $4.95 AC adapter which will allow me to conserve battery power while using the calculator at my desk or during lengthy executive conferences.

○ Please add the $3.00 padded carrying case.

Clip out Executive Order Form and mail with your check to the address shown below:

JS&A NATIONAL SALES GROUP

DEPT WMM   4200 DUNDEE RD.
NORTHBROOK, ILL, 60062 (312) 564-9000
©JS&A GROUP, INC., 1975

January 1975

OK WORLD, WE'RE READY

Laser Beam Mousetrap

"Build a better mousetrap and the world will beat a path to your door."

This is the story of two very unusual products. The first is a marketing phenomenon and the second a marketing experiment.

THE MARKETING EXPERIMENT

The marketing experiment has been designed to prove a well-known marketing premise. It was once said that if you build a better mousetrap, the world would beat a path to your door. So American scientists have developed the world's first laser beam mousetrap—a space-age triumph using the latest laser technology and American scientific genius.

If the premise is correct, the world should recognize this outstanding achievement and beat a path to our door. There is no technologically more advanced mousetrap in the world. If the premise is incorrect, then this marketing experiment will certainly prove it.

A REAL LASER

The laser beam mousetrap consists of a functioning laboratory laser with an ingenious wire hammer solenoid-activated spring mechanism. The entire system is mounted on an attractive polished walnut base which can be handsomely displayed in any office, board room, or rodent-infested area.

The laser is of the helium neon variety radiating in red at a wavelength of 6,328 ångstroms with one half milliwatts of power. All mechanisms are safely housed in a transparent acrylic container.

To activate the mousetrap, you place peanut butter in a small circular container located in the center of the trap. The laser beam is deflected down to the peanut butter, keeping it illuminated while the odor stays fresh. The wire hammer device is then cocked and held in position by a solenoid.

As the mouse nibbles the peanut butter, the laser beam is interrupted and a photo diode senses the mouse's presence and releases the spring-loaded hammer wire. Kerplow!

The mouse is then conveniently and rather rapidly put to rest.

The laser beam mousetrap is offered for only $1500 complete with a jar of peanut butter, complete instructions and a one year warranty—all during our special national introductory offer.

THE MARKETING PHENOMENON

The same company that invented the laser beam mousetrap is also in the midst of a marketing phenomenon.

The Holex Corporation has pioneered in the commercial application of laser technology and has done numerous laser experiments to create three-dimensional images on flat pieces of glass. When Holex placed these glass images in a gold-plated frame, not only did it make an unusual piece of jewelry, but it appeared to glow in iridescent colors enhancing the three-dimensional effect and creating an optical sensation for those who saw it.

Holex felt that laser pendant jewelry might make an interesting consumer item. To test it, they produced a few sample pieces which they sold for $50 each in a New York City jewelry store—well below their actual cost.

The hammer-wire mechanism is cocked and held in place by the solenoid.

The first production run quickly sold out. So did the second. It was then that Holex contacted JS&A and offered us the opportunity to offer the world's first mass-produced laser pendant in a large production run.

A small test run flyer was sent out to a selected group of our customers offering the pendant for $20. It received the biggest response we've ever received for any single product in our history. In addition, for every pendant we sold, we received an average of three reorders.

We called the results of our program a marketing phenomenon. Normally, a well-accepted product has a 10% reorder rate, but a 300% reorder rate was really an incredible statement about this exciting new product.

To capitalize on this marketing phenomenon, JS&A has made available its most popular two pendants, one called "Watch Movement," showing the inside workings of a watch, and the second, "Gold Dollar," showing a gold dollar good luck charm. Both objects come complete with necklace chain and gift box—all for the same low price of $20.

The pendants make great Mother's Day gifts, a gift for your employees, or a gift for anyone to whom you want to give a token of your appreciation or affection. It's truly an unusual and well-accepted gift idea that draws admiring glances and many compliments.

Laser technology is a relatively new technology. Its effects are being felt every day as new and more advanced uses for this science are being developed. JS&A is proud to introduce two of the newest technologies.

AN UNUSUAL OFFER

The laser beam mousetrap sells for $1500 and comes complete with peanut butter, instructions, and one year warranty. The laser pendants are offered for $20 each. (Illinois residents add 5% sales tax.) There are no postage and handling charges for either purchase. Credit card buyers may call our toll-free number to order. There is also a ten day trial period for each item. If you are not absolutely satisfied with your purchase, return it within ten days for a prompt and courteous refund. You can't lose.

PARTICIPATE WITH US

For each of you who participate with us and order either a laser pendant or a mousetrap, we will send you, three months after your purchase, a report on the results of our marketing experiment. We will tell you how many laser beam mousetraps were sold and our conclusions. Won't you join us and order either product at no obligation today?

The Laser Pendants are 1¾ inches in diameter and come complete with matching metal chain and gift box. When ordering, specify "Watch Works" or "Gold Dollar."

JS&A NATIONAL SALES GROUP

Dept. OO One JS&A Plaza
Northbrook, Ill. 60062 (312) 564-9000

CALL TOLL-FREE.... 800 323-6400
In Illinois call .... (312) 498-6900

©JS&A Group, Inc.,1977

April 1977

284

Pocket Yellow Pages

Let your fingers do the data entry with America's first computerized pocket telephone directory.

You're stuck. You're at a phone booth trying to find a phone number, and people are waiting. You feel the pressure.

To the startled eyes of those around you, you pull out your calculator, press a few buttons, and presto—the phone number appears on the display of your calculator. A dream? Absolutely not.

Space-age technology has produced the Canon Directory—a calculator that stores 20 of your most frequently called numbers in its memory and let's you recall them simply by entering the person's name or initials.

The keyboard has letters as well as numbers (like the touch-tone pad on a telephone), so it's easy to enter data and use. Want to call Jim? You enter J I M, and your display shows Jim's phone number. Even when you shut your unit off, it retains your complete directory in its large memory.

Ever forget to shut your calculator off when you slipped it in your pocket? No problem with the Canon Directory. The system was built like a liquid crystal digital watch. Its display can remain on constantly without draining the two long-lasting hearing aid batteries which you get with your unit. A low battery indicator also warns you well enough in advance when it's time to change batteries.

STORE IN CONFIDENCE

If you lost your little black book with all those confidential numbers, you might get in trouble. Not so with the Directory. Without knowing the specific initials or name, you can't access the numbers.

And then there's convenience. You carry your calculator with you anyway. Why not add the convenience of a telephone directory to a full-function calculator? When it comes to calculating, the Canon is no slouch either.

There's a fully-addressable memory, square root, and an add-on discount percentage system.

EASY TO OPERATE

Just enter the name and number you want stored and press a few buttons. That's all there is to it. Changing an entry is just as easy. You can also store credit card numbers, important serial numbers, birthdays, and anniversaries. For example, enter the next birthday or important date you should remember under "DATE." This date will appear each time you enter the word "DATE." By getting in the habit of doing that each week, the Canon won't let you forget. Or have you ever been stuck at a phone booth with no pen to write your messages? With the Canon, you can enter them directly into your unit—name·and number.

The Canon Directory is a new breakthrough in recent calculator technology. The large-scale integrated circuit is programmable by the user—something nearly impossible just a few short months ago.

TEST IT FOR A MONTH

Order the Directory. Quickly program it with your most frequently called numbers. (You'll be amazed at how many 20 numbers seem when you sort out your personal directory.) Then use it every day. Program those important dates, your social security number, the phone numbers of your favorite restaurants, airlines, or movie theaters. Test the batteries by leaving your unit on for a week.

See how easy it makes life. Then within 30 days, decide if you want to keep it. If not, no problem. Just slip it in its handy mailer and send it back. We won't be upset, and in fact, we'll thank you for at least giving our unique product a test.

JS&A is America's largest single souce of space-age products—a substantial company which has been in business for over a decade. Canon is the famous company that manufactures quality cameras, calculators, and other precision quality instruments.

If service is ever required, just slip your three-ounce unit in an envelope and mail it to Canon's national service-by-mail center. It's just that easy. Service should never be required since practically all components are on a single integrated circuit, but we wanted to assure you that a service program is an established part of Canon's program. The unit is 2¾" x 5½" and only one centimeter thick.

To order your own Canon Directory, send **$79.95** plus $2.50 for postage and handling to the address below (Illinois residents, please add 5% sales tax), or call our toll-free number below. By return mail you will receive your unit, a handy wallet-style carrying case, and a one-year limited warranty.

This year, let the sophistication of space-age technology and your fingers do all the walking. Order your Pocket Yellow Pages at no obligation, today.

June 1978

August 1978

George's Revenge

Drive your neighbors bananas as your children yell their heads off with the world's first voice-command pet truck.

George is a pet truck. If you talk to him, he responds. Just yell "George, turn right," and George turns right. Yell "George, go straight," and George goes straight.

George, however, is not a major breakthrough in advanced technology but rather an example of how space-age scientists have figured out a way to totally disrupt the American home.

For when George enters your home, you've lost your children. Instead of talking to you, they're on their hands and knees yelling at George. And at night while you're sleeping, if a sound disturbs George, there's a good chance that he'll turn on and drive right into your bedroom. That's George's revenge.

He'll also drive your neighbors bananas when the whole neighborhood gathers to out-yell each other right in front of your home.

It's not that George is bright. He's rather stupid. He only does the four things he was trained to do at the factory, and he does those four things in the same order.

George will start and turn right when you yell anything at him – and we mean almost anything. You can yell "George, turn right" or "George, you dummy!" and George will start his motor and turn right.

Then yell anything and George goes straight. Yell again and George goes left. Yell for the fourth time and George will stop. And repeat the yelling and George will repeat the same cycle. Like we said, George is stupid. He only responds to sounds, not to specific instructions.

George stands 9" long and is the world's first voice-command remote control pet truck.

Fortunately, George was programmed not to obey profanity. Unfortunately, George has not been programmed to attack burglars. But let's face it. George, with all his advantages and disadvantages, makes a great Christmas gift for any child with good lungs.

And George is definitely not expensive. $29.95 is rather cheap for a high class remote voice-command pet truck.

George will be sold only by mail this year, so make sure you order early enough for Christmas. Just send your check for **$29.95** plus $3.00 for postage and handling (Illinois residents add 5% sales tax), or credit card buyers may call our toll-free number below.

By return mail, we'll send you George (the 9-volt battery and the two "D" cells required are not supplied), complete instructions easy enough for a child to understand (which means there's a pretty good chance you'll be able to understand them too), and a 90-day limited warranty. If for any reason you are dissatisfied, you may return George anytime within 10 days after receipt for a quiet refund.

Your children will definitely jump for joy, and you'll climb the walls with George – the world's first voice-command pet truck. Order one at no obligation, today.

JS&A NATIONAL SALES GROUP

Dept. WJ   One JS&A Plaza
Northbrook, Ill. 60062   (312) 564-7000
Call TOLL-FREE **800 528-6400**
In Illinois Call .... **(312) 564-7000**
© JS&A Group, Inc., 1978

October 1978

Soviet Challenge

This is the computer that may change the course of chess playing history.

Can an American chess computer beat the Soviet Chess Champion? A Confrontation between American space-age technology and a Soviet psychological weapon.

The Soviet Union regards chess as a psychological weapon, not just a game. It is a symbol of communism's cultural struggle with the West.

So when Russian Anatoli Karpov competed against the Russian Defector, Victor Korchnoi, he had the entire Soviet Union's resources at his disposal, including a hypnotist and neuropsychologist.

Karpov won. And with it the world's undisputed chess championship. Karpov however, has never confronted American space-age technology and in particular JS&A's new Chess Computer.

So representatives of JS&A met with Karpov's representatives in Hong Kong in an effort to arrange a match between the Soviet Champion and the JS&A Chess Computer.

It wasn't easy negotiating with the Soviets. We offered them a $50,000 guarantee against royalties from the sales of our chess computers. But negotiations broke down.

Was the Soviet delegation afraid that American space-age technology would win? Were the Soviets fearful of negative publicity if Karpov lost to a $100 computer? Or were they fearful of a circus-type atmosphere that would degrade their prestige, even if he won?

Honestly, we don't know. We do know that our offer is still open, but we suspect Karpov will not accept.

Why did we challenge Karpov? Simple. We thought that having Karpov play against our computer would focus world-wide attention on our product. This attention would increase its sales and win or lose, we would sell more computers.

We had to sell more computers. We wanted to sell our unit for $100 even though it compares with units that sell for more than $300. But we had to do two things in order to sell our unit for $100. First, we had to manufacture it in Hong Kong where labor costs are very low. Secondly, we had to sell large quantities.

SOPHISTICATED DESIGN

The JS&A Chess Computer is designed to look several moves ahead to determine its next move. When we first designed it, it played five levels of chess. Level one was for beginners and as you played against the computer, you could increase its level of difficulty until the computer became more of a challenge. Level five was quite a challenge.

We thought we had the ultimate unit with five levels, until we developed our most sophisticated unit which has six levels. With six levels and all its previous features, the system is now a challenge for any Soviet Chess Champion.

The JS&A Chess Computer is a small unit that comes without a board or chess pieces. We felt that most players prefer their own board and pieces anyway.

LIKE PLAYING KARPOV

The system is the perfect way to sharpen your chess skills. It not only has six different skill levels, but if you are playing against the computer at level two and you are beating it, you can switch the unit to level six. It's like having Karpov as your new opponent – right during mid game.

To play against the computer, you enter your move on the unit's keyboard. You then wait until the computer examines all its options and selects its move. You then move the computer's chess piece to correspond with its request as shown on the display. A board layout is provided to show you where each chess piece should be moved.

SHARPEN SKILLS

If you already play chess, the JS&A unit provides a new chess dimension. If you haven't played chess, the system is a good way to learn and sharpen your skills.

The JS&A Chess Computer measures only 2⅛" x 4⅞" x 8⅞" and weighs just a few ounces, so if service is ever required you can slip it in its handy mailer and send it back to our prompt service-by-mail center. Service should never be required, but it is reassuring to know that service is an important consideration in this program.

JS&A is America's largest single source of space-age products – further assurance that your modest investment is well protected.

We suggest you order a JS&A Chess Computer on our 30 day trial period. Play against it. Raise or lower the level as you play and watch how the computer's personality can change right in mid-game – from a tough competitor to a push over.

TEST LEVEL SIX

Test our level six and see if you'd have much of a chance against the Soviet Champion Karpov. Then, after you've really given it a workout, decide if you want to keep it. If not, you may return your unit for a prompt and courteous refund, including your $2.50 postage and handling charge. There is no risk. Each JS&A Chess Computer comes complete with instructions and an AC adapter (no batteries are required).

To order your JS&A Chess Computer, send your check for **$99.95** plus $2.50 for postage and handling (Illinois residents please add 5% sales tax) to the address below or credit card buyers may call our toll-free number below.

The Soviet Union may have the World's Chess Champion, but JS&A has a very powerful Chess Computer and something the Soviets don't have – a pretty good advertising department.

Why not order a JS&A Chess Computer at no obligation, today.

Dept.WJ   One JS&A Plaza
Northbrook, Ill. 60062   (312) 564-7000
Call TOLL-FREE 800 323-6400
In Illinois Call .... (312) 564-7000
©JS&A Group, Inc.,1978

Mr. Karpov and our computer.

Karpov Accepts

Soviet chess champion agrees to endorse American chess computer in surprise answer to computer challenge.

The new $100 JS&A chess computer will make computer chess an affordable game for the American consumer.

Anatoli Karpov is the undisputed World Chess Champion. Last month, JS&A challenged Karpov to play against our chess computer. We offered him $50,000 and a percentage of each unit we sold if he beat our game.

Karpov rejected our offer and quite frankly, we were at a loss to explain why.

Our concept was simple. If Karpov played against our computer, he would focus worldwide attention on our product. This attention would increase its sales and win or lose, we would sell more computers.

We had to sell more computers. We wanted our unit to sell for $100 even though units with similar capabilities were selling for up to $400. But we had to do two things to keep our low price: First, we had to manufacture our unit in Hong Kong where labor costs are very low. Secondly, we had to sell large quantities to keep production costs down.

When we first announced our challenge, the Soviets rejected it. Could Karpov have been afraid to play against it? Or was the circus-like atmosphere that might surround the event not in keeping with the prestige of the coveted world title, even if Karpov won?

Quite honestly, we had no idea. So we asked Karpov for an explanation and got one. Here's what he said:

"I can appreciate your desire to sell the JS&A Chess Computer but you have missed an important point of the entire challenge. It took somebody to program the unit and since I am the world's chess champion, it is highly unlikely that the programmer person could beat me. You Americans have a saying, "Garbage in, garbage out."

Karpov continued, "Your unit is definitely a good product. I played several games at level six and found it to be a challenge even for me. What I like about your unit is that it is priced low enough so that most Americans can afford the unit and this will help promote chess."

The JS&A Chess Computer indeed has six levels of chess. Level one is perfect for beginners. Level six is a real challenge for any Soviet Chess Champion.

LIKE PLAYING KARPOV

The system is the perfect way to sharpen your chess skills. It not only has six different skill levels, but if you are playing against the computer at level two and you are beating it, you can switch the unit to level six. It's like having Karpov as your new opponent – right during mid game.

To play against the computer, you enter your move on the unit's keyboard. You then wait until the computer examines all its options and selects its move. You then move the computer's chess piece to correspond with its request as shown on the display. A board layout is provided to show you where each chess piece should be moved.

The JS&A Chess Computer is programmed for such complex functions as castling, pawn promotion and *en passant*. It also allows you to start in midgame, setting up any situation you choose. This is perfect for those players who wish to examine particularly intricate problems and allows for an infinite number of game variations.

SHARPEN SKILLS

If you already play chess, the JS&A unit provides a new chess dimension. If you haven't played chess, the system is a good way to learn and sharpen your skills.

The JS&A Chess Computer measures only 2⅛"x 4⅞"x 8⅞" and weighs just a few ounces, so if service is ever required you can slip it in its handy mailer and send it back to our prompt service-by-mail center. Service should never be required, but it is reassuring to know that service is an important consideration in this program.

JS&A is America's largest single source of space-age products – further assurance that

your modest investment is well protected.

We suggest you order a JS&A Chess Computer and use it for 30 days. Play against it. Raise or lower the level as you play and watch how the computer's personality can change right in mid game – from a tough competitor to a push over.

Test our level six and see if you'd have much of a chance against the Soviet Champion Karpov. Then, after you've really given it a workout, decide if you want to keep it. If not, you may return your unit within our 30 day trial period for a prompt and courteous refund, including your $2.50 postage and handling charge. There is no risk. Each JS&A Chess Computer comes complete with instructions and an AC adapter (no batteries are required).

To order our JS&A Chess Computer, send your check for **$99.95** plus $2.50 for postage and handling (Illinois residents please add 5% sales tax) to the address below or credit card buyers may call our toll-free number below.

Karpov told us (and this is a direct quote) "I have played all the rest of the American chess computers and find that the JS&A unit is the best value for the dollar. I will accept an offer to endorse the game, however, you can forget about your $50,000 offer and spend the money on advertising to spread the word."

Thank you, Mr. Karpov. We appreciate your honesty and your generosity and we promise to spread the word.

And you can help us America. Order a JS&A Chess Computer at no obligation, today.

Dept. WJ One JS&A Plaza
Northbrook, Ill. 60062 (312) 564-7000
Call TOLL-FREE **800 323-6400**
In Illinois Call .... **(312) 564-7000**
©JS&A Group, Inc.,1979

Endorsement Battle

A famous golf star endorses the Lanier. Our unit is endorsed by our president. You'll save $100 as a result.

We not only took the unit apart, we examined our competition as well.

Judge for yourself. That new Olympus micro recorder shown above sells for $150. Its closest competition is a $250 recorder called the Lanier endorsed by a famous golf star.

FANCY ENDORSEMENT

The famous golf star is a pilot who personally flies his own Citation jet. The Olympus recorder is endorsed by JS&A's president who pilots a more cost-efficient single engine Beachcraft Bonanza. The golf star does not endorse the Lanier unit for free. After all, a good portion of his income is derived from endorsing products.

Our president, on the other hand, does not get paid for endorsing products – just for selling them. And his Bonanza is not as expensive to fly as the golf star's Citation. In fact, our president also drives a Volkswagon Rabbit.

SOLD DIFFERENTLY

The Lanier is sold through a national network of direct salesmen similar to the IBM sales force. Naturally, these salesmen must be paid expenses and commission.

JS&A efficiently sells the Olympus through this advertisement – a very direct and inexpensive way to market a product.

With less overhead, no direct national sales staff, and no expensive endorsements, Olympus can sell its recorder for less money to JS&A. And with our company's efficiency, we can sell you practically the same recorder as the Lanier for much less – a savings of $100.

Is the Olympus better than the Lanier for less money? We weren't sure, so we took them both apart and what we found amazed us. Other than a slight size difference, the units were practically identical. For example:

CORELESS MOTOR

Both units have the new coreless motor. Conventional motors require a long and heavy solid core that is wirewound. In a coreless motor, the windings are on the outside or stationary part of the motor making it flatter, yet it has greater initial torque and more consistent speed than any other conventional motor.

THE FERRITE HEAD

Both units use ferrite for their recording heads – the same material used in precision studio recorders. This extremely hard, diamond-like material will last a lifetime and prevents oxide build-up.

A NEW KIND OF MIKE

Both units also use an electret condenser microphone with automatic level control. In an electret system, the impedence of the microphone remains constant, thus passing on the natural sound quality of all frequencies without distortion. The result is a clear recording with an extremely low signal-to-noise ratio, so you'll hear less objectionable background hissing or humming.

MANY SIMILAR FEATURES

Both units use the microcassette tapes that play 30 minutes per side. The Olympus measures only 1″ x 2½″ x 4⅞″ and weighs only 9 ounces. The Lanier is the same weight as the Olympus and measures only ⅞″ x 2½″ x 4″ – practically the same size.

HERE'S OUR PLAN

But prove it to yourself. Order an Olympus recorder from JS&A. After you receive it, call in your Lanier sales representative. Have him bring you a sample of his unit. (You might even check to see what kind of car the salesman drives.) Then make a side-by-side comparison. Compare both units feature for feature

Micro cassettes are the newest recording medium. Each cassette will record for 30 minutes per side.

and see how much better the Olympus sounds. Then carry them both in your pocket and on trips. Use them at meetings or while you drive in your car. Really give them both a workout.

Then decide. If you don't feel that the Olympus is as good a unit or better than the Lanier for $100 less, simply return the Olympus within 30 days for a prompt refund and then purchase the Lanier unit, keeping

one of our tapes as a gift. If you decide to keep the Olympus, consider yourself a smart shopper. Anyone who would take the time to read this advertisement and take the action to order and test the Olympus unit, deserves to save $100.

SERVICE AT ITS BEST

Both the Lanier and the Olympus units are solidly backed by efficient service organizations. Olympus has an outstanding service-by-mail facility so no matter where you live, just slip your unit in its handy mailer and send it in. Olympus is the same company that manufactures high quality precision cameras and optics, and JS&A is America's largest single source of space-age products – further assurances that your modest investment is well protected.

To order your Olympus unit for our comparison trial, send your check for $150 plus $3.50 for postage and handling to: JS&A Group, Inc., One JS&A Plaza, Northbrook, Illinois 60062. (Illinois residents add 5% sales tax.) Credit card buyers may call our toll-free number below. We will promptly ship your unit, one free tape, complete instructions, and one-year warranty. If you wish to order additional cassettes, you may order them for $3 each or $15 for a package of five (our minimum quantity).

CONSUMERS CAN BENEFIT

Endorsements are very helpful when you sell products. They attract attention and give consumers confidence that their purchase is also used by someone famous. But indirectly, consumers pay for endorsements. They also pay for a large sales force and less efficient marketing methods.

When you purchase an Olympus from JS&A, you pay for just what you get. A great product. Why not order an Olympus recorder at no obligation, today?

JS&A PRODUCTS THAT THINK

Dept.RA   One JS&A Plaza
Northbrook, Ill. 60062   (312) 564-7000
Call TOLL-FREE 800 323-6400
In Illinois Call .... (312) 564-7000
© JS&A Group, Inc.,1979

Has JS&A discovered a new way to move computers?

Computer Violence

I'll blow up my computer if somebody doesn't buy it.

I wanna sell my computer. Badly. So badly that if I don't get a decent price for it, I'll blow the thing up. Here's how it all started.

About six years ago, in 1975, JS&A purchased a Data General Nova II computer, a 600 line per minute Data Products printer and a couple disc drives.

Not knowing beans about computers, I was glad to let our computer salesman install the system and help us automate our entire order-processing operation. What our salesman failed to tell us was that our computer would not only save us money but would permit us to grow. And grow we did. 40% a year.

Now that wouldn't seem too bad except that our growth required more computer power. Our salesman quite efficiently came up with a proposal to add a few 80 megabyte Control Data disc drives, a few strange sounding boards like MUX and DUX and a bunch of terminals.

By that time we had quite a bit invested in our computer—over $300,000 and our computer salesman was quite a hero. We saved more money and our company continued to grow spectacularly. So spectacularly we again ran out of room in our computer and we once again turned to our ever-helpful computer salesman.

Add more terminals (we now had 16) a Data General Nova III CPU, another Control Data 80 megabyte disc drive (we now had three) and suddenly we found ourselves with a super little computer that would save us more money and let us grow even more.

More, that is, until the next year when we started growing at 50% per year. By this time we had close to $450,000 invested in the hardware and I was contemplating selling the monster. I wanted a computer I couldn't out-grow. I wanted one that I could forget about—one that would gobble up my company's growing volume with great speed and efficiency.

But my computer salesman wouldn't let me. "Joe," he said, "What you need is software. You've got plenty of hardware already." And he proceeded to recommend a complete conversion to a totally new software package.

I selected a software manager who promised me he'd have me up and running in six months—well before the 1978 Christmas season. He didn't. And we entered January of 1979 with a computer too small for our needs and software so screwed up that our computer finally coughed, gagged and dropped dead.

And it picked its demise in the middle of three consecutive blizzards that brought Chicago to a standstill. Computer repair people became as rare as snowblowers.

Well, we got out of the mess once our people could find their cars and get to work. We ended up doing everything by hand and we also used an outside service bureau to process orders. Our computer was finally put together, and we used it simply as an on-line look-up system to check out customer orders.

The other day I decided to sell our computer. It had served us well. We had taken good care of it through preventive maintenance programs and a lot of tender loving care. It was now time to sell it.

I called in a computer buyer who offered me $12,000 for the entire system. I threw him out. I then called in another computer buyer and he offered me $18,000. I threw him out. How could these businessmen expect me to fall for a hoax like that. The system cost me $450,000 and just the three disc drives alone cost over fifty thousand dollars new.

But then I soon realized that computers depreciate faster than some of the products I sell and that my system to an end user was worth at least $30,000 but to a computer buyer it wasn't worth much at all.

The more I thought about it, the sicker I got. My rotten computer had bitten me until it dropped dead just when I needed it the most. It cost me a fortune only to lose all its value just when we decided to part company. So I decided to offer my computer to some end user by offering it in this advertisement.

If I'm successful, I'll sell it for $30,000 or any fair offer. If I'm not able to sell it, I'll place it on a platform on an empty piece of property and blow it up. Five sticks of dynamite should do the trick.

My computer served me well. It helped my company grow, and it saved me thousands of dollars in the process. But there comes a time when you've got to dramatize an offer to make it interesting and build suspense to hopefully sell the product. I've never used violence before in any of my advertisements, but if I sell my computer, I've got a few Bone Fones I'd like to blow up too. Call for more details, today.

1981

Cadillac Garbage Truck

Here's why it paid to turn your luxury car into a municipal garbage truck thanks to a government mistake.

Even Cadillac owners have taken radical steps to take advantage of the opportunity.

Laws can sometimes get ridiculous. So it's not surprising to discover a law that encourages people to collect garbage.

Now collecting garbage may not appeal to you. And converting your luxury car into a garbage truck may appeal to you even less. Encouraging all this, however, is a product so appealing that thousands of Americans have bought this product–some even openly violating the law. Here's the story.

Over 40 years ago, a law was passed requiring passenger cars to be equipped with a headlight called the sealed beam. Older headlights leaked and let dirt from dusty roads enter the light chamber clouding the lens and dimming its brightness.

GARBAGE TRUCKS APPROVED

It soon became illegal to use any other light but sealed beams, although for some reason municipal garbage trucks were exempt from the law. Back then, the law was good.

Twenty years ago a company called Cibie in Europe developed a lighting technology using a quartz halogen bulb which doubled the brightness of headlights.

It was so spectacular that Europe adopted it overnight. The United States declined. For some strange reason (possibly special interests), the Cibie quartz halogen system, which was not a sealed beam, was only allowed on municipal garbage trucks. For cars, it was illegal.

But wait. To understand this emerging technology and the rest of this story, you've got to understand the difference between the sealed beam and the quartz halogen headlights. Please bear with us while we describe some heavy technical stuff.

HEAVY TECHNICAL STUFF

Picture a flashlight with a bulb, reflector and a lens that screws over the reflector. A European quartz halogen system functions the same way. When the bulb burns out, you simply change it like you would a flashlight bulb. But when a sealed beam headlight burns out, you throw the whole works away – the bulb, the reflector and the lens.

Now that you understand the heavy technical stuff, here's a lesson in lighting. If you learn the following, you'll know more about lighting than our Washington bureaucrats. Please continue reading.

There are only three things that make up a headlight: a light source, a reflector and a lens. The following describes these three things and compares the illegal Cibie quartz halogen headlight with the sealed beam.

THE LIGHT SOUCE

The Sealed Beam light source is a tungsten filament located in a vacuum similar to a light bulb. But since there is no perfect vacuum, the tungsten filament eventually combines with oxygen and slowly burns leaving black deposits on the reflector.

The Illegal Cibie Quartz Halogen light source consists of a tungsten alloy filament in a small quartz glass enclosure filled with halogen gas. The quartz glass withstands the tremendous filament heat (over 3,000 degrees compared to 500 degrees with sealed beams). Halogen gas, unlike oxygen, will not combine with the filament. What burns off the filament is actually suspended in the halogen gas. When the bulb cools down, the particles recycle back onto the filament. The filament actually improves with age. The light is hotter, brighter and whiter than the sealed beam light and lasts considerably longer.

THE REFLECTOR

The Sealed Beam has a coated glass reflector which darkens with age.

The Illegal Cibie Quartz Halogen reflector is metal, not glass, and goes through a progressive die stamping process because its exact parabolic shape is critical to maximum reflectivity. After forming, it is coated with two lacquer baths to ensure its corrosion resistance, and then aluminum vapor is exploded onto the surface to create its super reflective property.

THE LENS

The Sealed Beam lens is produced like any mass-produced glass product such as a pop bottle.

The Illegal Cibie Quartz Halogen lens is produced using techniques similar to camera lens design. Its flutes and prisms are computer-designed and quality-controlled using laboratory lasers. The end result is a precisely-controlled system which when installed in a car produces a white light which is evenly distributed over the road ahead and does not shine in the eyes of oncoming drivers. Nor in the rear view mirrors of those in front you.

Oh, one last thought. There are other quartz halogen headlights that use the quartz halogen bulb, but they are in a standard sealed beam enclosure and do not have the precision optics and parabolic metal reflector of the Cibie system. There's a spectacular difference so don't be confused.

There's only one more easy-to-learn fact worth knowing. Headlights come in one of four different sizes. There are big round headlights and small round headlights. There are big square headlights and small square headlights. It's just that simple. You need four of the small-sized headlights (a pair of hi-lo beams and a pair of high beam lights) or two of the large-sized headlights. Now you're an expert. But wait, there's a happy part to this story.

Cibie has developed a quartz halogen system for the American market which passes U.S. government regulations even though these regulations aren't necessary. The enclosure is sealed and the bulb is replaced externally from the enclosure. This means you can legally install these European halogen headlights without breaking the law and without having to convert your luxury car into a garbage truck.

Headlight installation should not scare you either. Installing a headlight is only slightly harder than installing the bulb in a light fixture. Or let your local service station install them for you while you wait.

We are so convinced that the Cibie quartz halogen headlights will make such a delightful change in your driving, that we'll give you a three-month, no-obligation trial period. This will give you plenty of time to install them, to use them and to experience the difference. If you wish to return them anytime within three months, you may do so for a full refund including a $5 payment for your trouble. Even if your headlights are brand new, we urge you to change them and see the difference. The increased safety at night will convince you of the incredible value.

During the winter months Americans often smash into each other as they overrun their headlights while driving at night.

JS&A is proud to expose this safety hazzard and to offer such an outstanding product and to make it exceptionally easy for you to order.

2 Large Round (8020CA09 4.00) **$55.50**
2 Large Square (8030CA09 4.00) 55.50
4 Small Round (8040CA09 4.50) 119.50
4 Small Square (8050CA09 4.50) 119.50

1981

292

Our production engineering team couldn't resist.

Pickle Power

An amazing new discovery may change the way we power our pickles.

JS&A has handled plenty of unusual products. Like our $1500 Laser Beam Mousetrap or even our Mickey Mouse Calculator. (Neither sold very well by the way.)

The electronic pickle, however, must take the award for being our most unusual product ever. But stop. Before you reach for your phone to order one, we'd better first describe what it does and how it's powered.

LOOKS NORMAL

The electronic pickle looks exactly like a pickle you'd find in any pickle jar. It's green and measures 2" in diameter by 5" in length. After you insert an AA-cell battery and press a small switch on the back of the unit, the electronic pickle becomes a flashlight.

"Now wait," you might say. "I've heard of the pet rock but the electronic pickle might be a little too much." And quite frankly, you're right. It's a stupid product that normally we'd never introduce if it weren't for those crazy batteries shown above.

The batteries are part of a new invention that can not only power the electronic pickle, but it can power any electronic product that uses D, C or AA-cell batteries. Let us explain.

HOLLOW TECHNOLOGY

The Dynamic Instruments AA-cell rechargeable battery shown above (that's the smallest battery) lasts for five years and is one of the finest and most energy-filled high-capacity batteries ever developed.

Let us say you own an electronic pickle that takes a C-cell battery. No problem. Simply place the AA-cell into that hollow C battery tube above and presto, you've got a C-cell.

Even if your electronic pickle is powered by a D-cell, you simply slip the C-cell with its powerful AA-cell into the D-cell tube and you've got a new D-cell.

SIMPLE CONCEPT

The concept is quite simple. Using one Dynamic high-capacity AA-cell battery to make your own C and D-cells means that you 1) always have the correct battery handy, and 2) you can recharge them easily with a simple single-size recharging unit that is supplied with the system.

The secret of the system is not only the hollow battery concept but also a new AA-cell

Insert the AA-cell into the battery compartment of the fully portable electronic pickle.

battery design that provides all the power you'll need for the C and D-cell.

So powerful is the AA-cell battery that with only one charge it will outlast 14 carbon batteries under a high 370-milliamp drain. And the Dynamic AA-cell battery can be recharged over 1,000 times. One dynamic AA-cell can replace 14,000 fifty-cent carbon batteries.

Of course, this example is not very realistic. Nobody would use 14,000 carbon batteries in any application. Alkaline or rechargeable batteries would definitely be more practical, but the savings are apparent regardless of what

battery you use for comparison.

One of the disadvantages with most rechargeable batteries is their high cost. With the hollow battery concept and the new Dynamic AA-cell, the savings start with the low price of the AA-cell and really become dramatic when you get to the savings with the D-cell units. Instead of stocking a variety of batteries, you simply purchase AA-cell rechargeables and a kit of hollow C and D-cells.

NOT YET AVAILABLE

The electronic pickle is not yet available. We were considering a patent until our production engineering team ate the prototype shown above.

But the batteries are indeed available right now. You can order a set of four AA-cells plus four of the hollow C & D-cell tubes for only $24.95. The kit also includes a small recharging unit which can also recharge the Dynamic 9-volt battery.

Your set of four AA-cells, C and D battery tubes and recharger cost only **$24.95** (0020CA07 3.00), the 9-volt battery is only **$8.95** (0021CA07 1.00). We'll send you the batteries, instructions and five-year limited warranty. Then really test the batteries when you receive them. Even your child can make a D-cell out of an AA-cell. Then if you decide to keep them, great. If not, return the complete package and we'll refund the entire purchase price including postage.

When our electronic pickle becomes available, we hope you'll already own our Dynamic battery system. After all, every good pickle should be powered for peanuts. Order your batteries at no obligation, today.

Mafia Auto Gadget

Announcing a great new product for a specially-targeted customer who doesn't want to be quite so targeted.

"Here's my keys Louie, go start da car."

Think of it. JS&A has over 600,000 customers. Some are famous movie stars, singers, song writers and politicians. Some might even be gangsters.

So it's not surprising that we have finally come up with a product that might appeal to our gangster customers. Here's what we mean.

One of the favorite ways gangsters have to eliminate each other is the car bomb. Simply explained, it's a bomb placed under the hood of a car and set off when the ignition is turned on. It's not very nice, but it certainly does the job.

GANGSTERS NOT STUPID

Gangsters, however, are not stupid. Often, they'll hire chauffeurs to start their cars while they stay at a safe distance. But plenty of chauffeurs aren't so happy about this arrangement either. Not so happy, that is, until the introduction of the Remote Bomb Igniter.

The Remote Bomb Igniter is nothing more than a portable remote control device that starts your car from as far away as 500 feet – far enough so that the impact of any explosion will be minimized.

Now all you gangsters and high-risk chauffeurs can comfortably and from a distance start your cars with complete peace of mind. You may lose your car, but you'll never lose your life.

GANGSTERS NOT IN MIND

When the Remote Bomb Igniter was first presented to JS&A, it was done so without gangsters in mind. The manufacturer thought that the product would be excellent for anyone who parks a car at the office all day and who wants to step into a cool air-conditioned car in summer or a warm car in winter.

In fact, the product was called Computer Start and not Remote Bomb Igniter, and the manufacturer thought it would be the ultimate gadget for anyone who really enjoys gadgets and wants to have something different.

We thought, however, that the cost was too high. Who would pay $325 for a gadget unless their life depended on it? And then there was the problem of installation. Our gadget customers would rather press buttons and read displays than crawl under cars to install a complicated device like that. And finally, some cars are difficult to start – especially in cold weather.

HOW WRONG WE WERE

But we were wrong. The installation takes a garage mechanic about two to three hours or between $50 for an American car to $140 for a Mercedes. Installation is really no problem.

And the price of many auto accessories exceeds $400 so our customers, many of whom drive pretty expensive cars, can easily afford one. And finally, the device does indeed work on even the most difficult-to-start cars in temperatures below zero. But here's how the device will work for you this summer.

Before you leave your car, you put your transmission in park, set your emergency brake and turn on the air-conditioning.

You're now sitting in your office. It's boiling hot outside, and the sun is turning the inside of your car into a pressure cooker. Soon it's time to leave the office.

You take out your slim pocket transmitter, press a button and your car starts, the air-conditioner turns on and the interior temperature starts to drop.

ELECTRONIC MIRACLE

What happened was another miracle of space-age electronics. The Computer Start responded by turning the starter for between 1.5 to 3.5 seconds depending on the outside temperature, and it will continue to turn the starter until the car starts. If the car doesn't start after several attempts, the unit will automatically shut down to avoid any battery drain.

Once your car is running, the Computer Start performs a few more well thought-out tricks. It will pump the accelerator at intervals to bring down the idling speed as quickly as possible to save gasoline. But what if you forget you started your car, and there it stands running merrily on? No problem. If you don't get to your car before six to twelve minutes, the unit automatically turns off the car.

There are thousands of different frequencies used in the unit's pager. So the chances of anyone else's pager starting your car is very remote. Then too the pager's distance limitation is 500 feet "line of sight." That means you have a maximum clear path of 500 feet from the pager to your car to start it. Going through walls limits the distance slightly although looking out a window won't. In short, if you plan to start your car from two blocks away, you'll be disappointed.

Despite this safety limitation, we found the Computer Start to be plenty of fun, a great convenience in hot or cold weather and a great way to warm up the car a few minutes before you drive away. In fact, it's perfect for fast getaways.

THE RIGHT TEMPERATURE

It wasn't long before we realized that our potential customers were not just gangsters but gadget connoisseurs – the car enthusiasts who want the ultimate auto gadget. Imagine walking up to your car with an important guest and to have it running and at just the right temperature? Even if you keep your car in a garage, there are times when you'll wish you had the Computer Start.

The Computer Start comes with instructions that your mechanic will easily understand and a one-year limited warranty. The remote pager, batteries and the the Computer Start system are supplied. Our current unit will not work on cars with diesel engines. However, we are coming out with a unit for diesels later.

But don't just wish you had one in your car. Order one, install it and enjoy a convenience that very few car owners have. And we'll send it in a plain brown wrapper, of course. Order your Computer Start at no obligation, today. **$325** (8060CA07 4.50) for cars with automatic transmission. **$325** (8070CA07 4.50) for cars with manual transmission.

1982

Our upset customer pointed out that our last blood pressure advertisement was lousy. And he was right.

Customer Explodes

We get lots of mail—mostly orders. But every once in awhile we get a letter from a customer who is upset with our advertising. Hal Speer of Sea Cliff, New York, was one of them.

Mr. Speer's letter started out, "Your new catalog arrived today, and I think I'd like to buy one of your blood pressure testers. But your copy omits a few things I consider important."

He then listed a bunch of questions we failed to answer. There were obvious things like, "Was the unit battery-powered? Was there a booklet on understanding the blood pressure readings? Was there an instruction booklet?"

UPSET WITH WRITER

And then Mr. Speer continued, "I like informative copy—even wordy copy—but I suggest you give your copywriter a product-familiarization lecture and then tell him (her) to let the customer know exactly what he'll get. If you'll answer my questions, I'll probably send in an order."

Well Mr. Speer, you're right. We absolutely goofed. In our desire to tell the story of how JS&A was indeed the first company to introduce electronic blood pressure monitors and how we won awards for this activity, we failed to cover the basics. So Mr. Speer, we're going to go one step farther. We're going to make you and our customers experts on blood pressure.

THE BLOOD PRESSURE STORY

Blood pressure is the force exerted by the flow of blood against the artery walls. This pressure reaches a peak with each heartbeat (systole) and then decreases between beats (diastole).

When you measure blood pressure, there are two important readings to take (such as 120 over 80). The 120 is the systolic reading while the 80 represents the diastolic.

Blood pressure ranges from a low of 90 over 60 up to 140 over 90. When your blood pressure goes up to and beyond 140 over 90

and remains there, chances are you have high blood pressure or hypertension (another name for high blood pressure).

NO OBVIOUS SIGNS

Hypertension is a very serious disease for two reasons. First, there are no obvious signs that you have it. So you may innocently have the disease until its late stages when it's often too late.

Secondly, when you've had it for awhile, the heart must pump harder. The heart therefore enlarges and eventually, under this extra burden, the heart weakens, loses efficiency and pumps less blood with each beat. Artery walls are injured, clog and eventually choke off blood to the heart, brain or kidneys, leading to heart attack, stroke or kidney failure.

Of the estimated 25 million Americans who now have hypertension, most don't know they have it. And hypertension—especially in its early stages—is curable.

GOOD COMMON SENSE

Owning a blood pressure monitor and checking your blood pressure periodically is a good commonsense way to protect yourself. And a periodic check might just be once a month. It's really up to you and your physician.

Ironically, just the act of regularly taking your blood pressure appears to help lower blood pressure as was proven in a study conducted at the University of Washington in Seattle.

JS&A offers two blood pressure units which in our opinion represent outstanding quality and value. One unit is only $69.95 and has an analog display (a needle that points to the correct readings as opposed to a digital read out).

ATTACH SLEEVE YOURSELF

You simply slip your arm into a cuff with a Velcro fastener. This Velcro fastener permits you to attach the sleeve yourself without assistance.

Once in place, you pump air into the sleeve with the attached rubber bulb until the needle goes beyond your estimated systolic reading. You then release the air from the bulb and the needle starts to drop slowly. When you hit the diastolic reading a red light goes on and you note the reading while the needle continues to drop. When the red light turns off, the needle is pointing to your systolic reading. That's all there is to it and it's really that simple to operate.

Our model 410B units sells for $139.95 and comes with a digital display of your diastolic and systolic readings plus a reading of your pulse.

There's nothing to observe. You inflate the cuff as you would with our model 310 and sit back as your readings are automatically displayed. After they are displayed, your pulse rate is displayed.

ALL BATTERY-POWERED

The units are all battery-powered with the analog unit using a 9-volt battery and the digital unit using four AA cell batteries. No AC current is required.

The cuff of each unit has a sound-sensing device which picks up the sounds created during systole and diastole. The electronic circuitry then interprets these sounds and visually displays them as either a digital readout or as a meter reading. Its design permits one-hand operation thanks to the large Velcro strip.

Each unit also comes complete with a handy carrying case, all batteries and complete instructions. A one-year limited warranty also accompanies each unit.

We hope our description in this advertisement is more in keeping with the JS&A style of advertising. We're human and occasionally we goof. Our products are tops but sometimes it takes our customers to keep our advertising people on top too. Thanks Hal—we really needed that.

Model 310 (7010CA08 4.00) **$69.95**
Model 410B (7020CA08 4.50) **139.95**

Space Shuttle

Experience the thrill of outer space with a seat on America's first commercial passenger-carrying space flight.

Photo courtesy NASA.

Each year, JS&A presents a unique surprise for the holiday season – a gift so unique, so unusual and so rare that only a few people will ever enjoy it. This year we've outdone ourselves. JS&A has officially petitioned NASA, the National Aeronautics and Space Administration, to be the first company to book commercial air travel on the Space Shuttle.

Although details have yet to be finalized and the exact launch date is still too far off to specify, JS&A has obtained enough information from NASA officials to give its customers our view of the scenario that may take place if you are among the lucky ones we select to participate.

COSTS ABSORBED

Your cost for the flight will probably be no more than a conventional first class round-the-world ticket on a commercial airliner or approximately **$5,450**. According to the few NASA officials we have talked to, most of the expense of the multi-million dollar launch will be absorbed by companies who will be placing satellites in orbit during the flight.

JS&A will randomly select the six participants from a listing of those interested parties who apply. We will supply details later in this article.

Passengers will first have to undergo a routine physical before flight confirmation can be granted. Once approved, you will attend a one week course conducted by NASA instructors to prepare you for what you will experience in flight. There will be techniques taught on how to handle weightlessness, eating, and sleeping. A host of other physical and mental exercises will be presented to prepare you for your flight. After your training program, you will be given a few days to relax, and then you will fly to Cape Canaveral to prepare for the launch.

Prior to launch, you will meet with newspaper reporters and TV commentators for both a press briefing and a question and answer period. You will then be driven to the site to examine the spacecraft and its systems.

COUNTDOWN TIME

It's then countdown time. You will first use the NASA launch pad washroom, then climb on board the Space Shuttle and assume your passenger positions. Since all clothes and requirements will be supplied, advance permission must be granted before you can bring any other objects on board. For example, if you are a ball-bearing manufacturer, you might want to bring a sample of your product with you and later claim that your ball bearings were on the Space Shuttle. Items, however, will be limited in size and weight.

Once on board, you will wait for the countdown to approach lift off. Finally, if all systems are go, you will lift off at 3½ g's (3½ times the pull of gravity) and become the first commercial passengers in outer space.

Sometime during the flight, you will be allowed in the cockpit where NASA astronauts will personally describe the flight systems to you. You can examine the on-board computers, the sophisticated guidance systems and the Space Shuttle's instrumentation.

During the flight, you will witness the release of satellites from the Space Shuttle's bay. You will see the satellites check-out procedure prior to initiating the burn that will place them in final orbit, and finally you will be able to take snapshots of all this activity.

NEVER BORING

The flight should never be boring. You will be asked to participate in a series of simple experiments to determine the future feasibility of commercial space travel and space colonization. Your assistance will be very important in these tests. The flight will last a few days and landing will occur back at Cape Canaveral on a special landing site for the Shuttle.

After landing, there will be a short medical debriefing by doctors and a national public appearance on network television right at the site. JS&A has granted ABC exclusive TV coverage of the event.

JS&A has also granted rights to companies interested in having their products carried on board the Shuttle and they include Brother Typewriter – as the launch's official typewriter, the Nimslo Camera as the official launch camera, and finally we have not yet decided on the official film for the flight although Kodak and Fuji are both still in the running.

After the press conference, you will then be free to rejoin your families and travel home. The JS&A public relations department will organize local homecoming festivities including, where possible, homecoming parades, local television appearances and full newspaper coverage. Special awards will be given.

NO FIRM ANSWER

As we mentioned, this is still in the planning stages and the exact dates, final permission and exact costs have not been finalized. In fact, although we have talked to several NASA officials, we haven't received a firm answer from NASA regarding our petition.

Nevertheless, we are continuing to prepare for the event starting with this issue of our catalog. All those interested in participating in the NASA Space Shuttle launch may do so by requesting a reservation certificate and commemorative poster of the planned event.

The official reservation certificate which will be suitable for framing will have a picture of the Space Shuttle in full color along with the words, "(your name) has been accepted for participation in the first planned commercial Space Shuttle." Then some fine print below will describe all the legal stuff required by JS&A to avoid potential lawsuits.

The commemorative poster will proclaim the proposed event with a picture of what outer space might look like millions of light years from earth. The poster will state "The New Frontier – America's first commercial passenger-carrying space flight. Commemorative Poster for JS&A by Mark Rickerson."

The poster was drawn by one of America's top space-scape artists, Mark Rickerson, and will be printed using a continuous tone full-color printing process on a high-quality paper.

This official reservation certificate and commemorative poster are available for only **$30** (0101CA09 3.00) or for only **$20** (0102CA09 3.00) for JS&A customers who purchase any other item from this catalog. Each poster will be individually shipped in a large cylinder.

If you're thinking of a really novel and different gift, we strongly recommend the official reservation certificate and commemorative poster for the person who has everything.

If you are sincere in wanting to participate in the first commercial Space Shuttle to carry passengers and do not want a poster or reservation certificate, please write us a letter indicating your interest, and we will advise you of the progress in our negotiations. Please keep in mind that it may take years before such a flight is launched and besides, who knows what NASA will say when they read this?

Commercial space travel is not here yet. But it will be. When the Wright Brothers first launched their flying machine, nobody dreamt of its commercial applications. Who could have imagined the huge 747 airplane or the enormous number of air passengers that routinely fly every day?

JS&A customers have always been two steps ahead of their time. They are always the first on the block, the first to learn the new technologies and the first to experience the products of the future. The Space Shuttle is no exception. Reserve a seat on the first commercial passenger-carrying space flight in history.

1982

The label modification device.

Juki Ooki

From the same company that stitched your jeans and put buttonholes in your relatives.

When the salesman called and told me that he had a revolutionary typewriter to show me, I asked for its name.

"Juki," replied Bob. "Juki?" I asked. "Yes, Juki," answered Bob. "Are you kidding me, Bob? Is it really called Juki?" "Really, Joe. That's what it's called. Juki."

Now I realize that a product can be a good product regardless of the name. But who would want to name a typewriter Juki?

So when Bob called, I asked him to bring background information on Juki along with a sample typewriter.

HIGHEST QUALITY

It seems that Juki is a Japanese company that started in business in 1938 making automatic machine guns. The company prospered. During World War II, if you or any of your relatives were shot with a machine gun, it was probably a high-quality Juki.

"How pleasant, Bob," I sighed. "I'm sure my readers would be delighted to hear all this."

"But wait, Joe," Bob responded. "That was the war. Juki went on to prosper after the war by making commercial sewing machines which dominated the world market. In fact, if you own a pair of Levi jeans, chances are they were sewn on a high-quality Juki."

LEAST DEFECTS

"Then Juki went on to win two Deming awards—the highest award a Japanese company could win. No other company has ever won two. The award is given to the company producing products with the least amount of defects. You can say Juki means high quality in Japan.

"Then Juki decided to get into the typewriter business by going against IBM in the office typewriter market. Do you remember the Avanti typewriter you carried in Catalog 13? That was made by Juki, and they became the largest maker of high-quality single-element typewriters after IBM. It was a real success story."

By now Bob was bubbling with enthusiasm. "Juki then decided to enter the American typewriter market with its own name especially after its success with Avanti. After all, Juki in Japan is like Mercedes is to Americans.

VANGUARD SELECTION

"And the typewriter they selected as their vanguard product is the Juki 2100—an electronic personal typewriter with daisy wheel printing elements. Strictly high quality, Joe."

Bob then opened up his briefcase and in a flurry of arm waving and cheap cornball dramatics unveiled what indeed was a beautifully designed, slim and light-weight typewriter. "Let me present the ultimate typewriter," boasted Bob.

"The Juki has a 12" paper width capacity with a maximum 9" writing line. Every key can be repeated. There are neat features such as express backspace, a return zone feature (which automatically returns the print element when you press a hyphen or space key after you reach the end of the line), automatic underlining and automatic centering.

SEVERAL AVAILABLE

"You can select any one of three pitches: 10, 12 and 15. And there's a 12-character buffer memory should you type faster than the typewriter speed of 10 characters per second. The daisy wheel printing elements are easily interchangeable and several are available. The cartridge carbon ribbons simply plop in."

By now Bob was almost foaming at the mouth. His enthusiasm, his excitement over what was obviously a very important product to him, was getting the best of him. "So there you have it, Joe. A perfect portable or personal typewriter for the person looking for quality, size, convenience, all the latest features and, above all, value. And now for the final surprise.

"You can also sell the Juki model with a special built-in printer interface (called the Juki 2200) which lets you plug your typewriter into a home computer and presto, you've got a letter-quality printer. And the printing head moves bidirectionally when used with your computer so your letters are printed out very quickly."

"Bob, you've done an excellent job," I responded. You presented your typewriter well and the Juki is certainly a product to be proud of. And I'm sure our customers would like to own one.....but Bob, it's the name Juki. I don't feel the name Juki has the same good ring that maybe an IBM would have. Smuckers even sounds better."

LOT MORE OOKIS

"Joe, I'm sure there's a way to get around it." Then suddenly, Bob grinned from ear to ear as if to say, "Joe I anticipated that reaction." He then pulled out a brown felt tip pen and started drawing something over the name Juki. When he stopped, I looked at where the Juki label had been and instead saw that Bob had redesigned the first two letters so it read "Ooki."

"Much better," I exclaimed. "We'll sell a lot more Ooki's than Juki's." And that's when we agreed to offer the new Ooki. Order a Juki 2100 or 2200 with interface. Then when you get it, see personally how easy it is to type with all its unique features, how beautiful it looks and how it makes typing fun. If you order the 2200, note the extra speed that the bidirectional motion of the printing element gives you.

PERSISTANT SALESMAN

After you've decided definitely to keep it, then take our new JS&A "Products That Think" pen that we'll supply free of charge and change Juki to Ooki. The pen is yours free just for buying the Juki during our special offer.

Bob's a persistant salesman with the ability to come up with answers to buyers' objections in almost impossible situations. But with a name like Juki, even Bob had his work cut out for him. Order one at no obligation, today.

Juki 2100 (6090F 6.00) **$279**
Juki 2200 w/serial interface (6091F 6.00)**325**
Juki 2200 w/parallel interface (6092F 6.00)**325**
Daisy wheels
   Elite-12 . . . . **19**
   Script-12 . . . . **19**
   Micron-15 . . . . **19**
6 Ribbon Cartridges **22**
6 Lift-off Tapes **8**
Note: Pica-10 daisy wheel supplied with unit.

1984

297

Nuclear Mail Box

It will survive nuclear explosion or we'll refund double its cost.

If you own a rural mail box and your home was nuked, it is highly unlikely that your mail box would survive. Who'd care anyway, right?

But, let's say you owned a typical rural mail box and your home wasn't nuked. Chances are that your mail box would rust within a year, corrode something horrible within two and have to be replaced within three. That's a three-year life if the neighborhood kids didn't smash it with their bats, explode firecrackers inside or blast it with a 22 caliber rifle.

Mail boxes are abused by people and weather and are made so poorly that they must be constantly replaced.

Enter George Korycan.

Like many Americans, George owned and replaced mail boxes. And like many Americans, George got fed up replacing them. So one day he sat down in his workshop and built the strongest, heaviest, most corrosion-proof mail box ever built on the face of this earth.

And when he presented it to us, we loved it. Here's why.

The Nuclear mail box is built to U.S. Post Office specifications. Its metal is ⅛" thick galvanized steel plate—enough to stop a bullet from ten feet. Before painting, each galvanized surface is first cleaned with acid and then each box is primed, sanded and then spray painted several times with battleship silver paint to give it a rust proof and hard finish that should never need replacing.

The mail box piano wire hinge goes across the entire width of the box to let you smoothly open the door. The red flag is made of .063" steel and protected just like the other components. Compare this 22 pound "tank" to the typical one-pound mail box you can buy at your hardware store for up to $20.

The U.S. Postal Service took six months to approve the Nuclear mail box. They put it through every test they could, including their 50-hour salt spray torture test and the appearance of the paint did not change. They had never seen a box like it before.

Owning a Nuclear mail box has several advantages. First, it's probably the last mail box you'll ever have to buy. Secondly, the mail box is weatherproof—wind won't blow open the door, moisture can't penetrate it and your mail will always be safe and dry. And each mail box includes a limited five-year warranty.

Order the Nuclear mail box and enjoy the peace of mind that comes with knowing that if anything ever happens to your home, or your city, at least you'll be able to get our catalogs. Mail Box (9001A 10.00). $99

1984

A/B split, running, 161-62

Advertisements: copy elements in, 113-28; graphic elements in, 27-29. *See also* Mail order advertisements; Print advertisements

Advertising Age, advertisement in, 3, 74-75

Advertising Secrets of the Written Word (Sugarman), cassette course with, 262

Airplane tails, collecting, 153, 158

Algren, Nelson, xiii

Allen, Steve, 67

American Heart Association, campaign by, 150

AOPA Pilot, advertisement in, 229

Articles, saving, 52-53

Assembly, explaining, 137

Assumed constraints, 53; examples of, 56, 57, 263-64; problems with, 55-58

Attention, gaining/holding, 27, 29, 35, 40-41, 98, 215

Auge, Peter, 72

Authority, establishing, 140-43. *See also* Expertise

Bally pinball game, advertisement for, 95-96, 118, 121-22

Bargains, attraction of, 139-40

Batman credit card, 89; problems with, 149

Battram Galleries, 37; advertisement for, 166-67

Beatles, 260

Believability. *See* Credibility

Belonging, desire for, 151-52

Big idea, preparing, 12, 71, 97, 98

Biological repair machines, hope from, 171, 172

Block diagrams, 95-96, 97, 98

BluBlocker Corporation/sunglasses: advertisement for, 48, 91, 241-43; curiosity about, 155; infomercials for, 127; selling, 153, 154, 168; specificity and, 167; storytelling about, 186; trial period for, 144

Bone Fone, 185; timing of, 150

Brain, stimulating, 176, 178

Brand names: credibility of, 137-38; familiarity with, 168-69

Brando, Marlon: Pocket CB and, 71-72

Bringe, Paul: on seeking assurance, 143

Burglar alarms, 18-19, 150

Burnett, Leo: advertisement by, 74-75

Business Week: personality of, 92; writing level of, 189

Buying environment: copy length and, 84; creating, 35-38, 40, 42-43, 45, 47, 60, 188, 207

Bylines, 91-92, 165, 186, 187, 216

Calano, Jimmy, 5; on technical explanations, 117

Calculators, 57, 120; curiosity about, 154; urgency about, 156

Canon Corporation, advertising for, 68

Caples, John, xiv, 170; emotional feel and, 70

Captions, 27, 93, 206; technical explanations in, 117; example of, 47, 226, 233, 237, 241

CareerTrack, 5, 117

Carter, Jimmy: credit cards and, 150

Cashin Electric Company, 50, 51

Catalogs, xiii, xiv, 1, 84-85, 92, 213-16

Celebrity endorsers, credibility and, 138

Chait, Larry, xiv

Charities, mailings from, 165

Cheever, John, xiii

Chess computers, selling, 72, 74

Cinamon, Harvey, 9

Cincinnati Microwave, 5, 149

Citizens band radios: fad for, 20, 148. *See also* Pocket CB

Clarity, considerations about, 120

Clichés, 24, 120, 170

Club, The: selling, 180-81

Collectibles, 158; selling, 152-53

Commas, use of, 107

Communication, 9, 259-60; emotional process in, 88-89; personal, 87-92

Compilers: examples of, 260, 261; originators and, 260

Comprehension, determining level of. *See* Fog Index

Computers, 158; assumed constraints about, 57; authority about, 142-43; writing with, 23, 82, 106-7

Concepts: combining products into, 72; developing, 75, 98; price and, 74; selling, 71-75

Conclusions, reaching, 175

Confidence, building, 199, 220, 222

Conrad, Pete: McDonnell Douglas and, 219-20, 221

Consolidated International, working for, 39

Consumer advocate, acting as, 249

Consumers Hero, 37, 48; advertisement for, 43, 59, 93, 108, 138, 144-45; personal letter for, 89, 90. *See also* "HOT"

Copy: amount of, 81-85, 103; compelling, 33, 63, 81, 82-83, 209; elements of, 113-29; example of, 47, 48-49, 50-52, 73; goal of, 4; psychology of, 4; reading, 31-33, 42, 65, 85

Copy sequence, 93-99

Copywriters, characteristics of, 11-12, 14, 23

Copywriting, 5, 9, 111, 196; direct marketing and, 14, 25, 93, 97; as mental process, 4, 24, 45; practicing, 23-25

Coupons, 128, 202

Creative staff, freedom for, 79-80

Credibility, 154; enhancing, 137-38, 205, 220; establishing, 166-67, 173-74, 200, 202, 206; hope and, 171, 172, 173-74; importance of, 136-38; piggy-backing on, 137; price and, 139, 140; specificity and, 166; technical explanations and, 117; testimonials and, 126-27; truthfulness and, 136

Cures: fear and, 181; preventatives and, 181-82; selling, 179-83

Curiosity, 63, 202, 206, 241; building, 154-55, 198, 199, 200, 237-40; as motivating factor, 155. *See also* Seeds of curiosity

Customers, knowing, 16, 17, 19, 21, 151

Cycle magazine, advertisement format from, 43

Deadlines, pressure of, 78-79

De Bono, Edward: lateral thinking and, 13, 58

DelGaudio, Richard: want ad by, 83

Dictionary, using, 13, 69

Digital watches, selling, 71, 82, 176

Direct mailing, 1, 61, 205; assumed constraints with, 56; personal communication and, 88

Direct marketing, 1, 14, 93, 97, 179; commercial approach and, 169; copywriting and, 25; goal of, 4-5; traffic and, 63

Direct Marketing, advertisement in, 3

Drake, Edwin L., 263
Drawings, purpose of, 27
Dunlap, Barbara: copywriting by, 213-16
Dworman, Steve: on curiosity, 155

Editing, 99, 128; aids for, 106, 107; crafting/polishing by, 95, 101, 105; elements of, 101-8; problems with, 108
Editorial 'we', using, 245
Effectiveness, 224; familiarity and, 169
Emotion, 96, 175, 185; appealing to, 138, 176; copy as, 65-70, 88-89, 221; storytelling and, 188
End result, visualizing, 77-78
Entrepreneur (magazine), ads in, 198
Environment: controlling, 37-38; copy length and, 84; creating, 35-38, 40, 42-43, 45, 47, 60, 207
Excitement, adding, 96, 105
Exclusivity, as motivating factor, 158-59
Experiences, ideas from, 12-13
Expertise, 16, 19-20; specificity and, 167. See also Authority
Eytinge, Louis Victor, xiii

Fads: belonging and, 151-52; exploiting, 146-49; publicity and, 148; timing and, 149
Failures, xii, 1, 12, 25, 261. See also Mistakes
Familiarity, 167-70
Features, explaining, 116-17, 132
Fields, Debbi, 264
Final drafts, perfecting, 107, 108
First drafts, editing, 24-25, 69, 101
First sentences: lengthy, 224; purpose of, 32, 45, 114; reading, 29-30, 33, 46, 47, 63, 65, 81, 93, 113; simple, 65; writing, 31-33, 95

Fisher, Irving, 263
Flow, 93, 95-96, 97-98, 199; editing and, 128
Flowchart, logical progression of, 95-96, 97
"Fluke of Nature, A" (Schultz), 188; writing, 205-11
Foch, Ferdinand, 263
Fog Index, 189-91
"Food Crunch," copy for, 41-42
Forbes, Steve: editorials by, 92
Forbes magazine: article in, 51-52; personality of, 92; story in, 261
Franklin, Howard: sales technique of, 17-18
Franklin Mint: collectibles by, 153; limited editions by, 158
Franklin Spelling Computer, 133-34, 256
Friedman, Milton, 260

Gates, Bill, 260, 264
Gender, addressing, 119-20
General knowledge, 23, 45, 77; importance of, 11-14, 27
Gerstman, George: on marketing seminars, 2
Gettysburg Address, writing level of, 189
Gimmicks, 71, 228
Ginger, encounter with, 60-63, 265-66
Girard, Joe: salesmanship of, 123
"Gold Space Chains" (Sugarman): controversy over, 119-20; writing, 245-47
Grammar: correcting, 101, 106, 107; forgetting about, 80; problems with, 108, 253, 256
Grapefruit, advertising for. See Schultz, Frank Lewis
Graphic elements, 111, 131; employing, 37, 53; human element and, 164; purpose of, 27-30, 113
Greed, appealing to, 39, 139-40

Group identity, importance of, 151-52

Guilfoyle, Richard: replicas by, 147-48

Guilt, using, 165-66

Gunning, Robert: Fog Index and, 189

Halbert, Gary, 14; personal advertisement by, 83

Harmony: buyer/seller, 40-41; creating, 42, 43, 65, 87, 164, 165; importance of, 41-44

Headings, paragraph. *See* Paragraph headings

Headlines, 29, 45, 77; attention-getting, 30, 98; critiquing of, 94; example of, 47, 48, 50, 51; integrity in, 136; patterning and, 98; purpose of, 27; reading, 63; writing, 72, 81, 93, 95

Health food: hope and, 173; prevention and, 181

Herman, Jerry: publicity for, 148

Hewlett-Packard, 263, 264

Honesty, 201, 206; importance of, 134-35, 199, 222; testimonial to, 202

Honeywell, 48, 225

Hope, as motivator, 170-74

Hopkins, Claude, 261

"HOT" (Consumers Hero ad), 48-49; writing, 249-52

Human element: relating products with, 163-65, 249; selling and, 179-80; storytelling and, 185-86

Humor, 121, 165, 229

"Hungarian Conspiracy" (Sugarman), writing, 237-40

Ideas: experiences and, 12-13; lateral thinking for, 13

Income Opportunity, ads in, 198

Incubation process, 75, 81, 98; elements of, 77-80; pressure and, 79; subconscious mind and, 80

Installation, explaining, 137

Instant gratification, power of, 157-58

Insurance, selling, 17-18, 19

Integrity, 30, 136, 206, 221; building on, 201; urgency and, 156

Interest, building, 82-83, 96

Internet, opportunities on, 259

Intuition, 80, 175, 176

Involvement devices, 131-34, 208

It's Better to Laugh (Levine), 185

Jargon, consumer, 249-52

Jobs, Steven, 263-64

Jogging machine, selling, 177-78

Jordan, Michael, 126

JS&A Group, Inc., 1, 17, 48, 73; copywriting for, 24, 31, 37, 50

Justification. *See* Purchase, justifying

Karbo, Betty, 197, 203

Karbo, Joe, 5, 23, 215; advertising campaign by, 104-5, 197, 203, 204; copywriting by, 197-203; death of, 203

Karpov, Anatoli, 72, 73, 74

Knowledge, 11; copy ideas and, 12; copywriting, 257; practical, 192. *See also* General knowledge; Specific knowledge

Korchnoi, Victor, 73

Land, Edwin: on mistakes, 12, 261

Language: colorful, 215; consumer, 249-52; technical, 117

Lateral thinking, 13, 58

Layout, overall, 29

"Lazy Man's Way to Riches, The" (Karbo ad), writing of, 23, 104-5, 197-204

Lazy Man's Way to Riches, The (Karbo book), 5, 23, 104, 197

Left brain, right brain vs., 80

Legibility, 113

Length: copy, 82, 83, 84, 85, 128; sentence, 121, 189, 190

Letterman, David, 236

Letters, personalizing, 88-91
Levine, Kathy: on storytelling, 185
Life Extension Association, award from, 150
Limited, The: Victoria's Secret and, 5, 216
Limited editions, 156, 158, 207, 211
"Lingerie for Men" (Victoria's Secret), writing, 213-17
Literary persuasion, 40
Logic, copywriting and, 67-68
Logos, purpose of, 28, 30
Long-copy approach, effectiveness of, 83-84

Madonna, 260
Magazines: first sentences in, 31; personalities of, 92; reading, 105-6
"Magic Baloney" (Magic Stat), 47 185; writing, 225-28
Magic Stat thermostat, 47-48; advertisement for, 165, 225-28; selling, 185, 228
Mailing lists/pieces, problems with, 61-63
Mail order advertisements, 2, 204; applying principles to, 195; copy length and, 84; instant gratification and, 157; writing, 262
"Mail Order Mansion" (Sugarman), writing, 187, 233-35
Marcus, Stanley: letter from, 212
Margoles, David, xiv
Market, broadening, 215
Marketing, 4, 5; knowledge and, 12; on television, 196. See also Direct marketing
Marketing Secrets of a Mail Order Maverick (Sugarman), 262
Mason, Archie, 94
Mass market, reaching, 158, 189
McDonnell Douglas, advertisement by, 219-22
Media tests, running, 150
Membership programs, 189, 211

Mental processes, understanding, 174, 175-78
Mercedes-Benz, motivation for buying, 66, 138, 151, 152
Messages: compelling, 265; educational, 243; emotion of, 67; location of, 33; personal, 208; psychology in, 131; receiving, 67
Midex burglar alarm, 68; advertisement for, 146; selling, 18-19, 126, 180
Minocqua, Wisconsin, 3, 159, 205
Miracell, 181; campaign for, 162-63
Mistakes: avoiding, 14, 142, 259; as learning tools, 12, 261. See also Failures
Models, using, 165, 247
Momentum, building, 36-37, 46
"More Stimulating Way, A" (Sony), problems with, 223-24
"More You Learn, The" (McDonnell Douglas), problems with, 219-22
Motivation, 261; curiosity as, 155; exclusivity/rarity/ uniqueness as, 158-59; hope as, 170-74
Mrs. Fields Cookies, 266
My Life in Advertising (Hopkins), 261

Name recognition, importance of, 137-38, 141, 168-69
National Enquirer, The, credibility of, 137
Nautilus Lower Back machine, advertisement for, 253-56
"Nautilus Spelling Sale" (Sugarman), writing, 253-56
Negative features/publicity, addressing, 47, 135, 219-21, 225, 228
New York Times, The, Schultz advertisement in, 211
New York University, lecture at, 68-69, 101

Nine-point puzzle, assumed constraints of, 56, 58
Notoriety, 154
Number 7, familiarity of, 169

Objections: avoiding, 221; raising and resolving, 118-19, 129, 137, 214-16, 219-22, 225
Obligation, creating sense of, 166
Offer summary, 127-28
Ogilvy, David, 170
Olsen, Ken: assumed constraints and, 57
Orders, asking for, 96, 128
Originators: compilers and, 260; examples of, 260-61
Overall layout, purpose of, 29
Ownership, feeling of, 131-34

Parade, Schultz advertisement in, 211
Paragraph headings, purpose of, 28, 114-15, 129
Pargh, Bernie, 2, 3
Patterning, using, 98-99
Periodicals. *See* Magazines
Persistence, 260
Personal satisfaction, feeling of, 177
"Pet Plane" (Sugarman), 165; writing, 229-31
Phone-tapping equipment, advertisement for, 148
Photos/photography, 29, 84; black and white/color, 178; purpose of, 27
Physical facts, 123-24
Pill, The: selling, 181-82
Pitch: length of, 83; making, 33, 209, 215
Pocket CB, 21, 28, 71-72, 74, 148
Pocket Yellow Pages, 68, 72
Popular Mechanics, assumed constraints and, 57
Positioning, 71, 75, 138
Practice, importance of, 23-25
Practitioner, 1, 260

Prevention: cures and, 181-82; problems selling, 179-83
Price: comparisons, 125-26; concept and, 74; considerations about, 28, 127, 139, 140; introductory, 157; limited-time, 156; lowering, 133-34, 140
Price point: copy length and, 84, 85; purchase justification and, 139; technical explanations and, 118; value and, 139
Print advertisements, 1, 131, 186; goal of, 4-5; personalizing and, 90-91; selling with, 40
Problem solving: assumed constraints and, 58; lateral thinking and, 13
Product explanations, 115, 116; simplicity in, 160. *See also* Technical explanations
Products: delivering, 154; drama of, 96, 146; evaluating, 181; failure of, 179; nature of, 17-21, 146, 179; presenting, 4, 75, 137; testing, 149
Prospects: identifying with, 200, 201; selling, 40-41
Psychological triggers, 111, 129, 131-74
Publicity, fads and, 148
Purchase, justifying, 96, 138, 139, 199

Quest/80 magazine, hook by, 52, 53
Questions, answering, 137. *See also* Objections
QVC, 51, 137, 168, 182; collectors and, 152-53

Radar detectors, selling, 5, 149
Raphel, Murray: Swiss Army watch and, 161
Rarity, as motivating factor, 158-59
Reader's Digest, writing level of, 189
Readership, increasing, 59
Reading gravity, force of, 46-47

Resistance, removing, 80, 145, 216

Resonating. *See* Harmony

Response devices: purpose of, 28; use of, 128

Return policy, establishing, 216

Rhythm, 121; editing for, 104, 128

Rickerson, Mark, 36

Right brain, left brain vs., 80

Rochlis, Jeff, 159

Rolls-Royce, as status symbol, 152

Rubik, Erno, 237, 238

Runyon, Damon, xv

Ruth, Babe, 1

Sackheim, Max, xiv

Salesmanship, developing, 39-40

Sales pitch. *See* Pitch

Satisfaction, feeling of, 177

Satisfaction conviction, 143-45, 199, 209

Sauer, John: advertisement by, 41

Saying too much, avoiding, 128, 178. *See also* Editing

Scare tactics, avoiding, 19

Schirra, Wally, 19, 126

Schultz, Frank Lewis: copywriting by, 205-12; grapefruit advertisement by, 65-66, 104, 117-18, 187-88

Schultz, Ray: on Sugarman, xiii-xv

Schwartz, Gene, xiii, 14

Scientific American, advertisement in, 46

Scott, Robert: catalog of, 84-85

Scrub Balls, advertisement copy for, 51-52

Second sentences, purpose of, 32-33, 45, 114

Seeds of curiosity, 265-66; using, 59-63. *See also* Curiosity

Selling environment, creating, 35-38, 40, 42-43, 45, 47, 60, 186, 207

Selling process: enhancing/stimulating, 128; personal, 209; in print, 45

Seminars, 1-5; charges for, 3, 261; participants in, 3, 5, 9, 10, 261; teachings of, 262

Sensor watch, advertising for, 15-16, 122-23, 125

Sentences: combining, 104; in first draft, 101; length of, 189-91; mixing lengths of, 121; short/easy, 31, 59. *See also* First sentences; Second sentences

Service, 17, 119; commitment to, 123; questions about, 96, 121-23

Sexual/sexist comments, avoiding, 119

Shaw, Artie, xiii

"She Fled the Table When the Doctor Said Cut Her Open" (Schwartz), xiii

Shipping methods, urgency and, 157

Short-copy approach, effectiveness of, 84-85

Simon, Fred, 94

Simplicity, 160-63, 209; power of, 160-61, 162

Sizzle, selling, 71, 200, 203

Ski Lift International, selling for, 166

Slippery slide, 63, 65, 81, 120, 249, 265; creating, 45-53, 198, 216; examples of, 47-49; satisfaction conviction and, 145; storytelling and, 185

Smirnoff, Yakov, 69

Smith, Fred: assumed constraints and, 57

Smoke detectors, selling, 72, 115

Snowmobiles, exclusivity and, 159

Sony Video Communications, advertisement by, 223-24

Space-age products, selling, 36, 37, 122, 140-41, 249

Space restrictions, meeting, 102-3

Specificity, 166-67; expertise and, 167

Specific knowledge, 11, 23, 77; importance of, 15-21; obtaining, 27, 45

Spelling: correcting, 106, 107; first draft and, 101; forgetting about, 80; problems with, 115, 256

Stanke, Mary, 3, 48, 107

Storytelling, 207, 213; educational messages in, 243; effectiveness of, 183, 185-88; using, 223, 225, 229-31, 233-36, 241

Style, 107; consistency in, 191

Suarez, Ben, 14

Subconscious: assumed constraints and, 56; incubation process and, 78, 79, 80; seeds of curiosity and, 59

Subheadlines, 30, 206, 224; curiosity-building, 98; example of, 47, 48, 50, 51, 73; purpose of, 27; reading, 29, 46, 63, 94; writing, 93, 95

Subliminal reactions, 124

Success (magazine), ads in, 198

Success Forces (Sugarman), 102

Sugarman, April, 9, 133; story about, 94-95

Sugarman, Jill, 9, 133

Sugarman, Judy, 107

Sugarman, Wendy, 3

Swiss Army watch, marketing, 161-62

"Tap Your Phone" (advertisement), 148

"Tcudorp" (advertisement), 75

Teachers, practitioners and, 260

Technical explanations, 15-16, 116-18, 176, 208; credibility and, 117; price point and, 118; purpose of, 116-17. See also Product explanations

Testimonials, 202; credibility with, 126-27; reverse, 126

Texas Monthly, Schultz article in, 211

'That' words, looking for, 104

"They Laughed When I Sat Down At the Piano" (Caples), xiv

Thinking: incubation and, 77-78; understanding processes of, 175-78

Think Tank, lateral thinking and, 13

Time, writing level of, 189

Timing, 245; fads and, 149; impact of, 149-50

Toll-free numbers, 29, 123, 124

Tools, problem-solving, 13

Traffic, 60; direct marketing and, 63; increased, 46, 59

Trial periods, 124-25; effectiveness of, 143-44

Trust, building, 116, 199

Truthfulness, 134-35, 214, 222; credibility and, 136; responsiveness and, 135

Tuning fork, analogy of, 101, 164

TV Guide, Schultz advertisement in, 211

Tweaking an ad, 169

Typefaces, 136; choosing, 32, 37, 113; corporate image and, 113; problems with, 160

Unique features, explaining, 96

Uniqueness, as motivating factor, 158-59

Unique selling proposition (USP), 71, 75

Urgency, 211; conveying, 155-57; effectiveness and, 156; integrity and, 156

Vague descriptions, curiosity from, 177-78

Valentine, Mike, 5

Value: establishing, 125, 138-39; justifying, 138-39; price point and, 139

Vibrations, positive. See Harmony

Victoria's Secret, 5; advertisement for, 213-16; The Limited and, 216

Video communications, selling, 223-24

Viguerie, Richard, 3, 10

"Vision Breakthrough" (Sugarman), 91, 186; reading level of, 190-91; writing, 241-43

Vitamins, hope and, 173

Walkie-talkies, 20-21, 71; fad for, 148

Walkman, 150

Wall Street Journal, The: A/B split in, 161-62; advertisement in, 17, 134, 138, 140, 148, 253; credibility of, 137; Karbo advertising in, 203; Schultz advertisement in, 211; story in, 261; writing level of, 189

Watergate Game, controversy over, 149

Watson, Thomas, Sr., 263

Weschler, Mike, 20-21

Whole-brain appeal, 175, 176

Winchell, Walter, xv

Wonderful-feeling hormones, stimulating, 178

Words: advantages of fewer, 103; eliminating, 102-3, 104, 105, 128; emotions and, 69-70; familiar, 169-70; length of, 189, 190, 191; misspelled, 253, 256

Wozniak, Steve, 264

Writing levels, rating, 189-91

Wunderman, Lester: on Sackheim, xiv

Your comments are important

I am always interested in your comments, feedback and suggestions on the book you've just read and I may also want to use them for advertising purposes. Please feel free to copy or tear out this form and mail it with your comments to: Joseph Sugarman, JS&A Group, Inc., 3350 Palms Center Drive, Las Vegas, NV 89103. Thank you.

I herewith freely allow and give right and title to Joseph Sugarman and/or DelStar Publishing, or their assigns, to use the following comments, feedback and suggestions either to improve this or any of Mr. Sugarman's books or as a testimonial in the promotion of this book in any advertising medium solely determined by Mr. Sugarman or DelStar Publishing. I also agree to allow the use of part or all of a testimonial as determined by Mr. Sugarman.

_____

Your signature   Date

Would you agree to appear on a TV testimonial? _____

_____

_____

_____

_____

_____

_____

_____

_____

Continue on back of page.

Marketing Secrets of a Mail Order Maverick
Stories and Lessons on the Power of Direct Marketing to Start a Successful
Business, Create a Famous Brand Name and Sell Any Product or Service

The story of the techniques Joseph Sugarman created and the results he experienced while selling thousands of different products to millions of people. Chapters include how to find a winning product, secrets for a successful ad layout, how to avoid typefaces that hurt response, how to buy media for less, testing a product's potential and hundreds of other insights that guide the reader to an understanding of what works and what doesn't. The lessons are alternated with entertaining and enlightening marketing stories from Sugarman's personal experience. ISBN 1-891686-06-2 (hardcover). 390 pages. $39.95

Television Secrets for Marketing Success
How to Sell Your Product on Infomercials, Home Shopping Channels and Spot
TV Commercials From the Entrepreneur Who Gave You BluBlocker® Sunglasses

The story of Joseph Sugarman's successful experiences with infomercials and the QVC home shopping channel. The book has useful tips on applying the principles of print direct marketing to make TV marketing work more effectively. He talks candidly about his failures as well as his successes, how he launched one of QVC's most successful promotions, how he created and built BluBlocker® sunglasses into a nationally recognized brand name, and how he used TV marketing to influence over 10 million viewers to buy his products. ISBN 1-891686-09-7 (hardcover). 310 pages. $39.95

The Sugarman Seminar Secrets Slipcase
A handsome slipcase designed to hold Joseph Sugarman's three books
based on his exclusive marketing course is **yours free.**

If you've already purchased this book or any one of the hardcover versions of the three Sugarman marketing books, you may receive, free of charge (other than the minimal per order postage and handling charge), a slipcase (a $10 value) designed to hold all three books in the series. Buy all three of the Sugarman marketing books and keep them in this handsome display case. Refer to them often. And start to build your library of Sugarman marketing books. Offer available only in the United States.

The Sugarman Seminar Secrets Boxed Set
Joseph Sugarman's three books based on his exclusive advertising
and marketing course in a special paperback edition, complete with
slipcase and at a special price.

Buy all three of the Sugarman marketing books in paperback and receive, free of charge, a handsome slipcase (a $10 value) as well as a $20 savings off the cost of the hardcover version. Available in paperback only as a complete set. $99.95

Order Form (See page 311 for details.)

❏ I wish to order the following books:

Advertising Secrets of the Written Word	$39.95	_____
Marketing Secrets of a Mail Order Maverick	39.95	_____
Television Secrets for Marketing Success	39.95	_____
The Sugarman Seminar Course Slipcase	FREE	_____
The Sugarman Seminar Course Boxed Set	99.95	_____

Postage & Handling **Per Order** 5.00

Total: _____

❏ Please put me on the Sugarman mailing list for announcements of books, seminars and marketing courses.

Name _____

Address _____

City, State, Zip _____

Daytime Phone: _____

❏ I wish to charge my credit card:

_____ Exp _____

Visa, MasterCard and American Express Cards accepted.

❏ I am enclosing $ _____

Make checks payable to **JS&A Group, Inc.**, and mail your order to JS&A Group, Inc. 3350 Palms Center Drive, Las Vegas, NV 89103. Offer available only in the United States. Call for prices in foreign countries.

Phone in your order: (800) 323-6400
Fax in your order: (702) 597-2002

Photocopy or cut out this page to mail or fax in your order.